Understanding Gender and Organizations

Mats Alvesson and Yvonne Due Billing

SAGE Publications
London • Thousand Oaks • New Delhi

First published 1997

SAGE Publications Ltd
6 Bonhill Street
London EC2A 4PU

SAGE Publications Inc.
2455 Teller Road
Thousand Oaks, California 91320

SAGE Publications India Pvt Ltd
32, M-Block Market
Greater Kailash – I
New Delhi 110 048

British Library Cataloguing in Publication data

A catalogue record for this book is available from the British Library

ISBN 0 7619 5360 4
ISBN 0 7619 5361 2 (pbk)

Library of Congress catalog card number 97–068907

Typeset by Mayhew Typesetting, Rhayader, Powys
Printed in Great Britain by Redwood Books, Trowbridge, Wiltshire

Books are to be returned on or before
the last date below.

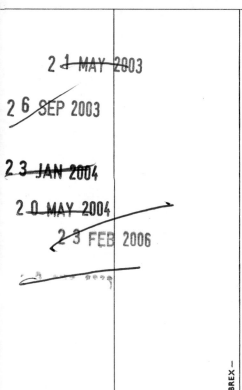

£14.95

Understanding Gender
and Organizations

Contents

Preface

Gender is a fascinating subject that can leave nobody untouched – even though many people are satisfied with their own convictions and 'truths' and are not interested in exploring the subject intellectually. It is also a very difficult subject, bound to frustrate the person who believes in absolute truths. Those who are not satisfied with apparently clear, stable patterns and simple explanations will look behind these and find variation, changes, ambiguities, contradictions and confusions. A specific difficulty in dealing with gender is that everybody has experience and intimate knowledge of the subject. This might create problems for the researcher who has problems with establishing herself or himself as an authority on the subject as many people consider themselves experts on gender. It might also create problems for the researcher because personal experience is not only an invaluable support in knowledge development, but also a source of taken-for-granted assumptions and bias, giving inquiry a predetermined, insufficiently reflective and self-critical direction. One's implicit beliefs and knowledge about men and women may prevent openness, curiosity and ability to be surprised. Good empirical research should lead to new insights and ideas. All research – social research is certainly no exception – must struggle with established wisdoms, and gender studies are certainly no easier to defend against accusations of embracing dogmas and biases than other politically and pragmatically 'hot' fields of social knowledge. The researcher/author – and the reader – must struggle carefully with this element. This book attempts to do so and aims in particular to inspire reflection and sensitivity towards gender issues.

Our reason for writing this book, therefore, is to provide a qualified, nuanced introduction and overview of the field of gender and work organization. We also aim at suggesting some ideas for theoretical development. We intend to focus more on ideas, theories and qualitative studies than rely on statistics and results of questionnaire studies. Rather than trying to provide 'facts' and 'truths' about gender issues in work organizations we aim for an interpretive, open and broadly critical, including self-critical, style.

We have greatly benefited from the comments and suggestions of colleagues who have read the whole, or parts, of a draft of the final manuscript: Joan Acker, University of Oregon; Ulla Eriksson, Anita Göransson and Lisbeth Johnsson, University of Gothenburg; Silvia Gherardi,

University of Trento; Wendy Hollway, University of Leeds and Elisabeth Sundin, University of Linköping.

Chapter 7 to some extent draws on an article published in *Scandinavian Journal of Management*, 1989, 5(2).

The preparation of this book has been facilitated by a research grant from the Swedish Work Environment Fund.

1

Introduction

Texts on gender and organizations often start by showing the sexist nature of contemporary society. Reskin and Padavic (1994), for example, start their book by referring to a US television programme in which two people, similar in age, qualifications and ethnicity, but of different sexes, apply for the same jobs. They receive highly different treatment. The male gets more offers and more qualified and well-paid jobs. The female is repeatedly less well treated in terms of employment possibilities. Other texts start by referring to common knowledge or statistics showing that women in general have lower wages than men even within the same occupation and at the same level, that women experience more unemployment than men, that women take more responsibility for unpaid labour, that they are strongly underrepresented at higher positions in working life, that they have less autonomy and control over work and lower expectations of promotion (e.g. Chafetz, 1989; Ve, 1989). There is massive empirical evidence on these issues (Reskin and Padavic, 1994) and those arguing for the existence of a gender order or a patriarchy, which gives many more options and privileges to men, particularly in working life, but also in life in general, have no problems in substantiating their case. Clearly gender – 'patterned, socially produced, distinctions between female and male, feminine and masculine' (Acker, 1992: 250) – is a key concept for understanding what is happening with individuals in their working lives and for understanding how people encounter encouragement, scepticism, support and suffering in organizational contexts. These viewpoints are based on ideas about fairness and social problems. They typically emerge from assumptions about women's interests in removing sources of inequality, through counteracting male dominance. The perspective is typically feminist–sociological.

Gender issues may, however, also be worth focusing on from quite a different point of departure: the business–managerial one. From a management perspective, there are reasons to be concerned about the ineffectiveness in terms of the utilization of human resources contingent upon contemporary gender pattern. Counteracting sex discrimination and conservative gender patterns would make possible a more rational way of recruiting, keeping, placing, training and promoting labour. Utilizing diversity – e.g. by employing and giving voice to men as well as women in terms of viewpoints and experiences – may also facilitate organizational learning and creativity. A flexible work force, untrammelled by conservative ideas about 'men's work' and 'women's work', that is what is natural and appropriate for men or women respectively to do, may be used more effectively. Therefore there are good reasons for management to address organizational cultures, structures and practices in terms of gender. To maintain ways of thinking and acting, as well as social structures, that prevent almost half of the labour force from being fully utilized in terms of their qualifications and talents may be said to be a prime example of irrationality. And although rationality in organizational settings – as in human life in general – is more often preached than practised, too obvious deviations from what appears to be profitable should have a fair chance of triggering changes, or at least attempts at change.

These two motives for taking an interest in gender and organization – injustice and profitable management – are strong and it is hardly surprising that gender studies, in general, are expanding, and that there is a rapidly increasing interest in this topic in organization and management theory as well as in organizational practice.

However, simple and straightforward empirical descriptions and arguments seldom work easily in social science. Social reality is complex and contradictory. In terms of management considerations, for example, it is possible that there is a surplus of talent in relation to high-level jobs and it cannot be taken for granted that top priority is given to encouraging and utilizing an increasing number of career-oriented people. Companies often benefit from women having learned that their place is in relatively low paid jobs, and the lack of ambition conventionally ascribed to women and their expectations of finding fulfilment in the family sphere facilitates adaptation to the many modestly skilled jobs available in contemporary working life (Acker, 1994). A gender division of labour which means that compliant and cheap female labour is accessible may be more beneficial for many companies than taking equal opportunities seriously, at least if the latter should call for major changes. In addition, the career-oriented person, giving priority to work over family matters, may be preferable in the business world, as a strong commitment to equality would often mean a re-balancing or downplaying of corporate matters in relation to family obligations and values. These complications are worth considering before assuming too much management interest in gender fairness. Even for managerial jobs it may be optimal for companies if most women are not strongly committed to promotion to top jobs. A manager of a large UK retail company said,

> what I can't have is sixty very ambitious people as store managers. I only want ten very ambitious people. Fifty I see as being hardcore managers, permanent in the areas where they are. And what I'm looking for, crudely, is thirty- to forty-year old females, with a good retail background, who are very effective and very efficient in their job but, because of their domestic circumstances, won't want to move. (cited in Cockburn, 1991: 49)

Rather than focusing on 'objective interests', as if there were such, it is better to explore how people in companies define priorities, think and act in this type of matter. Rather than trying to find the average we believe that studying complexity and variation contingent upon different industries, labour markets, occupations and organizational cultures and even specific situations is worth pursuing. Presumably there are very different opinions among executives about whether or not a progressive corporate practice on gender pays off. Although equal opportunities are increasingly espoused by more and more companies, this may often be more a matter of lip service for legitimacy reasons than serious business intended to permeate corporate practices.

In terms of universal gender discrimination in working life and society, the common picture briefly outlined above may, however, be too self-evident. Let us complicate the picture somewhat. First, men do not have a monopoly on privileges and women in some respects score more points on the goods of life. That men are much better paid, have far more formal power in organizations and hold the most prestigious jobs is beyond any doubt. But equally clear is that men's life expectancy in the Western world is much shorter than women's, they end up in jail much more frequently, lose conflicts about custody of children after divorces, are forced to do military service in many countries (which for some may be seen as a privilege, but for most it is a mixed blessing or strongly negative), and more men than women commit suicide, at least in Scandinavia.

In Sweden at the time of writing, half of the cabinet members are women.[1] Women are also well represented in parliament and in many top-level public sector positions, such as university presidents. It is clearly seen as positive, indeed important, to elect or appoint women to such posts. One may argue against the representativeness and significance of these examples, seeing them as purely symbolic examples of something done for reasons of legitimacy and to appeal to female voters. One cannot, however, disregard the fact that these jobs belong to the most powerful, prestigious and broadly visible in society. The impact in substantive but perhaps even more in symbolic terms should not be underestimated. The election of women and the espoused value of having women in top positions reflects people's basically positive attitudes to females in top positions in politics and many public sector organizations. This, of course, does not mean that there are no problems for women getting and functioning in top jobs, but it shows that there are also broadly shared 'pro-women' attitudes. (In business, the situation may be different.) Of course, people may express one opinion regarding relatively distanced holders of top positions – safely located far away from one's immediate life/work context – and another when it comes to women being their own managers. Attitudes are seldom consistent.[2]

One may argue that the above examples are only relevant to Sweden – and a few other (gender) progressive countries – and stress that, generally, women are if not totally absent then strongly underrepresented in top jobs in most countries (including the parts of the world that this book addresses, i.e. the Western world). But in most of the Western countries the number of women in top jobs is increasing, albeit slowly. The case of Sweden is not that atypical; even though the country is often believed to have a high degree of gender equality, the overall picture is highly contradictory and in most respects not in harmony with the espoused general positive view on female political leaders and public sector top administrators. The gender division of labour is as pronounced in Sweden as in most other Western countries. In most high-level jobs, male overrepresentation is very strong. Only about 10 to 15 per cent of higher middle[3] and senior managers and seven per cent of all professors are women.[4]

There is a much higher percentage of female managers in the USA than in other countries, but also in the USA very few women reach the top jobs (Reskin and Padavic, 1994). Although women's share of management jobs has increased, the gender hierarchy in organizations has not been altered substantially. Women managers are concentrated low in chains of command, they tend to supervise workers of their own sex, and their role in decision making is primarily providing input into decisions made by men (Reskin and Ross, 1992). Only one to five per cent of all top managers are women. (The numbers differ depending on how one defines a top manager.) That does not mean that women are necessarily disadvantaged in assessments and recruitment to top jobs. A study of applicants to senior executive positions in US federal government showed that women received significantly higher performance appraisals and were more often hired than male applicants (Powell and Butterfield, 1994).

If the reader now feels a bit confused, he or she has got the message. Our point, hardly original, is that gender patterns are complex, often contradictory. There is considerable variation in signs of biases against women and subtle social mechanisms and cultural ideas disfavouring women, and there are indications of the opposite. Case studies of organizations show much variation in the work lives of men and women, in terms of careers and work conditions as well as the structures, cultures and processes affecting options, actions, values, satisfactions and sufferings (Billing and Alvesson, 1994; Blomqvist, 1994). It is not easy to discover universal mechanisms or structures below or above empirical 'surface variation'. Efforts to impose a strong notion of a universal 'patriarchy' or 'gender system', as some scholars do, are problematic and are often not very useful for the understanding of organizational phenomena, since such a notion overstresses broad patterns and consistency and disregards variety and change.

For us, and this book, it is not only gender discrimination and obstacles to the realization of equal opportunities in work organizations that are important to illuminate. Nor is it solely male domination and female victimization and lost opportunities that are to be focused upon. Also of interest is the rich variation in the way organizations carry gender meanings and how men and women live their organizational lives. Work organizations are not just representative of privileges for men, compared with women, but they also – as they do for women – bring about conformism, constraints and suffering for many men. From the other angle, women experience joy and benefits not just from wage labour but also from everyday organizational life. Some of the constraints in organizations – such as the pressure to give priority to work over family – do not solely originate from male domination, but are also contingent upon the workings of capitalism and the idea of organizations effectively and competitively producing goods and services, making a high material standard of living possible.[5]

The exploration of gender-in-organizations, the mapping of what happens to men and women at workplaces, as well as of gendered organizations, and seeing organization cultures in terms of masculine and feminine values, ideas and meanings, may lead to the telling of many stories, with different morals. Many of these stories are explicitly and intentionally pro-women, opposing male domination and aiming at improving the conditions for women. This is the single most important theme to pursue and we tend to follow this route. But we also believe that it is worth addressing how women may act conservatively in relation to equality ideals, perhaps against their own interests, and how organizational cultures may affect many men in unfortunate ways. In addition, a gender perspective on organizations can give us important insights into how organizations function, for example in terms of leadership, strategy, organizational culture, groups, communication etc. In other words, the approach goes beyond questions about positive and negative outcomes of gender patterns. This variety of significant issues on the topic of gender and organization is, for us, part of what makes the subject so exciting.

Organizations and gender – a neglected area

Why consider organizations in terms of gender? There are many good reasons for taking an interest in each of these areas and also for combining the two. Organizations are central economic institutions that take care of the production of goods and services and of a major part of the control and care of the citizens. Most of us are in daily contact with (formal) organizations, taking part in organizational activities every day, working in them or relating to them as clients or customers. Organizations are workplaces, public as well as private, sites for childcare and education, institutions taking care of social services and health, and for most people organizations fill up maybe one third of their lives. Organizations are the context of, and decisive for, our paid working life and for our well-being, and it is therefore of great importance how they function, which logic (goals and means) dominates, which actors and groups set the agenda and how the relations between people are formed. Organization theory is accordingly a large and expanding field.

Organization theory – here broadly defined – has traditionally and up to the 1980s neglected gender aspects; employees have been viewed either from a supposedly gender neutral (male) perspective or from a point of view that considers only the male part of the employees as interesting

(Hearn and Parkin, 1983; Mills, 1988). In a *Handbook of Work and Organizational Psychology* (Drenth et al., 1984) one short article out of 42 deals with 'women and work', while gender aspects are not addressed in any of the other chapters. The massive literature on organizational culture in the 1980s, often driven by an interest in the meaning of life at the workplace, hardly considered gender at all. Also many recent books on 'people' in organizations hardly address gender, women, men, masculinity or femininity (e.g. Hosking and Morley, 1991; Legge, 1995). It has not been considered what impact this might have on the resulting analysis and interpretations. Neither the fact that only men (with a very few exceptions) have participated in the process of developing knowledge and understanding of organizations nor the possible impact of this on the research process have been taken into consideration. Men's expressed views on the world – or to be less inexact, primarily the views of elite groups of men – have been the only really significant contribution in the field of management and organization and have been considered valid for the whole of humanity, critics argue. Of course, the female sex in no way guarantees an interest in gender – the books just referred to have female authors[6] – any more than the male biological sex excludes an interest in the topic. But there is a tendency for a one-sex area in social science to neglect gender aspects. More broadly, one may question if and how a 'shift in perspective from men's to women's points of view might alter the fundamental categories, methodology, and self-understanding of Western science and technology' (Benhabib and Cornell, 1987: 1).

Masculine dominance in academic as well as organizational life has had an important influence on the kinds of questions raised and the answers subsequently produced in management and organization studies (J. Martin, 1994). Some subjects have not been considered at all or they have at least not been considered from a gender point of view. At the same time this established research is presented, and may for the 'naive' reader appear, as objective and neutral. It has been implicitly assumed and communicated that organizations are neutral to gender or that it is a man's world. The manager is assumed to be a 'he'. It is therefore rightly maintained that it is the life and work of men that has been considered the research standard, both within the human relations' school, strategic management research, cultural theory or any other known schools and fields of organization theory. This holds true for great parts of science as well. Research often uncritically reflects cultural beliefs. The traditional American concept of leadership may be described as 'a pastiche based upon a masculine ego-ideal glorifying the competitive, combative, controlling, creative, aggressive, self-reliant individualist' (Lipman-Blumen, 1992: 185). Arguably, the whole management field has a masculine bias (Collinson and Hearn, 1994, 1996); and according to Cullen (1994), even a seemingly more 'neutral' theory, such as Maslow's need hierarchy, may have a similar bias.

We shall just mention a few themes which call for attention to gender. How are organizations – as sites or scenes for human action and as materialized structures – central to the production of values, conceptions and gender relations? How are the values people bring with them when entering organizations influencing the way things are done within the organization? Are these values influencing the way relationships are established, how power is formed, distributed and exercised, and how organizations are viewed and developed? How are attitudes, conceptions, visions, interests, values and ideals related to the 'fact' that most organizations are populated with different sexes? Gender must then be appreciated both in terms of how certain previously established orientations associated with the sexes are imported into the workplace context and how gender processes in organizations actively constitute and shape gender.[7]

A gender perspective implies analysing the importance, meaning and consequences of what is culturally defined as male or masculine as well as female or feminine ways of thinking (knowing), feeling, valuing and acting. A gender perspective also implies an analysis of the organizational practices that maintain the division of labour between the sexes. The vertical division of labour according to sex can be intimately related to conceptions of the masculine/feminine, that ascribe to phenomena a gendered meaning that is contingent upon the cultural beliefs of what are typical or natural orientations and behaviours of men and women. Hence gender symbolism will be of special interest to the organization researcher, that is the tendency that jobs (or functions) are associated with a certain understanding of gender or have a certain gender aura around them, and that, in general, the (de)valuation of feminine work gives women a lower status and a poorer pay than men. For example, ideas and norms for leadership may express a strong masculine undertone which makes leadership appear to be more natural or easy for men than for women to engage in (Lipman-Blumen, 1992; Schein, 1973).

The use of a gender perspective on organizations would lead to a higher degree of sensitivity to contradictions and ambiguities with regard to social constructions and reconstructions of gender relations, and to what we consider to be discrimination and equal opportunities at the workplace level. It is important to stress that gender relations are not statically structured and defined once and for all but are emergent and changeable. Apart from studying discriminating practices and gender bias in organizations it is also important to study the elements of modern organizations that produce tendencies towards equality between the sexes. This last aspect has been very much neglected in gender studies. As we shall see later on, a great deal of the literature tends to be somewhat one-sidedly critical and 'negative'. 'Misery stories' and an emphasis on problems are popular. There are strong reasons for a critical approach, but arguably some modern societies and many organizations have social values and rules that promote the espoused interests and opportunities of women and do not only or mainly discriminate against them – even without the use of special legislation. These (social) rules are probably of greater importance to middle-class than working-class women. Modern societies praise themselves for being meritocratic and most (younger) people in Western societies probably claim to be in favour of an ideology that gives equal opportunities to both sexes, even though this is sometimes restricted to lip service. The possibility of letting organizations play a progressive and 'rational' part should not be excluded – even though this progressive and rational part has its limits; for example it may give women better options of employment and promotion, but it does not address wider issues such as the goals, values and interests that form organizational life in a capitalist society.

A gender perspective will not only mean dealing with the way men and women are constructed as individuals – how they are formed and reformed through social processes, how they act, how they experience their working life (as well as their private life), how they are supported and discriminated – but will also include a broader view on organizations. Some ideals and values could be seen as expressing male dominance, for example, companies that ruthlessly exploit nature, 'human resources', consumers, and so on. Ideals such as profit and maximum growth, aggressive competition, the tendency to make quantitative ideals (money) the ultimate measure of success, could be related to masculine conceptions and a male rationality. The limits of the explanatory/interpretative powers of a gender perspective are of course disputable, and it is certainly not the best perspective for the study of *all* aspects of organizations and working life. Being sensitive about the limits of its analytic and interpretive range hardly implies that women should cope with their under-privileged position in working life by a one-sided adaptation to structures, goals, languages and logics that have for ages been influenced by a strong masculine dominance. A gender perspective on organizations would imply studying these phenomena and focusing on fundamental questions of rationality, e.g. the structure and aims of the organization, maintaining a balance between a broad and an all-embracing view. The trick is to interpret gendered meanings sensitively in non-obvious situations without totalizing organizational life through seeing everything in terms of gender.

Besides studying general patterns and tendencies within organizations when we deal with the construction of gender it is also important to be aware of existing variations. Most researchers have analysed what they argue are the typical and dominant trends and patterns aiming at a general picture of gender and organization, even though diversity and multiplicity have received more attention recently.[8] Women and men have been socialized differently, they have different educations, occupations and experiences and they take part in the process of constructing and organizing the working place according to gender in different ways. Also, organizations differ very much when it comes to historical and reproduced gender biases in social practices, just as the gendered meanings that characterize different fields of work, functions, professions and positions differ (Billing and Alvesson, 1994).

Organization theories have been developed over the years by reinterpreting, more or less radically, former understandings (Reed, 1996). The human relations school from the 1930s stressed the social dimension of organizations. It stopped viewing work organizations as machine-like phenomena to be optimized almost regardless of the human dimensions and drew attention to attitudes, norms and group relations. The contingency theory opposed the former ideas of finding one ultimate superior form of organization and during the 1960s it started considering how differences in size, technology and environment influence the way an organization is managed and how it should be designed and structured. By the end of the 1970s critical perspectives emerged within organization theory. Instead of viewing organizations as results of a rational consensus about means and ends satisfying the needs and wishes of the majority of participants, power and the self-interests of dominating groups were stressed as important to the organization structure. Class aspects and social domination were in focus. During the 1980s the cultural dimension has been included, drawing attention to how the values and understandings of different groups influence the way they view organizations and act within them. Recently, also variation among societies in terms of how companies are organized has attracted interest and it has been apparent that Western ideas about management and organization are not exhaustive of business practices. Nowadays we have not only become conscious of, but almost take for granted, the importance of group norms, organizational environments, organizational politics and corporate as well as societal cultures.

After these new dimensions have been incorporated into the conventional 'know-how' they appear as self-evidently important, and it seems almost unbelievable that once they were not seriously considered especially significant to research and higher education. It is likely, therefore, that new central themes will emerge and qualify our understanding of the way organizations work and how people live and act within them. It is only recently that gender has moved into focus in organization theories, and in a few years it will probably appear as very narrow-minded that it was not until the mid 1990s that large numbers of researchers realized that organizations are not just composed of gender-neutral components, but populated by men and women, and that organizations are characterized by gender-related practices, values, goals, logics, languages, etc.

The idea of gender studies: sensitizing thinking

Most conventional general thinking as well as social research concerning gender aims at finding out 'how it really is'. Does leadership by women differ from leadership by men? What are the causes of unequal payment? Why are there so few females at higher organization levels? How common is sexual harassment? Which values are held by women and men respectively? One idea of gender research is to provide authoritative answers to such questions and to develop valid theories about these matters. There are, however, great problems with an approach aiming to establish the 'truth' in gender studies as well as social science in general. The problems are of a historical, political and methodological nature.

Gender is a historical phenomenon. Gender is understood, developed and changed differently in different cultural contexts and times. There is variety between, as well as within, societal cultures. Men, women and gendered practices are dynamic, at least in modern society: they were different a decade ago and they will be different in the future. Social science is part of, and contributes to, culture and thus affects how gender understanding and practice will look in the future. Social science is affected by the historical context and intervenes in the making of history as part of the general cultural understanding. Consequently, social science does not only study gender, but contributes actively to the construction of gender as well. Cultural ideas and social practices rather than genes account for the ratio of male/female housepersons, clerks, nurses, engineers and managers. Social science is fused with cultural ideas and contributes to their development.

All statements and reasoning about gender issues are informed by value judgements and are never politically neutral. The idea of studying gender is one political choice, as is of course the 'non-choice' (not paying attention to gender). To treat the distinction between 'men' and 'women' as crucial is another. One may see other distinctions – age, sexual orientation, work orientation, ethnicity, life style, religion – as equally important or even more so, or simply refuse to divide up humans into two sexes, seeing the significance of this distinction as problematic in social science as it obscures variation and misleadingly indicates that the categories of 'men' and 'women' are universal and homogeneous.

Also how one treats different phenomena and exercises judgement is politically informed. Does one, for example, choose to emphasize what may be perceived as relative equality or relative inequality in gender relations? In Sweden, within the same occupation, women on average earn one to eight per cent less than men, when age, education, position, working time and experience has been accounted for (SOU, 1993: 7). In a Swedish context this is typically seen as inequality by those referring to these statistics, but in many other countries, where the difference is much greater, the gap may be seen as a sign of a relatively high degree of equality.[9] Values also inform choices at other levels. How does one strike a balance between voluntarism and determinism in accounting for human action? To what extent is a particular gender division of labour treated as the outcome of 'free choice', and to what extent does the researcher emphasize constraints in the form of discriminatory practices or sex stereotypes that produce different kinds of preferences and work orientations among women and men? 'Free choice' is never a simple matter but may be understood in terms of how cultural prejudices and expectations operate as forces of power and produce certain gender-stereotypical orientations and constraints discouraging people from engaging in sex role-incongruent behaviour. On the other hand, the researcher cannot just assume that she or he 'knows best', treat women and men as ignorant 'cultural dopes' or passively shuffled around by societal structure and disregard their espoused wishes and preferences as simple outcomes of the operation of power or false consciousness. There is no clear-cut or easy way of dealing with such issues, but how they are treated undoubtedly reflects the researcher's values and priorities. How the researcher deals with these issues is never politically neutral. In social science generally, it is impossible to avoid either questioning or reproducing existing ideas and institutions (Alvesson and Sköldberg, forthcoming).

Gender research – like other social research, but perhaps even more saliently – is thus clearly a political project. It intervenes in the negotiation of how gender is understood and thus in the (re)production of gender relations and society. This does not reduce its intellectual value and significance. Its value is, however, related to other matters than the offering of 'neutral' truths accomplished through the use of a scientific apparatus. The potential value is as a source of intellectual inspiration and as an input in ongoing conversation about how one should live one's life and shape political institutions, including companies.

Methodologically, gender relations and dynamics must be seen as a particularly difficult subject area. The most significant aspects are hidden and elusive. How social processes and cultural understandings produce and re-produce certain gendered social relations may only rarely be observed. Interview accounts about these matters may be more or less reliable. They tend to be strongly affected by the interview context and may be seen as part of a conversation following social norms for interaction rather than mirrors of pure experience (Silverman, 1985, 1993). Responses to survey questions are notoriously unreliable when it comes to issues which do not have a clear and simple meaning. Most complex and interesting issues are difficult to grasp through standardized questions. The research subjects attribute their own meanings to the questions – meanings that may deviate heavily from the meanings intended by the researcher. A particular problem concerns the subjectivity of the researcher. Although scientists are never objective, neutral and distanced towards their research, gender issues in particular are among the most personally sensitive topics one may study, meaning that existential matters, personal background and convictions, including political sympathies, are more at stake than if one is studying, for example, formal organizational structures or mergers and aquisitions or any other 'dry' subject.

Without denying that there are sometimes clear-cut answers to questions about gender which have some validity outside local space and time contexts, the major contribution of gender studies is not to produce robust and unquestionable research results which claim to establish the truth once and for all. Empirical research is undoubtedly valuable and should be central, but one must be open to the ambiguities involved and the historical and situated character of the empirical object as well as of the constructed and interpreted character of so-called data (Alvesson and Deetz, forthcoming; Calhoun, 1992; Fraser and Nicholson, 1988).

Gender over- and under-sensitivity

The purpose of gender studies is, in our opinion, to facilitate advanced thinking and reflection about gender and, thereby, about social relations, society, organizations and working life in general. Such thinking may be discussed in terms of counteracting under-sensitivity about the meaning and significance of gender in various contexts.

On the one hand gender studies should therefore aim to 'sensitize' academic disciplines, politics, management and organization decision making and, in particular, everyday life interaction of organizational practitioners about the genderedness of thinking, feeling, valuing, acting, material and social practices and structures. The major task of gender studies therefore is to oppose the persistent under-sensitivity and gender bias inherent in a lot of academic and everyday life thinking and social practices claimed to be gender-neutral. As we said, organization and management theory and managerial and working life practice often disregard the issue of gender. This book will show this in some detail.

On the other hand, however, the opposite problem also sometimes occurs in gender thinking, an inclination to gender 'over-sensitize'. This refers to a tendency in some research as well as everyday life to see gender as relevant and decisive everywhere, to emphasize the gender dimension consistently without fully considering other important aspects and dimensions. A gender perspective which assumes that male domination or patriarchy is the mechanism behind all sorts of miserable phenomena will legitimize indiscriminatory critique. Some authors do not seem to consider that it is possible to overstress a gender perspective – or the critique that it normally implies. Alternatively this risk is regarded as not significant enough to be worth taking seriously. One could of course argue that no distinction in society is more crucial than the one between male and female, that no areas therefore are gender-neutral. According to this line of thinking, everything thus bears a significant gender meaning and reflects or constitutes gender bias, normally to the advantage of men or to forms of masculinities. This argument may, however, be accepted while still insisting on the problems with gender over-sensitivity. That everything could be perceived as having some gendered meaning or that it may be difficult to point out non-trivial areas or issues that are perfectly gender-balanced or gender-neutral does not imply that a gender aspect is worth emphasizing all the time. Also aspects including a grain of 'truth' may be overstressed. Any perspective runs the risk of being used in a one-eyed fashion, reducing all phenomena to issues of men and women or masculinity and femininity.

Gender over-sensitivity thus means not considering or too quickly disregarding other aspects or possible interpretations. It means an over-privileging of gender and a neglect of alternative standpoints. It makes gender the only decisive factor, and this way gender as a mode of understanding becomes totalizing. The metaphors of masculinities and femininities take precedence and repress other metaphors/perspectives as interesting points of departures for interpretations and theories. One could in this case also talk about gender reductionism: everything becomes a matter of gender and not much else.

There are different themes to consider in terms of gender over-sensitivity. One relates to the political function of gender studies. If the political aspect is stressed too strongly, it may be perceived as propaganda. There is an inherent dilemma in gender studies – as in much other critical work – between intellectual curiosity and academic criteria about constrained political commitment on the one hand and political engagement involving a wish to speak for the underprivileged and encourage social changes to their benefit on the other. This dilemma – or set of dilemmas – may be formulated in different ways: between gaining academic respectability and saying something important unfettered by academic norms and conventions; between open-minded curiosity and a wish to use one's privileged position and skills to change the world in a liberating direction; between a wish to be as honest as possible and a drive to facilitate one's political cause (or career prospects) through the selective reporting of (and at worst manipulating) findings, arguments and language.

Making strong political points may call for emphasizing simple, coherent, politically correct descriptions and arguments, and reducing the scope for investigating and writing about complexities and contradictions. In particular, it involves a specific kind of rhetoric. Recognizing and emphasizing signs of increased equality or conservative tendencies among women in, for example, occupational preferences or family life orientations may weaken the case for female politicians and academics as well as perhaps risking impoverishing the base for one's own career as a researcher of gender studies, as this is normally tied to the strength of a case for discrimination and suppression of women.

A related aspect of gender over-sensitivity concerns the seductiveness of gender concepts and ideas. They may be used to account for – or at least illuminate – all types of phenomena: from nuclear power to analytical thinking and creativity and language use. Instead of open-mindedly and self-critically using ideas about masculinities and femininities, these ideas may control the researcher. One may see gender and gender bias everywhere. One element here is the extreme intensiveness of the very personal and emotional character of gender. As mentioned above, gender issues involve much more of the researcher as a person than most subjects. This may be inspiring and enrich the research process – private experiences may be used productively as input – but there are also problems associated with over-sensitivity worth taking seriously. Balancing rich experiences with qualified interpretative and reflective work calls for self-critique and scrutinizing of one's own biases, use of vocabulary, selective memorizing, over-generalization from single cases and repressing alternative viewpoints. Or to say it more plainly, to be (pain)fully aware of the strong tendency not to believe it when one sees it, but to see it when one believes it (Weick, 1979).

It is hardly possible to state what is under- and over-sensitivity once and for all and seldom easy to evaluate when either of the tendencies imprints itself in a specific case. These terms have little to do with what is 'true' and 'false' and it is impossible to prescribe an appropriate degree of gender sensitivity. The terms signal problems worth reflecting on and talking about. Critics may be of help in pointing out imbalances. Sometimes the signs that somebody has fallen into one of the two traps of under- or over-sensitivity are strong. In the case of under-sensitivity for example, it is not an atypical experience during a lecture on gender that someone, sometimes a woman, protests against the claim that gender is significant in organizational contexts and suggests that 'we are all individuals'. This is of course not untrue, but the meaning of an 'individual' is hardly gender-neutral. 'Female' and 'male' individuals are encountered and do encounter themselves in various ways, involving expectations, constraints and rewards/punishments associated with dominating discourses about gender. In this section, we focus primarily on the issue of over-sensitivity, as this point is underscored in the gender literature and it is not the primary topic in the remains of the present book. Here are two examples.

A feminist friend met a woman whose (feminist) paper she had (anonymously) reviewed for a scientific journal. The paper was rejected and the author mentioned this outcome and attributed it to the journal's not wanting feminist papers. This conclusion seemed to be somewhat premature. The journal had sent this paper to be evaluated by people who encouraged and were positive towards feminist work (such as our friend). The paper was, however, rejected because it was simply not good enough ('logically flawed'), according to the opinion of people that, in principle, were supportive of feminist work.

The author in this case felt discriminated against because she was doing feminist work and this experience is undoubtedly valid in many cases, although perhaps decreasingly so in many countries. The problem is that one might end up attributing all kinds of negative outcomes to discrimination. One simply 'knows' that women and feminist academic works are often discriminated against. One is a woman, doing feminist work – ergo, one is the victim of discrimination if the paper gets a negative treatment when submitted to an academic journal. In this case, however, the paper may have had substantial scientific problems and was rejected for this reason (according to our informer).

Another example was that of a female professor at an American University who complained about sexual harassment when a reprint of Goya's 'Naked Maya' was placed in the lecture room (according to the Danish daily newpaper, *Information*, June 1994). This may be seen as taking the concept of sexual harassment rather far; little space is left for other considerations about the painting, such as the value of art or the preferences of others (men and women).

The story has another point too and also illustrates a case of under-sensitivity to gender. The Danish newspaper journalist (a male) describes the episode as a 'bizarre example' of developments in US society. This strikes us as somewhat unreflective. Even if the interpretation 'sexual harassment' by the female professor appears to be a too mechanical, puritan and intolerant way of reacting to the painting's presence in the lecture room, the label 'bizarre' suggests that the reaction is closer to pathological than understandable. Given the domination of males gazing at objectified female bodies and its consequences for gender relations and stereotypes, the 'bizarre' overreaction of the female professor could also be understood less pejoratively and more empathically. Her experience could be respected, even though the act of complaining and demanding a removal of the painting could be seen as a lack of consideration of other values rather than avoiding anything that may be perceived as sexually offending.

The gender literature includes many examples of empirical material which is used in a way that makes it relevant to discuss in terms of gender over-sensitivity and reductionism. We will comment more specifically upon this later in the book.

How can one minimize the risk of gender over-sensitivity? Of course, this is a matter for careful discussion between people in relation to specific instances. In academic work, feedback and the sharing of opinions may also lead to better judgement. One possibility is to broaden the interpretive repertoire – the set of concepts, metaphors, theories, ideas and other interpretive resources that one masters, or others expose one to, and which makes it possible to see and note different kinds of aspects and use a variety of vocabularies and arguments when approaching empirical phenomena or developing theoretical arguments (Alvesson and Sköldberg, forthcoming). Instead of solely reading and utilizing gender theory, other theories should be an active part of intellectual work. Marxist ideas on class, critical theory ideas on technocratic consciousness, the possibility that the one-dimensional domination of consumer societies is turning citizens into clients and submitting consumers to administrative control, as well as Foucault's notion of the interrelatedness of knowledge/power and the production of subjectivity, may be valuable (Foucault, 1980, 1982). Instead of just incorporating these ideas into gender theory and using them only to support gender interpretation, these other theories and aspects may also make it possible to produce other kinds of interpretations than the gender-related one, i.e. to use another vocabulary and stress other points than gender. The common impression after reading a gender study is that not much but gender really matters. Even though it is usually recognized that there are considerable differences within the category of women, differences associated with class, race and ethnicity are normally seen – or at least treated – as secondary, as representing variations of a general pattern. It is common that researchers 'add' class and race to gender as sources of oppression (West and Fenstermaker, 1995). Of course, the whole idea of gender studies is to focus on and develop knowledge of gender, but this main focus does not need to imply a sole emphasis on gender issues and a total neglect of themes conceptualized in other terms.

To take the problem of over-sensitivity seriously, gender studies should have access to other vocabularies and be open to the use of these. Alternative aspects and interpretations to those favouring gender as a concept should be routinely considered. What is hidden or downplayed by the use of terms such as masculinity(ies)/femininity(ies), patriarchy, sexual harassment etc. should be reflected upon and the research text be 'opened up' so that some of the cracks in the approach become visible, counter-acting totalizing writing. The reader is thus activated in relation to the text and alternative interpretations can be considered (cf. Alvesson and Sköldberg, forthcoming; Rorty, 1989; Steier, 1991). Of course, gender studies are not only a matter of using sound judgement concerning *when* to invoke gender concepts. More crucial is *how* gender perspectives are used and interpretations are made. That is the theme of this book.

This book thus aims to contribute to a more intensively multi-level reflective way of doing gender studies, in which the researcher (or prac-titioner) considers alternative aspects, vocabularies and interpretations and carefully considers and acknowledges the limitations and shortcomings of the line(s) of inquiry taken. Of course, all research involves elements of reflection, but often the researcher devotes much more time and energy to developing and persuading readers about the reliability of empirical results or the virtues of a particular theoretical point. This is important enough but disregards basic uncertainties and problems. Taking a broader perspective, where not only knowledge about gender and organization but also various ways of knowing, problems in developing knowledge in politically hot and personally engaging fields are taken seriously, a more careful, reflective mode of understanding may be adopted. In the present book, we try to encourage such work in gender studies. We therefore address some different levels: (1) empirical reality, i.e. women and men in organizations 'out there'; (2) existing theories and ways of developing knowledge neglecting or focusing on gender in organizations, i.e. the frameworks that dominate research and education; (3) more general theoretical problems and pitfalls in the basic approaches – among researchers and other people – towards this fascinating but complex and difficult area of knowledge. The third point is meta-theoretical and relates to the more general theme of how a more reflective social science may be developed. Gender and organization may be seen as an example of social science in general, and some of the ideas expressed here of potential interest for reflective work in other areas. Throughout the book we, however, maintain a gender and organization focus and do not elaborate on the more general aspects in social science.

In the book we comment critically on parts of the literature and even on widely held views within the subject area. This should not be read as if we are particularly sceptical to gender studies or that this field is more problematic than most others. A reflective approach means that established ways of doing social science are critically illuminated and a reorientation is suggested. Earlier work by one of us, in which various research areas, for example organizational culture or leadership, have been reviewed and lines of development suggested has not been more affirmative than what is expressed in the present text (e.g. Alvesson, 1993; Alvesson and Deetz, forthcoming; Alvesson and Sköldberg, forthcoming). As gender studies are often marginalized and are faced with little understanding, not to say hostility, from conservative and gender-ignorant circles, we are eager to avoid our intentions being misunderstood or misused. We feel confident that a critical–constructive approach also addressing problems in developing knowledge about gender, and shortcomings in substantial parts of the existing literature, will be beneficial for gender and organization studies.

On readership and limitations

We have had a rather broad and mixed audience in mind when writing this book. We hope that it will be of relevance for academic and student readers in all areas of social and behavioural sciences interested in gender, organizations and working life. Organization and working life are of interest in, for example, management, sociology, psychology, anthropology, public administration and education. We use literature from all these fields, and also from history and philosophy. We are, however, taking studies from economics into account only marginally. In relation to anthropology we use culture theory to a considerable degree but we do not cover 'foreign' societies as we concentrate on Western, industrialized societies. In relation to psychology the emphasis is more on social psychology than on individual psychology associated with psychoanalysis.

The book has a broad focus, but is more oriented to qualitative issues of meaning and understanding than focused on quantitative concerns about frequencies, correlations and explanations. This does not mean that we want to emphasize the conflict between the qualitative and the quantitative, that we are very negative to the latter, or do not take such research results into account. We also utilize and discuss quantitative research and think it has value in relation to certain questions. Our emphasis is, however, interpretative.

The book is a mix of research and textbook; in other words, we aim to present an overview of the field and introduce gender perspectives while still hoping to make research contributions, e.g. add novel critique, ideas and a developed theoretical framework to existing knowledge. The research contributions are more prominent in the final sections of the book.

The book is international in scope, but not in the sense that we aim for constant comparisons. Comparison across several countries often implies a quantitative approach, and we are somewhat sceptical about what statistics may reveal about subtle issues. The international orientation is expressed instead through our attempt to utilize literature from a variety of countries. A restriction is that throughout the book, with a few minor exceptions, we only address highly (post-)industrialized countries, similar to our own. We assume that most of what we are saying is of relevance for Western

European, North American and similar countries – although variations between these (and, of course, variations within countries) should be borne in mind. We live in Scandinavia and our text reflects this; some of our comments may also be heavily influenced by the area in which we are located. We do not consider the book as a whole to be very ethnocentric, however, as we have read vast amounts of North American and European literature – in the reference list in particular US and British texts greatly outnumber Scandinavian works. We frequently remind the reader – and ourselves – that empirical studies must be considered in terms of where they come from and the specific empirical terrain they cover, for example, US female managers in the 1980s rather than female managers *per se*, and through referring to the national origin of a particular text. (The time period referred to in a study is normally indicated by the year of publication, so it is seldom necessary to point out the time of the research to the reader.)

In the book we have given priority to certain areas, especially gender division of labour, work and organizational cultures, identity, masculinities and femininities, work orientations, socialization, leadership and promotion patterns. Some areas are included but receive less attention, including sexual harassment, unpaid work, family and work, race and ethnicity, and earnings. We also devote little explicit space to how planned change may be accomplished, although it will be clear that we have greater faith in consciousness raising and learning than in efforts to accomplish changes from above through the use of, for example, sex quotas. Our emphasis in the book reflects our interests, competences and societal context, but also the wish to achieve sufficient depth, which makes it difficult to cover 'everything'.

The outline of the book

Above we discussed why and when to use a gender perspective on organizations. In the following chapter we will outline the different perspectives found within gender research. This field of research has become increasingly complex. The traditional view focusing almost exclusively on women as a neglected group or category within organizations has been replaced by a situation where several perspectives compete and where few assumptions can be taken for granted or be left unchallenged. In Chapter 3 we will deal with gender segregation, the horizontal and vertical division of labour. We will discuss the phenomenon of gender labelling – how jobs and tasks are defined not as open or neutral in terms of gender, but as masculine or feminine and thus more congruent with the male or female anatomy respectively. A related issue is why male jobs tend to be more valued and, in particular, are better paid than female. A particular aspect is that top-level jobs are generally viewed and characterized as masculine. But why is division of labour according to gender and gender segregation still common, and why have so few women reached top-level positions? These are questions we will explore in some depth in subsequent chapters. In Chapter 4 we deal with how constructions of masculinities and femininities permeate social life, and guide and constrain people's behaviour, in particular through defining the identities of men and women. Arguably, understanding masculinities and femininities is an important key to understanding gender division of labour and other organizational phenomena. In Chapter 5 we treat organizational culture in terms of gender and also discuss the construction of masculinities (and femininities) in specific organizational contexts. We will explore how rites, material expressions of culture and language reflect and actively construct gendered meanings. As most organizations are 'created' and/or headed by men, masculinity is the dominant characteristic of work functions and cultures. This chapter therefore to some extent focuses on masculinity rather than femininity. In Chapters 6 and 7 the focus is on women in management, especially promotion and leadership. While Chapter 6 summarizes the development of, and current research situation on, women in management, the subsequent chapter reviews contemporary assumptions and ideas about women in management from a four-way perspective. We look at some alternative positions in accounting for women's leadership style, difficulties encountered by women in attaining managerial jobs and some of their problems, such as a high stress level, when working as managers. In Chapters 8 and 9 we discuss the field of gender and organization from a broader perspective, treating organizational issues on the border between gender and other critical perspectives. We discuss some basic problems in gender organizational studies and suggest some ideas for an organization analysis that is sensitive to oppositions, ambiguities and local variations in different organizations, this way advancing our understanding of organizations as complex and interesting phenomena, where people live different lives responding to different initial conditions. We also touch upon how gender studies may avoid being ghettoized and cut off from mainstream concerns – still neglecting issues of gender. Moving to something in between gender-blind and gender-one-eyed understandings of organizations is seen as a vital task.

Notes

1 Although women on average only have 16 per cent of cabinet seats in the EU, there are wide variations within Europe, from Sweden where women account for 50 per cent of the cabinet members, to 39 per cent in Finland, 35 per cent in Denmark, 35 per cent in the Netherlands, seven per cent in the United Kingdom and four per cent in Greece.

The proportion of women in national elected assemblies in the EU also differs very much. The percentage of female members in all the national parliaments varies from 25 to 40 per cent in Austria, Denmark, Finland, Germany, the Netherlands and Sweden to 12 to 17 per cent in Belgium, Ireland, Italy, Luxemburg, Portugal and Spain, and finally to six to seven per cent in France, Greece and the United Kingdom (European Network of Experts, 1996).

2 In terms of gender equality we believe it is safe to say that almost no one escapes contradictions and inconsistencies in the attitudes expressed in different situations.

3 Of male employees three per cent are managers, whereas less than 0.5 per cent of female employees are managers in the private sector; in the public sector six per cent of male and 1 per cent of female employees are managers, according to official statistics (SCB, 1996).

4 In Sweden, as in most other European countries, senior positions (professorships) are held by a limited number of university teachers; most faculty members are lecturers. When the above statistics about the low degree of female professors were published, they were interpreted by politicians and others as a clear indication of gender discrimination in employment practices and the parliament decided to have 30 professorships plus a number of junior positions reserved for women, in order to improve the imbalance. A more cynical interpretation would be that they wanted to do something that would serve as proof of commitment to equality. Then some investigators showed that the number of women appointed as professors was in almost perfect correlation with the number of women applying for the positions. In other words, a female applicant had the same chance of getting the position as a male applicant. This, of course, does not prove that universities are in fact gender-neutral. It is likely that there are complex patterns associated with the way science is constructed – often in dry, impersonal terms – and that various kinds of gender biases, perhaps more pronounced some time ago than at present, account for the limited number of female professors. Many academic cultures may be based on masculine values. This is not different from what is typical for most parts of working life, in Sweden and in other countries.

5 One may argue that capitalism, or at least certain versions of it, carries a heavy ingredient of male domination and that gender equality would mean abandoning or domesticating capitalism. Capitalism cannot, however, be reduced to male domination, but needs to be explored also in non-gendered terms.

6 They have, however, addressed gender in other writings (e.g. Dachler and Hosking, 1991; Legge, 1987).

7 Sex and gender are overlapping concepts. Sex is typically seen as referring to biological sex, i.e. the fact that nature produces people as men and women. Gender refers to how men and women are being formed through social and cultural processes. The distinction will be critically discussed later in the book.

8 Often diversity is reduced to considering the formula of gender, class and ethnicity (e.g. Ferguson, 1994). While acknowledging the risk of getting caught in complexity and detail, it is important to be aware of variation also within these sociological standard categories. There may be interesting diversities within black middle class US women, for example. People may also differ depending on which of their parents they primarily identify with: far from all identify with the parent of the same sex. Life style, nationality, sexual orientation, age, religion and family situation also account for variation as do individual differences.

9 Gender wage differences are more pronounced between women's jobs and men's jobs, i.e. in occupations dominated by males and females respectively. In Sweden, on average, women earn about 75 per cent of what men earn. In the UK women's average pay is around 72 per cent of men's (Rees, 1992) and in the US women's wages average 70 per cent of men's (Reskin and Padavic, 1994).

2

Different Perspectives on Gender

In the previous chapter we argued for a gender perspective and touched on some of the main problems in a general way. This chapter presents some alternative perspectives and their respective problems and difficulties.

Gender studies are dominated by feminism. There are various opinions about how this broad orientation should be defined. Most authors emphasize that feminist theory critically addresses the subordination of women with the aim of seeking an end to it. Chafetz, for example, defines a theory as feminist 'if it can be used (regardless by whom) to challenge, counteract, or change a status quo which disadvantages or devalues women' (1988: 5). Historically, feminism is connected to the struggle for women's economic, social and political independence. It goes beyond theory and research as it also refers to political and social practice. Here we are mainly interested in theory and research, so feminism should be read as feminist studies in this book, unless otherwise specified. Many contemporary feminists also think it is important to consider class and racial oppression as part of feminism.

We prefer the concept gender studies to feminist studies for several reasons. The most important is that gender relations can and should be investigated in other ways than strongly 'pro-female' ones, i.e. the objective of gender studies is not necessarily solely to support the presumed interests of all or some women and to deal with what is seen as disadvantaging (many or some) women. More diversified aspects of gender are also called for, including the study of men and masculinities, a growing although still undeveloped subfield. An isolated focus on women appears too narrow as women can hardly be understood without considering gender relations. It is also problematic, as we will elaborate below, as it tends to treat 'women' as a robust and unitary category. Diversity within the category means that it is not always obvious how certain conditions relate to the interests of different groups of women. Nevertheless, in this and other chapters we often talk about feminism as it is a dominant concept and orientation within gender studies and other authors frequently use this label. In many cases, it gives a more precise description of the orientation of an author and/or a school. The overlap between feminism and gender studies is sufficiently strong to enable us to use the words as synonyms in many contexts, even though the latter term covers a broader area and indicates a more open (and less committed) attitude.

The main part of gender studies seems to evolve around three major points: (1) the notion of gender is central to and relevant to understanding

all social relations, institutions and processes; (2) gender relations constitute a problem as they are characterized by patterns of domination/
subordination, inequalities, oppressions and oppositions; (3) gender relations
are seen as social constructions. They are not naturally given – offsprings of
biology – impossible to change but an outcome of socio-cultural and historical conditions, i.e. of processes in which people interpret and (re)create
the social world. Gender is the effect of social definitions and internaliza-
tions of the meaning of being a man or a woman. Gender can therefore be
radically changed through human action in which gender is redefined. Social
definitions and processes, not nature, form gender, according to most
feminists – although some also see biology as significant. The social nature
of how men and women are developed has motivated a preference for the
label 'gender' instead of 'sex'. The latter is often said to refer to biological
sex, while gender refers to the culturally constituted forms of masculinity
and femininity that produce the specific ways in which men and women are
developed in a particular society (see Chapter 1, note 7). The distinction is
somewhat unclear (Hallberg, 1992), as ideas about biology are social
phenomena – understanding biology is not just a matter of letting nature
speak for itself (Kaplan and Rogers, 1990) – and most people interested in
gender nevertheless take biological identity as a given point of departure and
talk about 'men' and 'women' as unproblematic, easily identifiable categories. Sex thus dominates. Therefore we are not inclined to stress the sex–
gender distinction, but follow praxis and use the former term when social
constructions are not very central and the bodies of women and men are
seen as the criteria for identification, while the term gender is used when
emphasizing the more social and cultural aspects. We see the terms as
overlapping, rather than distinguishable.

The various positions within feminism can be identified and classified in
different ways. A common way is to classify positions according to their
political standpoints; that is, distinguishing them according to the way they
view society and what they consider to be desirable changes, one typically
talks about liberal, radical and socialist feminism. *Liberal feminism* aims at
gender equality but does not seriously address or question any other aspects
of society than the ones which directly influence and disfavour women and
their opportunities. A slightly ironic interpretation of this position would be
that the idea is only to make upper-class women equal with upper-class
men, working-class women equal with working-class men and minority
men and women equal within the minority without considering other
possible forms of oppression and injustices in society. Society is seen as
worthy of critical scrutiny only in those respects which clearly disfavour
women's access to the same options as men and where men obviously are
oppressing women (e.g. sexual violence). For liberal feminists gender
primarily means strict comparisons of men and women and a commitment
to reducing differences unfair to women. *Radical feminism* rejects the male-
dominated society as a whole and claims that women – when freed from
the dominance of patriarchal relations – should aim to transform the

existing social order radically or even to develop their own social institutions. This radicalism is based on the assumption that women have
different experiences and interests than men and/or that women have
radically different orientations than those characterizing traditional and
contemporary patriarchal society. Radical feminism does not aim at
competing with men on equal terms or to share the benefits – top jobs,
higher wages, access to formal power – on a 50/50 basis, but wants to
change the basic structure of society and its organizations and make
competition a less central notion. *Socialist feminism* is partly inspired by
Marxist theory and studies society in a critical way with the ambition of
contributing to a radical change where new gender relations are included as
central elements. A significant example is dual systems theory which is
based on the idea of an alliance between capitalism and patriarchy in early
capitalism (Hartmann, 1979). This alliance is believed still to exist at a
social level today as men hold the formal positions of power in politics and
work life. While liberal and radical feminism mainly focus on improving
the living conditions of women – especially when it comes to career possibilities (for liberals) and sexuality and economic independence (for radicals)
– socialist feminism focuses on changes in society in a more general way
that will also benefit other unfairly treated groups, including groups that
are not restricted to only one sex (the poor, the working class). The
oppressive features of capitalism are highlighted. It also takes issues such as
ecology seriously, seeing exploitation of nature as an inherent characteristic
of capitalism and its dominating, masculinistic logic.

Another common way of classifying gender positions is according to the
researcher's view on *knowledge*. There are different ontological and epistemological positions, i.e. fundamental assumptions about the basic
character of social reality and in what sense one can develop qualified
understandings of it. The understanding of knowledge cannot be totally
detached from one's political standpoint but other elements are also
important, e.g. the understanding of the nature of language, of what
research methods are the most appropriate and what kind of knowledge
products are possible/most valuable: precise empirical description and/or
testing of hypotheses, valid theories, insights, change-stimulating arguments, practical advice and so on. One important dividing line concerns
whether gender is only an object of study or also a part of research,
explicitly or implicitly imprinted in theoretical frameworks and methodological ideals. Research ideals such as objectivity, neutrality, quantitative
measurement may, for example, be seen as gender-neutral or strongly
masculine.

We will follow Harding's (1987) distinctions and vocabulary here. She
classifies the dominating orientations into: gender as a variable, a feminist
standpoint perspective and poststructuralist feminism. It seems to be the
most commonly used framework for review purposes (e.g. Olesen, 1994).[1]
It identifies the three most common orientations, especially in the context
of organization studies. We will also incorporate some of the other

distinctions that overlap her three categories. Even though the evolution of gender research could be described in terms of phases, this does not imply that the development is one-dimensional or that one phase follows logically upon the other. In a certain way all phases are present at the same time and different subjects are rooted more or less firmly in different phases. Most research on organizations where gender is considered is rooted in Phase 1 (gender as a variable) even though this is at times combined with Phase 2 (feminist standpoint theory), while an expanding body of research has Phase 3 (post-feminism) as its starting point. Often this is, however, combined with elements of the political commitment salient in Phase 2.

Of course, all distinctions and ways of dividing up a complex, hetero-geneous and rapidly expanding research area are problematic. They inscribe order and obscure disorder, ambiguity and variety. Thereby they invite not only simplifications but also distortions. A number of authors and texts are difficult to press into the scheme. Combinations and syntheses are common and there are also orientations emphasizing other aspects than those focused upon here, for example, psychoanalytic feminism. We do believe, however, that Harding's model is of pedagogical value and adds to the understanding of the field of gender studies, at least for the newcomer.

The 'gender-as-a-variable' perspective

The first line of approach views gender (sex) as a variable and maintains women as a relevant and unproblematic research category. One is basically interested in comparisons between men and women in terms of inequality and discrimination and aims to explain such phenomena. Traditional (male-dominated) research within a number of different disciplines has disregarded women as a category and failed to pay attention to possible differences between the sexes (Acker and Van Houten, 1974). The gender-as-a-variable perspective investigates if, in what respects, under which circumstances and to what extent men and women differ in terms of subjective orientations (psychologies, ethics, values, attitudes) and how social structures and processes affect them. Various forms of gender inequity are measured and explained. Understanding gender requires that research pays careful attention to the specific conditions of women and does not take equality between the sexes for granted. We should therefore take possible differences between men and women into consideration when we want to understand different kinds of economic, social and psycho-logical phenomena, ranging from horizontal and vertical division of labour, class differences and salaries to work motivation, recruitment and selection, leadership style, and political and moral values. A large part of this research 'adds' women to the analysis of different phenomena.[2]

In the beginning of the 1970s, focusing on women and their conditions and how these differ from the conditions of men was a 'logical' conse-quence of the fact that women had been absent from or poorly represented in most previous research, both as subjects and as objects. Often, this approach shows a rather simple and unproblematic understanding of gender. It is very easy to classify people according to their (biological) sex, but defining the meaning and significance of this and finding out when, how and why men and women are treated differently can become a difficult task.

Variable research has been and still is a dominating trend within organization theory, especially within the field of women in management (WIM). It has been carried out since the 1960s, without much change:

> The majority of the women-in-management literature is still trying to demonstrate that women are people too. Consistent with the tenets of liberal political theory, it conceives of organizations as made up of rational, autonomous actors, whose ultimate goal is to make organizations efficient, effective, and fair. (Calás and Smircich, 1996: 223)

But other kinds of gender studies also use the variable approach as their starting point. For example, studies of gender wage discrimination or sexual harassment, and also studies that show how women are kept in an inferior position because of oppressive structures, and studies which show that differences in attitudes can be explained by differences in work tasks and job situations for men and women rather than by sex *per se* (Kanter, 1977).

The method of this approach can be quantitative as well as qualitative, but the former is probably most common. The variable perspective matches what Harding (1987) calls feminist empiricism; it finds that social inequalities and negative attitudes towards (or thoughtlessness about) women influence research. Feminist empiricism aims at making research more scientific – more objective, neutral and exact – by eliminating irrational (prejudiced) elements such as gender stereotypes hidden in the research design or in ways of reasoning. This view often ends up promoting a kind of gender-conscious positivism in which the sophisticated and non-biased treatment of the sex variable is emphasized. Even if some versions of feminist empiricism dissociate themselves from deduction, hypothesis testing and quantitative measurements, as is the case in certain empiricist qualitative methods, such as 'grounded theory', these versions can still be associated with a soft form of (neo-)positivism (Alvesson and Sköldberg, forthcoming; Guba and Lincoln, 1994).[3] Values such as objectivity and neutrality are held high, and assumptions about a robust reality out there which can be rationally studied through the rigorous application of the correct procedure are central.

Critique of the gender-as-a-variable approach

As mentioned, variable research is the dominating approach especially within management and psychology but also within other fields of gender studies. This approach has, however, been very much criticized, especially when it comes to the notion of science, the question of method and its rather restricted intellectual and political agenda. Nevertheless, neo-positivism has been and still is an unexpressed 'premise' in a lot of the scientific practices that make women (as well as other groups) the passive object of science and establish technical procedures as servants of truths and legitimizers of science as authority.

One type of critique is focusing on the naive view of language and the presumed possibility of mirroring objective reality through strict reliance on techniques. Critics claim that the results of trying to measure gender relations by means of questionnaires, observations of experiments or even (semi-) structured interviews are very unreliable. Formulations in questionnaires and interviews are typically interpreted in different ways by different people, and it is therefore difficult to know the intended meaning of a given answer. Even minor changes in the way the questions are formulated can make a big difference to the answers received. Questionnaires assume that language is transparent and that people's experiences, orientations and mastery of language are so straightforward that they can easily be expressed as responses in pre-structured formulations chosen by the researcher. On most issues, language and personal experiences as well as the very nature of social life are far too ambiguous to make such assumptions realistic (Alvesson and Sköldberg, forthcoming; Deetz, 1992a; Denzin, 1994; Potter and Wetherell, 1987; Shotter and Gergen, 1994; Silverman, 1985; Steier, 1991). When the possible answers are limited to those explicitly stated in the questionnaires, the questions and the response alternatives may not be appropriate to the actual experiences and meanings of the research subjects but only to the researcher's expectations. The problem is that language does not carry a clear-cut, simple and abstract meaning. Language use always depends on context and the interpretations of those involved. The idea that the researcher can control meaning and safely produce scientific facts through certain methods/techniques is naive. Language is simply not best understood as a medium that can mirror complex reality. Rather it portrays reality in a particular light, according to the language chosen, in what context it emerges and how it is interpreted by various readers.

In some cases the problems are particularly salient. In a lot of research about stereotypes respondents are asked to describe men and women for example in relation to management (e.g. Schein, 1975). The respondents are to choose between simplified and thus stereotypical response alternatives, preventing them from producing more qualified and nuanced accounts of how they look at the subject matter. Whether people in the study 'really' have stereotypical ideas or whether they are just 'victims' of a specific research design that make them appear in a certain way remains an open question.

A second problem with most variable studies is thereby touched upon: the artificial nature of the empirical material. Sometimes experiments are seen as the most rigorous method, because the researcher is supposedly able to control the variables involved and isolate pure effects, for example, of gender. In human studies, however, such research involves considerable problems. Often it may better be described as the study of the behaviour of students in simplified and artificial settings. It is thus a question of what exactly can be learned from laboratory studies. What seems to hold true in the laboratory does not necessarily correspond with what might be going on in the outside world. Similarly, responses to questionnaire items do not necessarily tell us very much about the social and psychological themes that researchers believe are revealed by marking crosses in questionnaires. (A similar criticism may be directed against interviews when accounts are treated as simple expressions of experiences and beliefs; see Potter and Wetherell, 1987; Silverman, 1993.) We are not suggesting that experiments or survey studies are of no value. They may often give us some valuable input to thinking and may be seen as arguments for why a particular view on a social phenomenon makes more sense than another one. But one should bear in mind the basic problems with this kind of research and not treat the results as the gateway to objective truth.

A third problem concerns issues of social totality and critical evaluation. Many gender-as-variable-oriented studies show only very simple statistical connections, occasionally claimed to be causal relations, whereas more comprehensive cultural patterns and structures or dynamic processes are not considered. The societal totality, where equalities/inequalities and sex-biases are established, is left outside or marginalized in studies focusing either on behaviour in an artificial setting (laboratory) or on counting responses to questionnaire issues. The variable approach leaves relatively little room for questioning the subject matter in a more critical way. The ideal of science as neutral, non-political and objective is increasingly seen as naive and outdated. This view appears as a mystification that misleads the public and constrains and self-disciplines the researcher. According to the critics, gender research should acknowledge and make room for personal and intersubjective experiences as well as judgement and reasoning about social context (totality) and not limit or subordinate the research to an 'apparatus' based upon rules, techniques and procedures. Questionnaires, data processing and tables thus do not provide a good picture of the phenomenon being studied. Arguably, abstract, technical, formal, seemingly 'author-free' writing associated with objectivistic research ideals presents the phenomena it aims at addressing in such a way that they become unrecognizable and little deeper understanding is achieved.

A fourth major problem with the variable view is that it often involves the researcher in objectifying and controlling the research subject. As mentioned above, the person constructing a questionnaire or an experimental situation typically defines the issue at hand and a narrow range of possible responses, and thus 'forces' the research subjects to respond to the questionnaire or to behave in the laboratory within a particular set of constraints, depriving them of using language in any non-trivial way to describe meanings, feelings and cognitions. We have discussed the methodological problems above. Here we want to address the ethical problems involved. The subordination of the research objects to the researcher's definitions of what is important, which questions should be answered or which stimuli responded to, reproduces the existing social inequalities and passivization of certain groups, including many women, and that is exactly what a lot of gender research, as other critical research, is trying to overcome. Many feminists are concerned about the ethics of the relationship between researcher and researched and want to minimize the asymmetries and power relations involved (Acker et al., 1991; Davies and Esseveld, 1989; Finch, 1984; Olesen, 1994). The restriction, and thus silencing, of voices other than those legitimated by elites, including researchers, is consequently an important drawback of a lot of variable-oriented studies, according to critics. For political and ethical reasons, less constrained, constraining and objectifying research methods should be used.

More generally, variable studies are often characterized by imitating established ideas and models in social science without adding very much in terms of novelty or taking more sophisticated ideas on gender into account. As Calás and Smircich evaluate the research on women in management, 'it is difficult to find any gender-specific theoretical development among these works. The questions that are asked, and the research approaches that are followed, mimic those developed and utilized in research that does not emphasize gender' (1996: 223).

It should be added that the variable approach is not necessarily limited to quantitative measures; qualitative methods are also possible. Sometimes the pretence of objectivity, and a technocratic view on method, is less pronounced and the space for research subjects to express their meaning is greater. However, much variable-oriented qualitative research basically shares the commitments of quantitative neo-positivism (Alvesson and Sköldberg, forthcoming; Guba and Lincoln, 1994). In both cases variable studies maintain a fixed definition of women and men and focus on comparing these and the given conditions. Our critique therefore is also valid for the neo-positivistic qualitative studies which assume that 'data' collected and analysed through the rigorous adherence to technique and procedure lead to the production of truths. In any case, the quantitative approaches are predominant within the gender-as-variable perspective. This is especially the case in the USA but also in academic psychology more generally. We must add that not all the problems mentioned are present or significant in all variable-oriented research. In general, variable-oriented research tends to be based on neo-positivistic ideas about the separation of theory and data – or at least treats theory and data as if separation is possible – and most such studies are at least to some extent plagued by the problems discussed above.

We will not discuss what we believe to be a just criticism of neo-positivism any further but refer to some of the existing literature on the subject (e.g. Alvesson and Sköldberg, forthcoming; Denzin and Lincoln, 1994; Hollway, 1989; Morrow, 1994; Potter and Wetherell, 1987; Steier, 1991, etc.).

The feminist standpoint perspective

This perspective stresses the importance of a broader and more profound documentation and theorizing of women's situation and experiences. Gender is seen as a fundamental organizing principle of patriarchal society; social relations (of all kinds) are heavily structured by hierarchical differences in the social position of men and women. The feminist standpoint perspective proceeds from an assumption of the existence of specific experiences and/or interests of women that differ radically from those of the majority of men, at least with regard to how these experiences and/or interests are formed and expressed under contemporary (patriarchal) conditions. Many researchers are aware of the possibility, indeed likelihood, of variations in terms of women's espoused interests or manifest orientations across time and culture, but they de-emphasize this point in favour of women-alike or shared experiences arguments. Below the variation of surface manifestations of groups of women, some common logic or basic themes are seen as uniting them. Widespread oppression and devaluation of women are regarded as central features of society and its institutions.

While feminist empiricism often matches liberal feminism, the feminist standpoint perspective rather matches radical and socialist feminism, even though it could also, to a certain degree, be combined with a more liberal political standpoint. Some of those who strongly emphasize early psychological development as the origin of feminine orientations are more liberal than radical. The political relevance and commitment is, however, much more emphasized within the radical and socialist approach.

> Feminist theorists must demand that feminist theorizing be grounded in women's material activity and must as well be a part of the political struggle necessary to develop areas of social life modeled on this activity. (Hartsock, 1987: 175)

Science is not merely a question of searching for 'the truth' (or even of research grants and promotion); even more important is the question of being socially engaged and stimulating social changes. The scientific respectability and justification is therefore secondary to the production of knowledge with a social and political relevance and impact. The purpose is to contribute to emancipation from oppressive social conditions. Harding (1987) calls this position *the feminist standpoint*. The empirical standpoint research focuses on making the lives of women visible, viewing women as more than variables to be considered in comparison with men, presenting women mainly as victims, but also as active participants essential to the creation of their own lives. Research tends to be pro-women and the focus is often strongly on women, rather than, as in variable research, on comparisons of men and women. Hartsock proposes 'theories for women – theories which begin from the experience and point of view of the dominated. Such theories would give attention not only to the ways women are dominated, but also to their capacities, abilities and strengths' (1990: 158). Women tend to be seen as a combination of victims and fighters of oppression, as morally good and/or as carriers of particular insights (e.g. Spender, 1981). When men are considered it is often at a rather abstract level associated with patriarchal structures.

This perspective assumes that there is something that characterizes women as such and that women – irrespective of differences associated with class, age, ethnicity, etc. – have something in common. This unique and unitary femaleness is seen as originating from a variety of sources, for example positions in the relations of production (reproduction), a universal status as the second sex, where men are culturally defined as the first and as superior, a specific female sexuality, experiences associated with childbirth and childcare and/or a language that generates a certain feminine 'logic', common feminine values or a general way of relating to the surroundings. Care or rationality of care (Sørensen, 1982), love power (Jonasdottir, 1991) and capacity for mothering (Chodorow, 1978) are all common notions in this regard. Specific qualities tend to be associated with women: sensitivity, nurturance, emotional expressiveness, social orientation and social skills. Most researchers are now sensitive to the notion of essentialism – the idea of defining women in terms of a universal, stable basic quality – and want to avoid biological explanations or lines of inquiry emphasizing the existence and social significance of biological differences *per se*. Nevertheless, standpoint feminism implies that biology is viewed as being of some significance, without having definite, determinating impact. Cockburn (1991: 162) is probably representative in saying that we should not ignore biology and in arguing that 'the social practices that structure gender relations neither directly express nor are without reference to natural biological differences'. She emphasizes childcare as of particular significance for the orientation of women.

Many authors focus on an abstract system or structure rather than individuals or specific actions and conditions when accounting for gender relations.

> Patriarchy as a political structure seeks to control and subjugate women so that their sexuality, childrearing, mothering, loving, and laboring are curtailed. Patriarchy as a system of oppression recognizes the potential power, which derives from the necessity of society to reproduce itself. By trying to affect woman's sexuality, their reproductive capacities, and their labor by individual men and society as a whole. The sexual organization to control women reflects the priorities of patriarchy. (Eisenstein, 1981: 14–15)

To the extent that men – and not an abstract system – are viewed as of interest, they are sometimes seen as the enemy, or at least as carriers of patriarchal structures and values. They then often appear as evil-doers, primarily engaged in the domination of women. Men are seen as homogeneous in certain vital respects. Although it is recognized that men differ – as women do – and that men dominate other men, it is emphasized that 'men in organizations are . . . part of the social category of "men" and the gender class of men' (Hearn, 1993: 150). They have political interests in common with other men, benefit from being men and may, when they occupy senior positions, 'be leaders and articulators of men's interests against women' (p. 150).

In principle, feminist standpoint research has a larger range – addresses a broader set of issues – than the gender-as-a-variable perspective. All significant aspects of society are, in principle, seen as gender-relevant. The institution of science is – like all other sectors – heavily gendered. According to standpoint feminists, traditional science is influenced by masculine assumptions, priorities and central notions, giving the enterprise a narrow and constrained orientation. The predominant principles and rules of science are seen as essential parts of patriarchal dominance, preventing the exploration of vital social issues, such as an in-depth understanding of gender, including the experiences of women. The ideal of positivism – the dispassionate, neutral, objective, analytic, number-crunching researcher – is viewed as expressing a masculine bias (Jaggar, 1989). Often, standpoint researchers are not very eager to stress science as a central base and criterion for their writings.[4] Instead of arriving at the ultimate 'truth' or insight, input into rethinking and political consciousness-raising may be crucial guiding values for standpoint researchers. The question of whether women have different understandings of reality, whether they are attracted by, or would benefit from, alternative ways of creating knowledge, has therefore been raised by researchers, leading to an interest in feminist methodology (Harding, 1987; McGrath et al., 1993; Olesen, 1994). The goal of emancipation, an interest in personal experiences and of connecting everyday life with an underlying social order (Acker et al., 1991; Smith, 1989).[5] The feminist standpoint approach maintains that including the experiences and interests of women is necessary to reduce the knowledge bias, for example in organization studies. While the gender-as-a-variable perspective (feminist empiricism) views sexist research as bad research, as specific examples of how biased ideas interfere with research in terms of design, focus and reasoning, the standpoint approach considers almost all traditional research to be sexist if it does not take the interests, experiences and insights of women seriously. This opinion, however, creates some problems for standpoint researchers. To maintain a feminist perspective in science is not at all easy in the light of the dominating notions.

> [A] feminist standpoint is not something anyone can have by claiming it, but an achievement . . . To achieve a feminist standpoint one must engage in the intellectual and political struggle necessary to see nature and social life from the point of view of that disdained activity which produces women's social experiences instead of from the partial and perverse perspective available from the 'ruling gender' experience of men. (Harding 1987: 185)

In terms of methodology, alternative approaches giving more room for personal experiences and critical insights are usually preferred. This normally implies a qualitative approach, even though a lot of qualitative methodology is very much focused on techniques, protocols and other means of de-subjectifying the entire enterprise, thereby possibly also male-biased. The idea is that research founded on women's experiences and interests will have something special to offer. Harding, for example, states that the personal experiences of women are a 'significant indicator of the "reality" against which hypotheses are tested' (1987: 7). It is believed that the marginal status of women enables them to develop certain kinds of insights. It is argued that an excluded and exploited group can provide science with more adequate and critical descriptions and interpretations than is possible when only the point of view of a more privileged group, i.e. men, is available. The female experience 'is a more complete and less distorting kind of social experience' (p. 184), because women have a double consciousness: they have knowledge of the dominant (male) culture as well as their own. The standpoint position claims to provide alternative insights compared to those established, well-known and, therefore, taken for granted.

This perspective is usually related to – and justified by – claims about women's concrete and unambiguous experiences of discrimination and oppression. Ferguson (1984), for example, argues for a feminist attack on bureaucracy, that is, the common way of structuring organizations and the underlying rationality that has been very much influenced by a masculine rationality characterized by individualism, hierarchy, lack of emotions, impersonality and a competitive mentality. Ferguson promotes a critical understanding of the repressive character of modern organizations based on 'the concrete and common interests of women' (1984: 27). Cockburn advocates a women's movement in organizations in order to strengthen women's position and self-confidence 'so that we can re-introduce our bodies, our sexuality, and our emotions on our own terms' (1991: 159).

Within organization studies, standpoint research is primarily expressed in the form of critical investigations of organizational practices (e.g. Cockburn, 1991; Ferguson, 1984) or in studies of feminist organizations – organizations oriented to the needs and goals of women using principles and means viewed as feminist (e.g. Brown, 1992; Morgen, 1994). The latter include combining the private and the public, considering life as a whole also in the context of work, building upon feelings of community and using democratic means of coordination.

A version of feminist standpoint theory is the (pro-feminist) male researcher who is less focused on women *per se*, but is interested in patriarchy and masculinity as oppressive forces. What may be referred to as an 'anti-masculinity' standpoint tends to associate men and masculinities with privileges and domination of women. This orientation may ironically be referred to as 'male masochism', as its representatives portray men in critical and pejorative terms. In Hearn, for example, men appear to be primarily engaged in the domination and control of women, experiencing joy from beating other men in games and wars (domination of women is, however, according to Hearn, not joyful as it is taken for granted) and inclined to use violence against women in organizations (1993: 153). Men come through in the text as rather negative characters: the metaphor of the aggressive brute may enter the mind of the reader.

Critique of the feminist standpoint perspective

The main problem of this perspective, according to critics, concerns the ontological basis for claiming a specific standpoint based upon 'women's' experiences. To what extent can women's experiences be said to be uniform? Based on ethnicity, nation, class, age, profession, sexual orientation, religion, and so on, women, and men for that matter, are very different. Different historical periods and different cultures change the notion of man and woman and the connected experiences. Even when it comes to individual backgrounds, life styles, courses of life and political and ethical standpoints variations are considerable (Chafetz, 1989). Within a specific category of women, for example US white middle-class women in their thirties, some are heavily consumption-oriented, others less so, some appear to think that children are the most important thing in life, while others see work as equally significant or as the prime source of satisfaction. Some women are pro-, others are anti-abortion. Even though the voting behaviour of women differs somewhat from men in many countries, they tend to be somewhat more leftist – possibly contingent upon women more often being employed in the public sector and benefiting from the welfare state – but they, like men, vary, from radicals to conservatives. The claim of speaking on behalf of all or even a larger group of women is therefore questionable, sometimes even criticized for being an ethnocentric expression of white middle-class women (e.g. Mohanty, 1991).[6] Critics thus claim that feminist researchers have repeated the criticized universalization and narrow perspective prevalent in what they see as masculine research, only exchanging traditional notions with female experiences that are often understood to be generalizable and superior.

The standpoint feminists argue that the oppression of women and their status as the secondary sex is a universal feature and that all, or at least most, women to some extent have such experiences (e.g. Daly, 1978). But oppression is not a simple, straightforward and one-dimensional phenomenon. It may be interpreted in many ways and take many different forms, being neither uniform nor similar for women, nor in many areas restricted to them. At a universal level such terms become too abstract and remote from the rich variety of complex and contradictory experiences. Research that is based on 'concrete and common experiences' of women (Ferguson, 1984) easily ends up with a narrow scope, as the experiences may vary tremendously.

Feminists are of course aware of the fact that the category of woman is heterogeneous and that gender never appears in the abstract, but in the context of a variety of social and material situations. Considering all variations such as race, ethnicity, class, age, profession, sexual orientation and individuality would make the whole issue very complex and make the text very difficult to follow. Therefore, it is often hard to avoid, in research and discussions on gender, as on race, ecology and class, '. . . a flattening of the world and a silencing of other voices . . . all human characteristics, relationships, investments and viewpoints unrelated to the binary are suppressed' (Gergen, 1994: 61). Some authors of books, in which more aspects can be treated than in an article, do, however, succeed in addressing some of the variation within the overall category of women and also, to some extent, that of men (e.g. Cockburn, 1991).

One way of handling the diversity problem would be a differentiated approach departing from specific groups of women, for example, elderly skilled British female factory workers or young black female MBAs in a particular US industry. The experiences and perspectives of these specific groups can then possibly be defined and studied, if one is open to their unique as well as possibly diverse experiences and accounts. Also within a social category, diversity may be prevalent. For example, in a study of Swedish female civil engineers and MBAs of the same age, 55 per cent answered that they had felt themselves discriminated against (negatively treated) at work on at least one occasion because of their sex, while 58 per cent answered yes to the question, 'Are there situations in which you think you have been differently treated because of your sex in a positive direction?' (Wahl, 1992: 298–9). (Of course, the questions are independent. One may sometimes be positively, sometimes negatively treated contingent upon any characteristic.) There is also considerable variation within negative and positive sex-based work experiences respectively.[7] These figures indicate considerable variation in terms of the experiences associated with gender at work. This is also illustrated in research carried out among Swedish female physicians in which one head physician said, 'I have little in common with 25 year old junior physicians with small children' (Sahlin-Andersson, 1997).

Of course, if a few other dimensions (age, industry, ethnicity, immigration status, family status, sexual orientation) are considered, some of the hetereogeneity may be accounted for, with the risk of the attention to gender issues being weakened and the general relevance getting lost in favour of the details of the highly special situations. Still there may be insights of relevance far beyond the specific focused group or setting. Variations and shared experiences/orientations could be investigated within a manageable, and in certain respects homogeneous, group. Alternatively, one could restrict the focus to a relatively limited set of experiences/ conditions seen as typical for a relatively broad group of women, such as conflict between work and family for female professionals. This is in line with the methodological suggestions of some standpoint researchers that one should proceed from the specific location of (a group of) women. But if the interest is in a group of women (engineers in pharmaceutical companies, parents with mentally disturbed children, UK voters, for example) there is an a priori tendency to read into and emphasize something universally female in the group being studied (e.g. being oppressed, communitarian, nurturing). In other words, even if a distinctive standpoint for women does not necessarily imply 'a general attribute of women as a class of persons', it is still assumed that there is 'a mode of experience that is distinctive to women' (Smith, 1989: 34) and that this indicates something close to universal. Even a more local version of studying female perspectives and experiences therefore has difficulty in avoiding some of the problems mentioned.

There is often a contradiction between wishing to make a politically relevant contribution on the one hand, and on the other, acknowledging the ideal of expressing only what is implied in, or at least gets reasonably strong support from, specific empirical material.

Fletcher (1994) suggests that the feminist standpoint approach is interpreted not as exclusively grounded in experiences of all or even many women, but as forming a counterpoint to mainstream understandings. This means that 'the fact that not all women speak in "women's voice" as currently defined, and that some men do, is beside the point'. The alternative to stereotypical male models is developed, however, through 'listening closely to women's experience' (p. 81). The rationale for this counter-argument to critics of the feminism standpoint is somewhat confusing. One could propound a feminist perspective without a grounding in claims about women's experiences, and pay the price of losing the legitimacy and force of such grounding, but if one does refer to women's experiences, it appears to be important to explain which women and which experiences, and to address the problems and possibilities of generalizations.

A problem with the idea of genuine experiences and in particular the idea that feminist research is mainly about, or proceeding from, an exploration of women's experience concerns the vague, ambiguous, often contradictory and always constructed nature of experiences. Experiences are not just out there in the subjectivities of women, waiting for the emphatic and egalitarian feminist researcher, in a dialogue, to stimulate their straightforward expression and subsequently 'mirror' them in research publications. Experiences may be made sense of, constructed and told in many different ways. Depending on the assumptions and interest of the researcher and the dynamics between her/him and the interviewee, very different accounts (or stories) may be produced. Experiences can not only be expressed in different ways, but are also affected by the vocabularies and interpretative frames that guide how one makes sense of the world and talks about one's experiences. We must consider that discourses at macro as well as micro levels influence the accounts produced by interview subjects. Experiences and accounts of discrimination are not independent of talk about gender inequality in society at large. In a social context in which such vocabulary is unknown, females may be more inclined to experience what may very well be interpreted as stereotypes and discrimination as 'natural' for women. Frequent discussions on gender inequality, for example in the mass media, on the other hand may lead to over-sensitivity to any sign of the absence of equality, perceived as disadvantageous for, and as discrimination against, women. But also what takes place in the interview situation is crucial for the way experiences are recounted. The interaction and language used by the researcher in the interview does not so much tap the subject about her genuine experiences but is also productive in constructing these. The assumptions, style and vocabulary of the researcher greatly influence what comes out of the interview. The researcher is active in constructing an account – or story – of the interviewee. Researchers must carefully consider the complexities involved in the constructions and accounts of experiences and cannot simply rely on accounts of experiences as the crucial element in developing knowledge (Hammersley, 1992; Silverman, 1985, 1993). Critical assessment and theoretically informed interpretation are always necessary. The risk that these tend to confirm one's point of departures and assumptions is significant – and a broad reading of gender studies indicates that relatively few findings deviate from established wisdom in the field; although qualitative work may be more problematic in this regard than quantitative studies, as it is a little easier here to produce selective interpretations based on assumptions and expectations.

There is a tendency in some feminist standpoint research to give a strong privilege uncritically to women's experiences, seen as carriers of superior insights. Elshtain's critique of 'systematic know-it-allism' is relevant here. It is characterized by an 'unquestioned inner authenticity based upon claims to the ontological superiority of female being-in-itself' (1981: 129). A similarly focused critique concerns the tendency to put a female way of knowing against a male, dominant version.

> There is no male science, or female science. True, the experience of women differs from that of men. I would rather state this differently: some women's experiences (in plural) differ from some of men's. Does this mean that their scientific methods have to differ? (Coser, 1989: 201)

A strong tendency to look for one perspective capable of explaining all oppression is related to the whole idea of assuming something universal about the situation of women as the point of departure for a general critique of dominating social relations. This is usually thought to be work/ economy (capitalism), patriarchy, sexuality, childcare or language. The cause of the oppression is described as a phenomenon that has always existed and is relatively independent of limited historical contexts (e.g. patriarchy). Looking for the universal explanation of asymmetrical gender relations simplifies it and does not take the enormous variations of gender relations seriously enough.

The concept of patriarchy, embraced by many but not all standpoint researchers, appears to be particularly problematic in this respect, tending to function as a totalizing concept reducing historical and cultural variation to the status of different versions of the essence of patriarchy.[8] Even though some contemporary theorists talk about patriarchies, i.e. in the plural (e.g. Hearn, 1993; Walby, 1992), it is clear that the essence of male domination over, and the victimization of, women is given a universal status and that this aspect is privileged over other ways of understanding society. Assumptions that 'men have political interests with other men' (Hearn, 1993: 150), and that the contemporary society is a patriarchy, 'a system of social structures and practices in which men dominate, oppress, and exploit women' (Walby, 1990: 20), (1) underestimate the role of subjectivities – interests and orientations anchored in their ways of being rather than in abstract, elitist sociological categorizations; (2) neglect enormous social variations within the categories of men and women; (3) underestimate what the large majority of men and women have in common (e.g. interest in clean air, peace, good housing, safe transports, unpoisoned (healthy) food, low criminality, good schools, low unemployment, low inflation, preferences for autonomy and variation at work, etc.); and (4) simplify the notion of 'interests'. This is, of course, not to deny that some men share some political interests or that women frequently are dominated by men.

It is easy to agree that being a male is a significant symbolic resource in many areas of life in general, and especially in work organizations, and that women and women's work are often devalued, but there are also situations and areas where men do not enjoy the privileged position that they do where formal power, status and income are concerned. In the context of work organizations, the lower life expectancy of men may indicate that not only the good things in life, but also certain strains have an effect on the work and life situation of men more than women. Studying oppression, hierarchy and discrimination are certainly core themes for gender studies, but not the only relevant themes to study. Defining women primarily as victims of patriarchy freezes the intellectual project too categorically.

The most significant problem with a lot of standpoint thinking is that its broad-brushed view on patriarchy, men and women, means that variation, complexity and contradiction are lost from view. By assuming and searching for the feminine viewpoint one too easily finds confirmation. Aspects of organizations falling outside what is addressed by the dominance–resistance–victim vocabulary tend not to be seriously considered.

The question of variation is exactly what the third perspective of feminism revolves around.

Poststructuralist feminism

Poststructuralist feminism (postmodernist feminism), sometimes shortened to post-feminism, questions the gender categories that were taken for granted by the two perspectives previously described.[9] Notions like men and women, the male and the female, are no longer viewed as fundamental, valid points of departure but considered to be unstable, ambiguous and attributing a false unity (Calás and Smircich, 1992b; Flax, 1987; Nicholson, 1990; Weedon, 1987). One might rightly ask what is the common significance of 'woman' when applied to a 70-year-old, retired Brazilian schoolteacher as well as a 14-year-old girl from the New Delhi slum, a Norwegian female prime minister, a black single mother of several children in South Africa, a young MBA career woman on Wall Street and a lesbian upper-class middle-aged artist in Victorian England? There are hardly any interesting common social and cultural characteristics or meanings for these 'women'. Even the biological sex of these women has different and maybe even contradictory meanings in different situations: in the gynaecological clinic, in relation to (non-)marriage and sexuality, children, family, different employment situations, in political elections, etc. Because of these considerations some researchers think unitary notions such as 'woman', 'feminine gender identity' and 'mothering' are problematic as they imply a false unity and suppress divergence and variety (Fraser and Nicholson, 1988). The general understanding that language is not simply a mirror of reality but has validity only within, and in relation to, a specific local situation–context, seems to support this standpoint. The meaning of 'woman' is not universal, but varies with the language contexts – discourses – in which it is used. Also other favoured concepts such as masculinity, dominance, hierarchy or discrimination may indicate a misleading unity – if the use is not governed by an appreciation of the local context giving these words some meaning in particular instances. This understanding is intimately connected to the poststructuralist understanding of language, as something more and other than a neutral and simple reflection of reality. Deetz (1992a; 1992b), for example, stresses that the words 'man' and 'woman' do not simply represent a given reality 'out there', but communicate a certain way of making people aware of what is the case 'out there'. No use of these notions is ever neutral. The distinction reveals that the identity of the subject is constructed as woman or man, and that people are defined as objects with certain rights and characteristics. When the chain of definitions (signifiers) has become a net the woman can be viewed as mother in a family relation, as wife in a marriage relation, etc. In every case, the way possibilities and limits have been defined by institutional dispositions provide the individuals with advantages as well as disadvantages. The distinction, however, remains arbitrary. Definitions are arbitrary in the sense that distinctions based on gender can be neglected or become irrelevant or questionable from one moment to the other, and the relational system of concepts can therefore be generated differently.

This understanding of language not only has consequences for addressing what is naively seen as specific and robust categories, but has drastic consequences for our attempts to develop knowledge in the traditional sense of the term. Methodologically, all observations and interview accounts are contingent upon the vocabulary and distinctions applied and there are always alternative ways of representing phenomena. This means that social reality as well as 'inner life', for example, attitudes and feelings, become problematic and difficult to account for in any self-evident or objective way. All descriptions tend to be seen as arbitrary and stand in an ambiguous relation to any phenomenon 'out there'. That words used to describe, for example, feelings or values say something definite or clear is not accepted, at least not without reservation.

Female experiences – like all experiences – are therefore not seen as robust, language-independent concepts and points of departure. According to Flax (1987) gender must be understood as a social relation, as this is the only way of identifying women and men as parts of specific societies. Apart from some aspects of anatomy the notions of men and women (masculine/ feminine behaviour, work, etc.) are generated and defined in various ways in different situations. A specific women's standpoint is therefore seriously questioned by this perspective. It is argued that 'the most important single progress within feminist theory is the fact that gender relations have been questioned. Gender can no longer be viewed as a simple and natural matter of fact' (Flax, 1987: 627).

Poststructuralism is an intellectual movement – or rather, several rather heterogeneous streams – that has been very influential within social studies since the late 1980s. The understandings of language, individuals, how science works (or doesn't work) expressed in poststructuralism and related writings (particularly by Derrida, Foucault, Lyotard) have had a significant influence on parts of gender research. Many maintain that there is a considerable overlap between a poststructuralist perspective and a feminist position (Flax, 1987; Nicholson, 1990). Like the poststructuralists and many others prior to them, feminists have also revealed the political power of science and argued against the illusion of objectivity and neutrality.

The poststructuralist critique represents what has been called the *self reflective phase* in the evolution of gender research. The 'self' being reflected on is, on the one hand, the constructions of men and women and, on the other hand, the theoretical traditions drawn upon within gender research (the 'self' of the research community). The perspective thus introduces a general scepticism as to universal understandings whereas differences and variations become central notions. Any attempt at a true or ultimate understanding is rejected, as are most uses of statistics, based on the idea that representing reality in numbers indicating 'the truth' means that diversity is suppressed.

According to poststructuralism the world is a fragmented place, and analytical notions of race, class, gender, woman and man are therefore also fragmented. Since the categories are differentiated within themselves they cannot be used as common, unambiguous concepts. Every attempt to generalize notions that do in fact cover a wide range of variations and differentiations is therefore most questionable. As notions, women and men are linguistic constructions and should therefore be dissolved in order to reveal the underlying diversity and complexity. Talk about men and women does not simply reveal objective reality but is part of discourses uncoupled or loosely coupled to any possible reality out there.

While both empiricism and the standpoint perspective try to find a stable ground for a feminist science that is, at least in some regards, superior to traditional research, poststructuralism questions the very idea of finding a universal ground for reason, science, progress or even the subject. The feminist search for 'truth' – or the 'genuine' female standpoint – is seen as just one more attempt to conquer reality, and it prevents researchers from addressing ambiguities, diversity and fragmentation and understanding how reality is rhetorically constructed rather than discovered by social researchers. Rather than developing valid knowledge based on a firm methodological standpoint or a strong political commitment, sensitive listening and providing space for alternative voices is celebrated.

As opposed to other gender researchers the poststructural feminists stress the arbitrariness and vulnerability of social constructions. Gender as a label and a guideline for identity and experiences is viewed as arbitrary and contradictory. Gender identity and gender-related ideas about social and individual phenomena must therefore be understood as dynamic, indeterminate phenomena. Static and specific definitions and correlations are of no use and must be replaced by such questions as, What is, in the local situation, defined as masculine and feminine? What does such labelling obscure? What is the significance of these definitions when it comes to creating and recreating subjectivity, that is, the feelings, cognitions and self-image of a person? In other words, what are the effects of language use? What is the dynamic of gender relations? What is expressed by the notions of gender? The point that specific and final answers are not possible probably remains the most important. All answers must be understood as not only historically limited, but also locally oriented. Gender and gender relations differ at different times and places. To repeat, 'men' and 'women' – like other signifiers – have only a precarious, temporal meaning tied to the context in which these words (signifiers) are used.

The theme of stressing the local and avoiding the universal, totalizing in language use and theorizing has then two aspects related to different levels: one concerns the level of generalizability, where the local means awareness of history, culture and social variation; the other concerns the dynamics of different micro-situations, meaning that all language use changes with micro-context and it becomes impossible/difficult to 'generalize' or compare meaning even across micro-situations *within* a specifically defined, limited setting. The meaning of 'female' may, for example, change many times during a work day, even from moment to moment.

Acker (1989: 78) asks, 'How do we put together the myriad standpoints of women?' From a poststructuralist perspective this question should be given a critical meaning, not intended to search for a positive answer, but to encourage critical reflection on how this is actually done, that is, how order is created and fragmentation suppressed. The poststructuralist avoids putting standpoints together, thus hiding the diversity; instead the myriad should come through in research texts and *not* be put together.

For poststructuralists the gender perspective cannot be specifically related to men and women in organizations. Instead, discourses about men and women – as expressed and constituted in the use of language – become central. A discourse may be defined as a set of statements, beliefs and vocabularies that is historically and socially specific and that tends to produce truth effects – certain beliefs are acted upon as true and therefore become partially true in terms of consequences. Different discourses produce different effects. There are no independent objective truths existing 'before', or independent of, a discourse.

Viewed as an important phenomenon in society that saturates all cultural relations, fragmented gender relations and discourses may be traced in the basic structures of social institutions and our general concepts of goals, rationality, values, and so on. Gender can therefore be useful as a perspective on, or a metaphor for, understanding organizations, for example. The gender dimension could be stressed on a more abstract level than the actually existing relations between men and women, for example, one is not counting bodies or taking accounts of experiences as 'truths' or even valid viewpoints. Calás and Smircich (1992a: 227) suggest a radical reinterpretation of organizational thinking in terms of gender: 'We will examine how the idea of "gender" can become a strategy to question what is commonly presented as organization theory. We would also like to start discussing how this leads us to a different way of writing "organization".'

This kind of feminism disregards the level of the individual subjects and replaces the interest in forming essential ideas about gender by, for instance, an interest in trying to make dominating organizational and management relations visible by illustrating them in terms of masculinity, or rather masculinities. Talking about 'corporate strategies' could for example be seen as a way of expressing/enforcing a masculine identity by using terminology from the military (Knights and Morgan, 1991). This kind of research strategy avoids the problem of defining men and women based on biological criteria and also bypasses the assumption that there are experiences tightly bound up with this biological equipment. To the extent that men and women are of interest to study, it is the discourses in which they are constituted that are relevant to explore.[10]

The purpose of research is thus not to develop 'truths', but to show the contradictions and problematic claims of efforts to establish truths, to open up and destabilize cultural meanings and beliefs that appear too rigorous and unproblematic. Discourses defining 'women' and thus tying and subordinating these subjects to this signifier – locking subjects into the fixed identity of being a 'woman' – are critically examined.

Within the general commitments of poststructuralism – giving privilege to language, diversity, fragmentation and the local – one may distinguish between a *strong* and a *weak* version. The former pays exclusive attention to a discursive level, where the social reality is cut off and sceptical analysis of rhetorical claims is made in texts. All accounts – interview statements, conversations in everyday life, academic texts – may be seen as texts to be analysed in terms of structure, how claims are supported by rhetorical moves and undermined by contradictions, repressed meanings and alternative representations. This branch, here broadly defined, is called deconstruction and aims at showing the false robustness of claims. It is a relatively strict approach, antithetical to empirical work and empirical claims, at least as this is normally understood. In feminism it is primarily used for the critique of texts expressing dominating views on women (e.g. Calás and Smircich, 1991; Martin, 1990). The weaker version sees language as precarious and loosely coupled to social reality but maintains an idea of some relation, although an uncertain one, between words and a social reality beyond language. Texts may throw a certain light on social conditions. Something 'out there', apart from language use, 'exists'. Ideals such as fragmentation, diversity and an emphasis on the local means that one holds back strict theorizing and the prospect of generally valid points, including universal concepts (class, race, men, women). Empirically oriented work takes the accounts of interviewees seriously, but these are seen as multifaceted and context-dependent, not arising from a uniform subject (a consistent and integrated individual) mirroring genuine experiences and viewpoints. Accounts have a narrative quality, following their own logic of story-telling. Discourses form the subjects' experiences and accounts, which are open for a variety of representations (descriptions) and interpretations. For the purpose of the present book, it is the weaker version of poststructuralist feminism that is of relevance (cf. Fraser and Nicholson, 1988).

Critique of poststructuralist feminism

The poststructural critique has turned upside down a number of dominating ideas within gender research, and it is especially popular among those who take an interest in theoretical and philosophical questions. Researchers more inclined towards empirical research have been more sceptical and found the orientation unhelpful, not to say destructive.

One line of critique maintains that the ideal of diversity and variations is strongly exaggerated. Most researchers now probably accept that it is not reasonable to consider our universalized and abstract notions of gender, reproduction, sexuality, marriage, man, woman, etc. to be adequate when applied to a wide range of different cultures, groups in society, historical periods etc. But this does not exclude some generalizations which could be relevant or even necessary in order to say anything of any interest.

> In our determination to honor diversity among women, we told one another to restrict our ambitions, limit our sights, beat a retreat from certain topics, refrain from using a rather long list of categories or concepts, and eschew generalisation. I can think of no better prescription for the stunting of a field of intellectual inquiry. (J.R. Martin, 1994: 631)

Bordo (1990) also finds the emphasis on diversity problematic as it easily leads to a mechanical and coercive requirement that all enlightened feminist projects should take race, class and gender seriously. One cannot include many axes and still preserve analytical focus and argument, she argues. In addition, the ideal of diversity would mean that research does not stop with adding class and race to gender. The list of what diversity may draw attention to is endless: sexual orientation, ethnicity, age, family conditions, occupation . . . these categories may also, and quite contrary to poststructuralist ideals, be seen as unitary, macro, a priori. Discourses involving these variables may, from a poststructuralist point of view, call for deconstruction – showing the fragile and contradictory nature of the way they are used – rather than be understood as positive and authoritative guidelines for what should be explored. Another objection to poststructuralism does not question the value of the approach as such but its current relevance to feminist studies. Di Stefano (1990) finds poststructuralism a valuable inspiration for reflections within academic fields that have already obtained a certain stability and strength. This, according to Di Stefano, is not the case with feminism, and the disturbance of ideas and notions that is usually the result of poststructural reflections could therefore have very destructive consequences. Bordo also feels that poststructuralism would seriously harm the critical potential and political impact of feminism and argues that it is too soon to let our institutions 'off the hook via postmodern heterogeneity and instability' (1990: 153).

Another criticism is that the importance of language is overestimated at the expense of empirical studies. Gender is being reduced and considered as nothing but a discourse on men and women; all that can be done, therefore, is to destabilize ideas and terms. It is difficult to maintain that anything 'is' in any 'positive' sense, that something is actually the case. No statements claimed to convey truth are accepted as such, but are treated as claims always less robust than they appear to be. This way everything is in danger of becoming relative – or becoming common sense expressions that are only reasonable from a very specific point of view and use of language. At least the stronger forms of poststructuralism could be seen as expressing a kind of language reductionism. The linguistic aspect is privileged – in the stronger version the non-linguistic is expelled from inquiry – and everything else becomes a commonplace and almost uninteresting object of science (Alvesson and Sköldberg, forthcoming). Against this view of language as self-contained, social conventions giving language an agreed-upon meaning in combination with social shared understandings of the context-dependencies of language use may be said to lead to statements being able to say something 'valid' (empirically anchored) about something 'outside' language.

A lot of the critique of poststructuralism concerns its (lack of clear or focused) political implications. Identifying suffering and problems 'out there', for example, in organizational life, and suggesting lines of thinking improving the life conditions of people is discouraged by poststructuralist thinking. This may be subversive in problematizing and deconstructing dominant discourses, thus opening the way for alternative ways of relating to the world. But poststructuralism may equally well be used against observations and accounts of discrimination, suffering and unjustice. Any form of critique with a claim to express the truth or a better judgement may be disarmed. Poststructuralism tends to leave the existing social reality outside its agenda and may be criticized for encouraging esoteric and conservative orientations, an expression of the narcissism of academic 'text workers' (Sangren, 1992). The research agenda becomes narrow, of interest solely for people fascinated by academic authorship and texts and uninterested in the lives and problems of people in general.

In practice, most feminist poststructuralism in social science avoids the extreme poststructuralist position that totally ignores humans as beings of flesh and blood and regards all accounts of oppression and injustices as mere linguistic expressions. Instead, most researchers have some interest in political issues and in promoting change. Fraser and Nicholson (1988) are inspired by poststructuralism and criticize mainstream feminist research, but find that studies making empirical claims are legitimate and reasonable if they are aware of and acknowledge their historical and contextual limits; that is, if they avoid the problem of overgeneralizations and fixed categories. They thus adhere to a 'soft' or 'weak' version of poststructuralism. Its relevance for social research is thus maintained but the approach easily becomes a bit muddled. Sometimes authors move between a strong and a weak version in an unfortunate way. This mixture of the philosophical position and a more robust feminist perspective addressing reality 'out there' – although a reality that is constructed by the researcher and open to a variety of representations and viewpoints – is a common attitude among feminists who take an interest in poststructuralism. The risk of too salient inconsistencies, however, is hereby considerably increased and the perspective easily becomes self-contradictory and confused. Weedon (1987) for example sometimes expresses rather conventional, objectivist statements – typically when she wants to characterize patriarchy and the injustices done to women – while more often arguing along a poststructuralist line which radically doubts the validity of statements and discourses which she views as working against women's interests and opportunities.[11]

A critical–interpretive perspective

The three sketched perspectives in Table 2.1 reveal different and important dimensions of gender research. The most central differences, probably, concern their focus on the importance of political involvement and their expectations as to the possibility of obtaining, by means of good research, dependable and valuable knowledge of reality 'out there'. The writers of this book tend to subscribe to a middle position in this table; a position that could briefly be described as critical–interpretive. This critical–interpretive perspective should be seen as a loose, basic orientation rather than a distinct, clearly elaborated theoretical position. Used as a general framework this orientation can be very useful when trying, as in the case of the present book, to describe and comment on the field of gender research rather than promoting distinct viewpoints. This demands a certain amount of straightforwardness regarding preferences and bias among the presented theories, and a clear line of thought that allows for coherence within the text but still counteracts personal preferences from influencing the presentation of the different theories in an unfair way. Neutrality, however, is never possible in such questions, and instead an effort should be made to treat criticism of all theories in a serious way, even when they concern

Table 2.1   *Comparing the perspectives*

Politics	Conception of knowledge ideal		
	Robust truth, validation of theories/hypotheses	Positioned truth, valid points, insightful arguments	Avoiding 'truths', resistance through opening up/ deconstructing
Political engagement		Feminist standpoint	
Doubting, sceptically committed		The position of this book	Feminist poststructuralism
'Cool', constrained commitment	Variable perspective		

standpoints one approves of and would usually defend. The critical–interpretive perspective could also be the starting point of empirical research, but in this case it would have to be combined with more specific theories.

The characteristics of our version of a critical–interpretive perspective are influenced by insights produced by poststructuralist feminism as well as other modern philosophies of science, hermeneutics and variations of critical social studies (Alvesson and Sköldberg, forthcoming; Deetz, 1992a; Denzin and Lincoln, 1994). A certain, not to say considerable, amount of scepticism is part of this influence. As opposed to poststructuralism, we tend to find that some degree of scientific rationality is possible. Empirical studies may be taken seriously, which does not exclude a concern for differences, variations and considering 'undecidabilities'. Moreover, we find it is important to say something of relevance to the world outside a specific, narrowly defined local context. Language is a significant and problematic theme for reflection in research, but it also offers the possibility of illuminating important phenomena and seeing them in constructive perspectives. Carefully used, language opens up more than it closes in terms of constructive understanding, although the element of closure (the use of a specific vocabulary discourages alternative understandings) cannot be neglected. Theory – in the sense of a framework and vocabulary offering a line of interpretation and understanding sufficiently abstract to work across empirical situations – is desirable and necessary. The risk of absolutism, however, should be handled (1) by incorporating elements that allow for reflections on language, perspective dependency and one's own rhetoric, and (2) by alternating between alternative perspectives and interpretations, letting these confront each other (Alvesson, 1996a; Alvesson and Sköldberg, forthcoming). These two methodological principles overlap and facilitate each other. Rorty's (1989) ideas on irony are relevant in this regard. The writer should be aware of the fact that alternative interpretations are always possible and should therefore maintain a certain distance from his/ her own writings – so that neither the writer nor the reader are led into believing that they are witnessing the final and ultimate 'truth' or the superior interpretation.

Now we will deal, in a more detailed way, with the characteristics of our favoured approach. An essential element of our perspective is a social and political involvement, which implies an emancipatory interest – although we are modest about its potential and well aware of the dangers in critical research such as elitism and negativism (cf. Alvesson and Willmott, 1996: chapter 7). The critical–interpretive perspective, however, tries to avoid the desire to stimulate social changes being one-sidedly privileged, and does not take it for granted that research can do much more than suggest questions to be reflected on and discussed without any clear-cut political objectives, offering arguments, illustrations and raising question marks (not evidence) for certain understandings. In this way research contributes to a larger and more reflective sensitivity towards gender questions. As opposed to many traditional feminist ideas of describing the 'true' nature of the patriarchal society in a broader way, this position is, on the one hand, more doubting as to what an adequate description of the multifaceted and varied character of actual society would be and, on the other hand, also more humble as to its own contributions in this regard. There are very few safe truths on the subject matter and these tend to concern relatively simple issues.

Instead of being strongly politically committed and risking the political–propagandist aspects getting priority, the critical–interpretive approach tries to avoid a highly selective use of examples and a vocabulary that scores extra rhetorical points rather than stimulating critical reflections. Describing women as victims and (many) men as brutal oppressors can, at times, be fair and important, but this kind of thinking grows out of proportion in some feminist literature and studies of masculinities – normally, though, worded in a more sophisticated way. We will give examples later on. Other, less negative, aspects of gender relations could also be worth considering in a serious way.

The critical–interpretive approach identifies with unfairly treated groups and wants to bring forward their voices and interests – although not without critical interpretation. Possible alternative meanings – in relation to dominant ideas and understandings – are exposed by studying different ideologies, ideas and discourses, helping to clarify social phenomena and ideas in a new way in order to provide a broader foundation for understanding and dealing with gender relations. Simplified and one-sided descriptions of asymmetrical structures of power and interests should, however, be avoided. We find any universal notion of patriarchy problematic. Expressions such as 'women's interests are subordinated to the interests of men' (Weedon, 1987: 2) are far too general and thereby partly misleading. Other general observations can be opposed to this kind of expression, making the whole picture considerably more complicated – for example that men have shorter lives than women. Secondly, more specific studies of, for instance, workplaces show large variations as to how gender relations are organized. This of course does not exclude acknowledging that

Weedon's proposition could, in many specific cases, be relevant and that gender studies should be critical to forms of male domination. However, a less totalizing and more local understanding is preferred, one that is sensitive to variation and contradiction in superiority/subordination as well as to the meaning of 'interest'.

It is thus important to maintain that gender relations vary considerably not only between different societies, cultures and other macro-categories (lesbians, class, ethnic groups, age, profession, country), but also within and across these categories. Research should be sensitive to these variations, and within organization research it could be relevant to consider how different branches, workplaces and occupations, or even different situations and processes within the same workplace, constitute and express gender relations. An interpretive sensitivity does not, however, imply stressing differences and variations as far as possible, as in the case of poststructuralism. There is as little reason to give privilege to diversity and fragmentation as guidelines for inquiry as there is to emphasize generalized patterns. Instead of avoiding universal categories altogether, they are used in a locally defined situation but with the ambition of finding patterns as well as variation in the local case. One should be very careful when generalizing or using universal concepts such as men, women, patriarchy. Not only local grounding but also middle-range conceptualizations – universalizing across micro-situations but not across history, class and society – should be seen as a valuable ideal.

The interpretive perspective tries to get a deeper understanding of limited empirical phenomena. Questionnaires and similar methods are considered of little value in exposing complex connections of meaning. These methods can be useful for comparing simple, non-ambiguous, comparable relations such as salary, educational level, possibly formal positions (even though titles and statistics can often be misleading and may tell us little of social status and work tasks). The interpretive approach uses qualitative methods when trying to capture images, ideas and understandings as well as more subtle practices. Ethnography is the preferred method. This method aims at an intimate and deep understanding by combining long-term observations of everyday life with unstructured (loosely structured) interviews. Empirical studies are considered important even though it is admitted that they cannot provide us with any ultimate truths; results are always contestable and open for reinterpretation. Researchers have a tendency to find what they expect. At the most, empirical studies can provide us with a basic understanding and input for further, more differentiated considerations and theories. Empirical material can also be used as a more or less strong argument for a case of how one should represent and understand a specific piece of social reality (Alvesson and Sköldberg, forthcoming).

Another central aspect of the research approach is the element of criticism of the ideas and meanings expressed within the social groups and situations that are being studied. Instead of embracing a non-evaluative attitude towards the meanings produced by the subjects being studied, as most interpretive research tend to do, this approach allows for critical viewpoints that can stimulate reflections on these ideas, values, experiences and practices. Critical investigations are thus not only directed towards abstract categories such as patriarchy, capitalism or class society, but also embrace the subjectivities and the 'politically incorrect' feelings and orientations of people. Challenging and stimulating rethinking of established ideas, theories and social practices is important.

Critique is also important in relation to different gender research approaches. Many feminist researchers believe that criticism should be restrained; instead they stress the importance of support and acceptance (for example, J.R. Martin, 1994). Feminists should stick together at least until it has become a more established field of research, they say. Hirsch and Keller (1991) suggest that the long-time tendency among feminists to suppress awareness of diversity and conflict may reflect poor skills among many women, perhaps especially white US middle-class women, to cope with constructive conflict. Although some researchers agree with a lot of the poststructuralist criticism, they reserve the critique for more established and perhaps stagnated targets (Di Stefano, 1990). A critical–interpretive approach does not share this opinion. Contemporary feminism is increasingly characterized by debate, critique and the acknowledgement of conflict. The time has indeed come for critical studies of the different approaches to gender research. Gender research is sufficiently broad and powerful; the literature is huge and rapidly expanding; the field has a sufficiently long history and in most of the countries that this book relates to (Scandinavia, Western Europe and North America) its legitimacy and political support is also sufficiently established to allow for and motivate a more thorough critical research. Neglecting this would be a disservice to gender research for two reasons. In the first place, critique is essential as a correction to bad ideas and, thereby, an inspiration for reconsiderations and more careful empirical studies and theoretical developments. Critique stimulates development.[12] Secondly, the idea that community and support are essential to feminist research and that it is too frail and unstable to be able to withstand critique only promotes a questionable and problematic identity. As Elshtain notes, the repeated evocation in feminist discourse of images of female helplessness and victimization blocks self-critique and self-reflection:

> The presumption is that the victim speaks in a pure voice: I suffer therefore I have moral purity and none can question what I say. But the belief in such purity may itself be one of the effects of powerlessness, and that belief, congealed in language, is endlessly self-confirming. It loses any edge of self-criticism, and a feminism that cannot criticize itself cannot, in the last analysis, serve as a bearer of emancipatory possibilities that can never be fixed and defined, once and for all. (1981: 136)

The resistance to questioning and critique of and within feminism (gender studies) agrees with stereotyped notions of women – considered to have difficulties handling critical feedback – thereby promoting the asymmetries in working life that have been documented by feminist research, for example the lack of support experienced by women in career development and promotion. It also prolongs a tolerance for problematic ideas and styles that contribute to low respect and impact and thus a shaky identity, whose fragility is said to call for constraints in critique.

It should be remembered, however, that 'rough' discussion patterns can sometimes be related to scientific, male-dominated, conventions.[13] The critical approach should therefore be careful when promoting the value of criticism, and it should be very aware of the risk of becoming a question of fighting for positions and prestige, thereby losing its constructive element (Gergen, 1994). It is therefore important to reflect on the tone and style of the critique. Self-critique and confrontation of one's favoured line of interpretation with counter-ideas and alternative interpretations becomes important (Alvesson and Sköldberg, forthcoming).

A final point concerns language. Not only the choice of vocabularies, but also how one views language, is crucial in all research. Language is not a simple medium for transporting meanings; it is a system of differences where some meanings and relations between meanings are hidden. A word like masculinity, has for example, no simple and absolute meaning. There is no one-way relation between the notion and some cultural or social reality 'out there'. This does not mean that the term is unable to describe a social phenomenon or stimulate thoughts about social reality, extrinsic to language, but it is important to recall the hidden and suppressed meanings that give the notion an arbitrary and relative meaning. Masculinity pre-supposes femininity which again presupposes masculinity. The meaning is unstable and dependent on context and perspective. The fact that the relationship between language and reality is not simple and one-sided is sometimes used by poststructuralists as an excuse for focusing on language alone, on deconstructing texts only and in this way avoiding the question of 'extra-textual' (social and material) reality as such. On the other hand conventional researchers, including variable researchers and to a large degree standpoint researchers, tend to avoid the complications of philosophical questions on language by ignoring them and treating language as a tool for communicating 'facts', genuine experiences and abstract, general theories. A critical–interpretive approach must find its way between these two positions. Language is ambiguous. All descriptions and ways of talking about subjects and things are in a certain way arbitrary and liable to redefinitions. Language does not mirror anything outside, it re-presents. But language has the ability to accomplish shared understanding – if only in a precarious form. Researchers should therefore consider their use of language very carefully. Alternating between different vocabularies – using theoretical as well as empirical/low-abstract terms – could be a useful way of not subordinating the researcher and the reader to a particular vocabulary (and way of thinking). The ideal is to present theories and reflections in a way that generates open-mindedness. This is difficult to do and it must be seen as an effort and ideal rather than something that is (fully) accomplished. Dealing specifically and exclusively with language is, on the other hand, not essential to a critical–interpretive point of view. Language is important as a theme for reflection and as the object of study but less significant than the ambition of making empirical studies and generating interesting interpretations and theories. Language will of course always be a part of this, but it is not necessarily treated as the most important. It is definitely not seen as the sole and exclusive concern – impossible to go beyond.

Theory, in the sense of abstract ideas and concepts integrated in a framework for understanding, having some empirical relevance, is of course an important part of all research. The diversity of societies, cultures and groups implies that universalizations of theories and notions should be avoided. It is easy to agree with the idea that theories should be locally and historically situated. Both the researcher and the reality s/he studies are influenced by the societal and political, as well as the local, context. What exactly is implied by this is, however, open to interpretation. It is difficult to define a specific historical time period about which it is possible to produce (not too general) statements. The degree of local contingency or universality also depends on the issue. Some psychological circumstances can be relatively stable and basic, and a possible biological influence could not be excluded either. But in this respect too, interpretations and theories depend very much on the historical context of the researcher. Also the meaning and effects of biology are social constructions (Kaplan and Rogers, 1990). When it comes to social phenomena such as working conditions, sex-typing of jobs and national politics it is more apparent that the theory must be very sensitive to the local situation.

An important theme running through all kinds of research is defining its limits and the legitimate field of research. What kind of questions can it even try to answer? In this regard we think that the field of gender research should be carefully expanded beyond the limits of the variable approach. And this expansion should be combined with critical considerations as to how and when notions of gender are broadened too far, so that they are made to be all or nothing. Assuming that gender is everywhere, and/or that it is useful to question everything in terms of gender, involves a risk of absolutism. Gender is often an interesting and productive approach to various phenomena, but sometimes other terms and vocabularies may provide a better understanding. Intellectual imperialism and its partner reductionism represent a serious threat in all research, and gender studies are no exception. Some research and thinking simply neglects how gender always exists in a matrix of other ways of dividing people and society and that some conditions affect men and women more or less equally (e.g. ecological issues). Gender research should therefore be accompanied by self-criticism and modesty, for example, admitting that the gender vocabulary is no more absolute or self-evidently reliable or valuable than any other vocabularies, which sometimes have more to offer. The researcher may, therefore, broaden and enrich the interpretive capacities through developing an interest in other fields of research, as well as trying to get acquainted with their vocabularies (Chapter 9).

A research 'agenda' based on all three perspectives?

From a theoretical point of view the three approaches or perspectives seem easy enough to distinguish, but researchers often make use of a mixture of two or maybe even all three of them, or work with other ideas and points of departure. Sometimes, the differences between the three perspectives are not so much viewed as categorical and absolute, but rather as different aspects that could all contribute to the same research programme (Cockburn, 1991). Especially within qualitative empirical research the three approaches do not always appear in pure form. (As mentioned above, quantitative studies based on the feminist standpoint perspective are rare and the post-structuralist approach is also very sceptical about the quantification of social phenomena.)

At least at a superficial level, elements from all three perspectives could, to a certain degree, be considered within empirical studies of specific research areas. For instance, when analysing labour market and organizational conditions the following questions could be raised. How are the sexes divided according to work tasks and social positions, that is, what does the horizontal and the vertical work division look like? How are privileges distributed? How do recruitments, selections and promotions take place seen from a gender perspective? Asking these questions implies making anatomy the decisive distinction and accepting the variable approach. This, however, does not exclude a subsequent broader approach, and the results from the anatomy-based questions could therefore be followed up by the following questions. Are some experiences gender-specific? What are the predominant relations of power and dominance for men and women? Do the actual power relations, priorities and ideologies favour one gender rather than the other (normally men or a certain group of men)? Or is power unstable and multidimensional, including also female forms of power and male subordinacy? How is gender being constructed by organizational structures and processes, that is, how are men and women 'created' within the organization (how is their gender identity being influenced) by means of language, patterns of interaction and social practices? How can the organization – objectives, practices, values – be described from a gender perspective? Can ideas, values, actions and practices be interpreted in terms of masculinities/femininities, for instance, carrying male and female values and meanings respectively? If so, what kinds of masculinities and femininities dominate and, if there is not hegemony, how do they interact? Why do we (as researchers and other kinds of developers of knowledge) define something as masculine or feminine, and what do we gain or lose from using these concepts? Does the language used express gender bias? How do discourses on gender interact with different forms of subjectivity, and what is made possible or impossible by the dominant discourses and attempts to develop resistance against them? To what extent does it make sense to talk about dominant patterns or should fragmentation, inconsistencies and ambiguity be emphasized instead?

This whole cluster of questions goes far beyond what could be asked within a specific study, but some of them could be combined, thus reflecting aspects of all three perspectives. These are, as mentioned, expressed in specific theoretical and empirical studies but not always in a very clear form, and many different combinations are possible. If the approaches are to be reasonably consistent, however, they cannot be combined in an arbitrary way. There are profound differences between the variable, the standpoint and poststructuralist perspectives which mean that the specific approach of an individual researcher is committed to one or a combination of two of these and not to the other(s). It is, of course, not possible to combine totally different world views or political commitments. In general, eclecticism, the free borrowing from different sources, easily leads to shallow and confusing projects. One cannot count and compare bodies of men and women (in relation to other variables), nor focus on the experiences of women as carriers of particular insights and simultaneously view 'women' as a signifier without trying to give a stable and unitary meaning to 'women'. Normally, one main position forms the starting point and minor inspirations from other perspectives can then be included subsequently. If all the suggested questions are included in the same study, the variable idea of counting and comparing bodies of men and women can provide a general foundation, while the following more complicated questions aim at more central research perspectives. Comparisons of men and women (defined in terms of bodies) could give some ideas for the examination of female experiences and disadvantages as well as for the study of discourses on 'men' and 'women'. It is very rarely possible to include all questions in just one study, even an ambitious and longer one; giving priority to some at the expense of others is inevitable.

Notes

1 An alternative, but overlapping classification would be distinguishing between feminist rationalism, feminist anti-rationalism and feminist post-rationalism (Di Stefano, 1990). The point of focusing on rationalism is to stress the central meaning of a dominating, masculine logic and indicate ways of dealing with it. Another approach is to combine political, theoretical and epistemological dimensions as grounds for dividing up the field. Calás and Smircich (1996) do so and include six versions of feminism in their review article: liberal feminist theory, radical–cultural feminism, psychoanalytic feminism, socialist feminism, poststructuralist feminism and third world/(post-)colonial feminism.

2 Apart from making women visible as a specific category within different empirical studies, it is also a question of pointing out important but disregarded contributions by women to, for example, politics, art, science and administration (see Keller, 1974; Lerner, 1986; Stivers, 1993). Or it can be a question of drawing attention to activities and themes that are seen as mostly related to or problematic for women, for example, household work, childrearing

and sexual harassment. Arguably, certain research areas have been disregarded contingent upon the traditionally low representation of women in research.

3 Neo-positivism means that science is seen as a search for objective, neutral knowledge in which data and theories tested against data are seen as central. Scientific knowledge is viewed as cumulative. Laws or law-like patterns are searched for, as are causal relations. Present versions of positivism partially recognize some of the problems with older conceptions – problems with neutrality and impossibilities of fully separating theory and observation, the preliminary nature of knowledge – without changing the basic commitment.

4 This position they share with a number of different critical schools that view the dominating notions of science and method as conservative, technocratic and limited and try to justify their research approaches in alternative ways (Alvesson and Sköldberg, forthcoming).

5 One may distinguish between a more theoretical/political and a methodological/empirical version of standpoint feminism, exemplified by Hartsock (1987) and Smith (1989) respectively. The second version emphasizes the importance of locating research in particular experiences. Here the focus is on the need for a located, empathic rather than an external, explanatory approach. Smith (1989: 34) writes that 'rather than explaining how and why people act (or behave) as they do, we would seek from particular experience situated in the matrix of the everyday/everynight world to explore and display the relations, powers, and forces that organize and shape it'. We will not, however, go any closer into similarities and differences.

6 One may even go further and say that the level of representativity is often restricted to the quite limited group of white middle-class, leftist, feminist public sector professionals.

7 We should add that many of the positive examples, for example, getting additional attention, may be less significant than many of the examples of discrimination.

8 There is no absolute relationship between standpoint theory and the use of the concept of patriarchy. Some standpoint feminists do not talk about patriarchy and the concept may be used also by researchers not adhering to the standpoint perspective. There is, however, a strong connection between an inclination to capture contemporary society as a patriarchy and the adoption of a standpoint perspective.

9 Poststructuralism (sometimes labelled postmodernism – we treat the concepts as overlapping) is a theoretically and philosophically sophisticated stream. Our intention is not to review the core ideas in a way that does the complexities full justice, but only to summarize some vital aspects of relevance to social science/gender studies that maintain an empirical interest in social phenomena and do not move into literature criticism, philosophy or – something poststructuralism sometimes seems to border on – the esoteric. For reviews of poststructuralism (postmodernism), see e.g. Dews, 1986; Poster, 1989; Rosenau, 1992; Sarup, 1988.

10 From a strict poststructuralist position there are reasons to open up the idea of the 'masculine' nature of 'corporate strategy'. This would mean showing the fragility of notions of 'masculinity' or 'strategy'.

11 For example, she asks 'why women tolerate social relations which subordinate their interests to those of men' (1987: 12) and talks about 'power relations in the family, in which men usually have more power than women' (1987: 38).

12 In a sense all researchers acknowledge the significance of critique. Critical evaluations are a cornerstone of scientific activity. In practice most have mixed feelings, and many probably celebrate strong critique of other approaches while simultaneously being less sympathetic to critique of their own camp or branch of research, unless the critique accepts all basic premises and only addresses details. Within feminism, some people explicitly say that many forms of critique are harmful for the field (e.g. J.R. Martin, 1994).

13 When saying this, we are well aware that we run the risk of reproducing categorical and stereotypical ideas. We try to reduce this risk through careful expressions ('can sometimes be related to . . .' rather than the more categorical 'is') and in occasional notes (like this one) in which the problem, which should be taken seriously throughout the entire book, is pointed out.

3
Gender and Work

Today's labour market is often characterized as being highly segregated, horizontally and vertically.[1] Women and men work in different sectors and job areas and men occupy 85 to 90 per cent of the positions at the top levels of working life. The concept of segregation implies that the division of labour is not based on 'natural' skills or on the 'free will' of individuals but that it needs explanation, especially because the segregation also results in inequalities, mainly that women are concentrated within low pay areas, whereas men's jobs are better paid and offer better promotion prospects. The division of labour into 'female' and 'male' work areas is broadly considered to be a vital element in the subordination of women.

Many explanations are available when we wish to understand the gendered division of labour historically and in the present day and the resulting inequalities between the sexes. We deal with and discuss explanations at different levels: the macro-level, the meso- and the individual (micro-) level. In this and the following chapters we introduce and subsequently develop a more local cultural approach as useful for understanding gender and work.

A brief history of work

Most cultures seem to include systems of meanings and norms prescribing different activities and characteristics for women and men. Women's work throughout the ages is described by Novarra (1980) as six tasks which pre-date the money economy and which are necessary for the human race to survive and life to be tolerable, and these functions are still women's main work areas today. These are: to bear children; to feed them and other members of the family; to clothe people; to care for the small, the sick, the elderly and the disabled; to be responsible for the education of children; and to take care of the home (including making products of use to the home). Men have shared, in varying degrees, the tasks which are needed to sustain and continue the human race, such as hunting, farming and fishing, but our image of men's work is not currently or historically drawn from the six tasks, argues Novarra (1980).

In the pre-industrial family women and men both produced goods for the household and women also took care of the home and the people living there. Work was then not regarded as separated from private life. People produced from day to day what they needed for their existence. Wage labour was a rare phenomenon. Today most of us are dependent upon selling our labour power for wages, and if we are unemployed we are dependent upon financial support, primarily from the state.

Although women's and men's tasks overlapped in the pre-industrial era there were rather strict ideas about women's work and men's work within the specific community. What exactly is (and historically was) regarded as typically feminine or masculine to a considerable extent varied from country to country and even from one region to another. Within certain work areas there was even a taboo against the other sex doing the job; in France and Sweden for example, milking cows was exclusively regarded as women's work until this century. Men risked ridicule, from women as well as other men, if they milked cows (Shorter, 1975), and the mythical aura around milk made it unthinkable even to drink it if men had been involved in its production. Besides, prestige was connected to the work men did, and men lost status and power if they did women's work. It was easier for women to do men's work than the other way round. Men had more to lose. When women did men's work they were not harassed in the same way. However, it was difficult for women to achieve the status connected to men's jobs (Göransson, 1996).

On farms in Sweden it was largely men who produced the raw materials while women did the refining (Göransson, 1978) but there were also areas where women and men worked together, e.g. with the harvest. What was thought to be women's or men's work varied according to different economic and ecological preconditions (Löfgren, 1977), for instance, if men went off hunting or fishing women took over responsibility for the farm in the meantime. Women were considered as capable as men of taking care of the farm work. In the southern part of Sweden (in the eighteenth and nineteenth centuries) in large-scale agriculture there was a stricter division of tasks, with women doing work close to the farm and inside it, and men working in the field.

It is not possible to say why some work was women's and some was men's; to do so would imply a specific historical investigation of the cultural local meanings which are attached to the respective job tasks. It also takes a lot of research to discover why jobs change gender. Sommestad (1992) discusses why dairying (in Sweden) changed from being a female area of competency for many hundreds of years to becoming a male job in the 1930s. Her study clearly shows that the gendered division of labour has nothing to do with economy/biology but is historically constructed and that work is labelled female or male on the basis of historically changeable interests and assumptions. The re-labelling process takes some time of course – it is not done in a matter of days. In the case of dairy work, the introduction of machines into the production process and the development of a scientific approach to milk meant that the associations between milk and women eroded. Milk was now also connected with machines and technique. The inclusion of milk in a technological–scientific tradition led to a transcendence of the gap between milk and masculinity. Milk was no longer something mysterious, taken care of by women (connected to breastfeeding), but could now be regarded as a result of a chemical process/ solution which is seen as appropriate for men to work with. When milk became scientific it lost its exclusive association with the female body and intuition and this gave men the opportunity to be involved with the hitherto taboo-laden female milk. In the UK dairying also used to be women's work but was likewise taken over by men when cheese making became more scientific (Davidoff, 1986).

It is difficult to say whether women's and men's work were regarded as equally important as some researchers tend to believe (e.g. Baude, 1992; Illich, 1982; Reskin and Padavic, 1994), while others advocate that whatever women did was regarded as less important than men's work (Hirdmann, 1988). Segregation remains today, and although the sexual division of labour is very variable there are some areas which are culturally defined as male or female respectively and dependent upon the ideas within the communities about what is suitable work for women and for men.

The industrial revolution (which started in Western Europe in the eighteenth century and continued over the following 200 years) transformed the way work was done. The work of craftsmen, for example, which was male work, was industrialized and the production was now controlled by capitalists. Many former self-employed craftsmen and farmers were forced to sell their labour power on the market. Some parts of women's production of useful items in the home were now also to be carried out on a market basis (such as textiles), first in cottage industries and later in factories, and many of these jobs were primarily reserved for (unmarried) women. In the early industrialized countries men became the large majority of the labour force while women's main responsibility was to take care of the home.

The breakthrough of industrialism and capital's need for cheap and plentiful labour power made it possible for (and/or forced) women on a greater scale (mainly working class women and children) to join in the production process, in areas unrelated to their former work in the home. This, however, carried the contradiction with it, as Engels maintained (1972), that the proletarian families were being dissolved (whether women worked or not) because, on the one hand, women could not earn anything if they fulfilled their duties in the family and, on the other hand, if they worked in industry they were unable to fulfil family obligations. Engels said that this was true of women in all sorts of occupations, from medicine to law.[2]

In the early period of industrialization in many countries women and men faced unregulated working conditions – for example in England there were no regulations about the length of the working day or opportunities for maternity leave. Some restrictions on the length of the working day for women were made in the 1840s in England (10 hours a day), and in the 1870s the Health of Women Act did restrict the working hours to 56.5 hours per week for women, children, and young persons employed in textile factories (Lewis and Rose, 1995). Protective labour laws were eventually carried through in other European countries, in the late nineteenth and early twentieth centuries. These provided women with some protection, maternity leave, etc., and limited the length of the working day. In many countries women were also banned from night work. Because women's labour was indispensable both for industry and the proletarian household economy, it was important that the protective labour legislation made it possible for women to reconcile paid work with family demands. 'Women's protection was not rhetorically linked to their working conditions, as in the case of men, but rather to their sex' (Schmitt, 1995: 128). The underlying discourse on women's work was then linked to their motherhood and family roles, thus confirming that housework and childcare were women's duties. More historians have debated the power of these discourses on protective labour laws for women and have concluded that when they were applied to women only, on the one hand they created special categories of workers (thus consolidating segregation) and on the other, in practice, they produced divisions among women, because they affected some categories of women more than others. This legislation served the purpose of 'reconciling the competing needs of women and families to meet a broader set of social purposes including sustaining the family wage male breadwinner ideology; supporting a sexually segregated labor market; and enhancing the possibilities of survival for future generations of workers' (Kessler-Harris et al., 1995: 23).

Industrial development also made it possible to produce on a large scale what used to be produced by the household. The development of the means of production and the needs of capital to find new markets meant that work which used to be done in the home by women (spinning, weaving, knitting, baking, butchering) was also done on a commercial basis. The industrial development made it possible to produce all consumption goods faster and cheaper than was possible in the home. Female-dominated industries increased in the late nineteenth century. One example from Sweden is bakeries, where there were (strictly) male ('soft'/white bread) bakeries and female (ordinary bread) bakeries; only in four per cent of these were men and women working together (Baude, 1992).

Because the family was no longer a production unit and could not meet its own reproductive needs any longer it became important to earn enough on the market to support the family. Women's wages were lower and perhaps more uncertain than the husbands' and the latter took on the role of the main providers or, as it was to be called later on, the breadwinners. A majority of married women became dependents and house-keepers/home-makers, and the labour force became predominantly male. This family wage model was endorsed by protective labour legislation in the late nineteenth century in many countries and is believed to have asserted woman's primary role as a mother and childrearer and also subsumed her role as provider (Kessler-Harris, 1995). In other countries, however, a family wage was never accepted by the employers and women had to accept whatever job they could get, as the families could not live on one income.

Many middle-class women only had paid work until they married, when they were primarily expected to take care of the house and children and be dependent on their husbands' wages. In working-class families women would often have to have paid work after marriage as well, in order to provide the family with what it needed. Married (middle-class) women's withdrawal from the labour market was contingent upon the idea of a woman's proper place being in the home and a man's in the world of commerce (away from home). Work and family life were in many countries regarded as two separate spheres.[3]

> Reinforcing these beliefs were stereotypes of men as strong, aggressive, and competitive and of women as frail, virtuous, and nurturing, images that depicted men as naturally suited to the highly competitive nineteenth-century workplace and women as too delicate for the world of commerce. (Reskin and Padavic, 1994: 21)

Another reason why many married women did not work was that it was not always possible for them to get work – for example during the depression years in the 1930s women were discriminated against in many countries. In the USA 84 per cent of the nation's insurance companies, 65 per cent of the banks and 63 per cent of public utilities had restrictive rules preventing married women from holding any jobs (Campbell, 1984: 110, cited in Alpern, 1993). State and local governments passed laws barring women from public employment; they were joined by the federal government in 1932 (Stivers, 1993). In Sweden too, unions accepted the dismissal of married women (Wikander, 1991). It should be noted, however, that not only women but also black men were discriminated against; in the 1920s in the USA 'racism in the federal government began to push black women and men out of white collar job opportunities' (Harley, 1990, quoted in Stivers, 1993).

Although many of the gender arrangements of early capitalism were a continuation of the work pattern in the pre-capitalist economy, capitalism has had a crucial role in maintaining, consolidating and reconstructing patterns of segregation and sex-typing (Bradley, 1994: 152). In the early industries men and women competed for the same tasks, but in the new industries as well as in the public services work was 'designed' according to one or the other gender (Göransson, 1996). By designating jobs as women's work, it was possible to employ women more cheaply because of the lower social value already put on their work, and capitalists also benefited from men trying to reserve jobs as male jobs, as that resulted in the relegation of women to low-paid female jobs. For example domestic services, agriculture and light industry (textiles, tobacco and clothing) were women's jobs, while men worked within the manufacturing industry, engineering and commerce. There were also jobs which men eventually took over. 'The invention of a new machine or technique provides a rationale for men to redefine an old female occupation as a man's occupation, thereby increasing its social standing and driving women out to the margin' (Bradley, 1993: 16). As a result of the industrial revolution (and mechanizations) in Britain men eventually took over female specialities like baking, brewing and spinning (Bradley, 1993).

Some jobs which used to be men's jobs also became women's jobs eventually, e.g. clerks, tobacconists and weavers. In 1871 clerks in the UK were almost all men, while in 1930 women constituted over 40 per cent of the clerical workers. In 1911 clerks were placed in the highest of 5 social classes, class I. By 1930 clerks had fallen to class III, according to the official ranking of occupations (Kirkham and Loft, 1993). In 1870 in the USA, three per cent of the office clerks, stenographers, typists, bookkeepers, cashiers and accountants were women, whereas in 1930 women made up 95 per cent of all typists and stenographers, two thirds of all office clerks were men, and almost half of all bookkeepers, cashiers, and accountants (Reskin and Padavic, 1994). According to Stivers (1993) it was not lack of qualifications that accounted for the small number of women in the civil service in the USA in the late nineteenth century but discrimination in hiring. In the period from 1884 to 1894 women constituted between 28 per cent and 43 per cent of those passing civil service examinations, but only seven per cent to 25 per cent of those were actually hired (Aron, 1987: 110, referred to in Stivers, 1993). During World War I there were significant changes in the participation of women in the public sector services, in factories, in paid and unpaid work, and women demonstrated that they could do the work as well as the men they either replaced or collaborated with (Stivers, 1993).

In both (war)periods (World Wars I and II) in the countries at war women had access to jobs which were ordinarily men's jobs. Reskin and Padavic (1994: 51) cite slogans designed to attract women to blue-collar jobs: 'If you can run a sewing machine you can operate a rivet gun'. They mention for example that women worked as conductors on the trams, and that they were building and flying cargo planes. When the war(s) ended women were laid off and transferred into low-paying jobs such as assemblers and clerk–typists and it was not until the 1970s that women were admitted into traditionally male occupations, according to Reskin and Padavic (1994). Although Bradley (1989) regards the two world wars as important challenges to sex segregation, because it was liberating experience in itself that women were able to demonstrate that they could do all sorts of tasks (from managing offices to maintaining railways), she concludes that wartime experience had little long-term impact on the structure of segregation. After World War II many women were channelled into service jobs, and many employers (in the USA) introduced marriage bars. Married women again became dependent on their husbands' wages.

In some countries, like the USA, Sweden and Denmark, the 'period of housewives' culminated around the 1950s, after which more and more women (including married women) had paid work. The increased labour demand was due to economic growth and, in the Nordic countries, to the expansion of the welfare state where childcare became a responsibility of the state; in the beginning of the 1960s around 40 per cent of Swedish,

Finnish and Danish women were active in the labour market – by the 1990s this number had almost doubled. The number of women in the labour force differed very much in Western Europe, the closest number to the Scandinavian figures being West Germany with 36 per cent of women in the labour force (1970). There are (and have been) differences in family politics in the Scandinavian countries compared with the continental countries. Married women especially in Sweden and Denmark were accorded individual rights and were supported by the state in their economic independence whereas married women in continental Europe were, and are, regarded as dependent on their husbands (Borchorst, 1993). These differences in the policies of the state combined with different cultural gender ideologies have probably influenced mothers' participation in the labour market particularly.

Contemporary work, horizontal and vertical division of labour

A very large part of the paid work women do today is allied to the traditional six tasks we mentioned earlier (to care for children, the sick, the elderly and the disabled, to clothe people, to be responsible for the education of children and to take care of the home and so on), although many of these tasks in our part of the world have now to a great extent become professionalized, institutionalized, industrialized and commercialized. We could mention for instance food processing, restaurants, hotels, textile industries, nursing, social and health workers, teaching, furnishing, decorating and cleaning. Around 75 per cent of female workers within the member states of the EU are concentrated mainly within what is loosely described as the service sectors. (Itzin, 1995, estimates that in the UK 90 per cent of women are employed in the service sectors.) There is a female dominance especially within the education, distribution and health sectors, with one third of all working women employed in these three sectors. Nineteen per cent of women work in industry and six per cent in the agricultural sector (Fakta Europa, 1993). With regard to the last of the six tasks, taking care of the home, most women today feel that they hold most responsibility for the home and for the children, and a number of them work part-time or take leave when the children are small.[4]

The early traditional division of labour contributed to the present sex-typing of jobs or gendering of work in the late twentieth century. By the end of this century most industrialized countries have a labour market that is divided into sectors according to sex. Women play a dominant role within the social security, health and service sectors, teaching and the retail trade while men predominate in the technical fields, trade, transportation and administration and national defence (Bradley, 1989; Reskin, 1984). Women's occupations have changed little in the course of the century; their characteristics are surprisingly similar. 'Most have a strong welfare or "service" element or they reflect domestic functions directly' (Scott, 1986:

162). The occupations of secretary, telephonist and sales assistant, nursing, teaching, laundry and cleaning jobs, dressmaking and cooking accounted for 67 per cent of total female employment in 1911 in the UK and 66 per cent in 1971 (Joseph, 1983, referred to in Crompton and Mann, 1986). Many traditional ideas on male and female labour were only loosely coupled to biological–functional conditions. One should bear in mind the difference between a reasonable tendency for a job to be dominated by one sex and the exclusion of the other from it. In a few jobs, for example, ambulance driver and fireman, it makes sense if the jobholder is able to lift a relatively heavy weight. The fact that many women are physically weaker than the average man should not lead to the exclusion of all women, however – some women are sufficiently physically strong and therefore qualified for these jobs. Generally, sex-related physical qualifications are of no significance for most contemporary jobs.

The horizontal segregation of the labour market is often said to be characterized by the position of women in the secondary labour market (cf. Fine, 1992). The work situation is more insecure, with fewer career possibilities, and the jobs also have lower prestige (Giddens, 1989). Half of all work areas are possible to characterize as female or male (in Scandinavia) which means that 75 per cent of the employed at the workplace belong to the majority sex and less than one fifth of the work areas have a balanced division of labour (SCB, 1996). The vertical division of labour – with women holding only one to five per cent of the positions at top level and about 10 per cent of higher middle management positions – is connected to the horizontal division of labour as 'women's jobs' often offer fewer possibilities for advancing to higher levels.[5] (We discuss different explanations for the limited number of women in higher managerial jobs in Chapter 6.)

In the EU 47 per cent of all women worked in 1989, compared with 75 per cent of all men (Gonäs, 1992). Sweden and Denmark are the two countries where women work the most, around 80 per cent compared to Great Britain, Portugal, France, Germany and the Netherlands where about 55 to 60 per cent of women work, and Ireland, Luxembourg, Spain, Greece and Italy where about 40 per cent of women have wage labour. In the USA 65 per cent of women were in the labour market in 1989.

The higher rate in the Scandinavian countries is, among other reasons, the result of a higher participation rate among women with children under school age than in other countries due to a higher rate of public childcare opportunities.[6] In Denmark, 48 per cent of children under the age of three were accommodated in subsidized day-care (1990), and 85 per cent of children aged three to seven in day-care centres (Schunter-Kleemann, 1995). Compare this to the UK where one per cent of children under five are in public childcare and France where 20 per cent of children aged one to three are provided for in public childcare. In the Scandinavian countries the expansion in the needs of the family and the extremely high tax pressure – to pay for the welfare state which is also the major employer of women – has made it very difficult to cope at least at what is considered to be a reasonable level unless there are two wages (or 1.5 wages: 30 to 40 per cent of women work part-time). Most women regard it as self-evident or indeed obvious that they should work during marriage, and maybe make interruptions for shorter periods when the children are small. This is supported by state policies; for example the taxation system is no longer household-based but based on the individual. The family wage and the era of the housewives is over, not only as a material possibility but also as a relatively compelling norm and as an espoused preference among the large majority of women. One could say that the social construction of what is 'normal' and 'good', in Scandinavia at least, is to have wage labour or earn an income as a self-employed person, not to be a housewife. In other countries ideologies are probably different; with respect to the European Union Schunter-Kleemann has identified six welfare regimes reflecting different cultural views from the 15 different countries in the EU. In the *Bulletin on Women and Employment in the EU* (1996) the member states are divided into strong, modified and weak male breadwinner states. In the strong male breadwinner states it is assumed that there is a male bread-winner and a dependent wife (childcare in the family is encouraged and taxation is based on the household), while the weak male breadwinner state is based on an assumption that all adults work or want to work (childcare and paid leave systems are provided), for example, in Sweden, Finland and Denmark. The modified male breadwinner state includes contradictory elements from both the strong and the weak systems, for example household taxation and childcare provision (e.g. France) or individual taxation and hardly any childcare provision (e.g. the UK).

Despite women's entry into the labour market it is still women who are mainly responsible for the housework and care of children. This double role, partly paid work and partly unpaid work in the home, has been labelled the double day. Quite a lot of women work part-time; in Sweden and Denmark about one third of all women work less than 34 hours, compared with about one tenth of the men (in 1994). In the USA it is 26 per cent of women, five per cent of men. In Great Britain almost 50 per cent of women work part-time, whereas in the Mediterranean countries only about 10 per cent of women's employment is part-time. The figures, however, conceal that the definition of part-time is very different in these countries.

In every country women (in general) earn less than men; on average women's wages are 25 to 30 per cent lower than men's (Fakta Europa, 1993: 35). The lower pay is often explained as a result of the devaluation of women's work (e.g. by Reskin and Padavic, 1994), and in general it is believed that 'the more women in an occupation, the less both its female and male workers earn' (p. 9). Reskin and Padavic (1994) mention for example that in the USA most dentists are male, whereas most dentists are female in Europe; in the USA the wages are very high, whereas they are average in Europe. Pfeffer and Davis-Blake (1987) also found that increases in the proportion of women in a work area (college administrators) resulted in lower wages. Reskin and Roos (1990) show that although the loss of status in former male-dominated occupations is reinforced by women's entry it could for example be technological changes demanding different skills which start the erosion of the status and the lowering of wages. Wright and Jacobs (1995) found, however, that an increase in the ratio of women in computer work did not affect wages. Finally, Jacobs (1992) found a narrowing of the gender gap in wages among managers. The increase of women in management and the resulting improvement of their situation with regard to wages compared to men's is explained by Jacobs not as a result of a growth in women's labour experiences (as some economists would claim), but because 'women are catching up to men more because they are getting a better return on their attributes than because they increased their human capital investments' (p. 174).

We are faced with the possibility that there are no simple and straight-forward explanations or universal truths about the relationship between a certain proportion of one sex and the level of wages. Similar situations (a high number of women and small wages in a job) may have different historically specific explanations and cannot be treated as identical. Although much of women's work is devalued and paid badly, other circumstances than just the sex of the workers within the area may have 'caused' this effect. As we have seen, women and women's work are not always devalued. When we use the concept of gender division of labour or segregation, we should be aware of the relativity connected to this; there are great variations. These variations are perhaps easier to illustrate when we make a comparison with countries outside the Western world, where class for example in many cases matters much more than sex.

Scott (1986) made a comparative analysis of the gender division of labour in four different countries (Britain, Peru, Egypt, Ghana), and she demonstrates 'the gender embeddedness of the division of labour' and the variability in patterns of segregation; for example in the case of Egypt the only occupations dominated by women were domestic service and nursing. Egypt has a much higher proportion of women in professional and white-collar work than Peru, or even the UK, and the 'vertical distribution of women workers is weighted toward the top rather than the bottom, especially in wage and salaried employment' (p. 173). These differences in the degree of segregation are explained by Scott as being due to variations in family structures, religion and the role gender ideology has in the institutions structuring the economy. In the case of Egypt the 'moderniza-tion' of Islam gave elite women access to education and employment within sex-segregated and high-status institutions. The idea within the wealthy classes that all paid work is degrading gave women from these classes access to high-status work as the women's social honour could then be maintained. 'Secularization, institutional reform and changes in the class and status system were necessary before market forces could "liberate" women's labour' (p. 173).

Jacobs and Lim (1992) examined trends in sex segregation by occupation and industry in 56 countries from 1960 to 1980. There were tendencies to declines in sex segregation in a majority of countries, although this was not clear-cut, as there was no consistent trend towards an increase or decrease in segregation in developed or developing countries. Jacobs and Lim found that in a majority of countries men were more likely to share an occupation and industry with women during the period than women were to share the same occupational (and industrial) group with men (p. 450). Bradley (1993) believes that technological change and economic opportunities are significant for men wanting to take over or invade women's jobs. In the USA for example, midwifery has been taken over by men (obstetricians) whereas in the case of most countries in Western Europe this is still considered women's work.

In general women seem to be in spheres of the labour market which do not provide them with the same opportunities that men have, either with regard to power and status positions or to pay. The division of labour is explained by many as a result of the labour demand from employers. Within industry for instance, employers have long recruited a specific sex to a particular work area (Dahlerup, 1988; Brittan, 1989) – women to jobs designated as women's jobs. A number of women have, however, moved into men's jobs while men seem more reluctant to do women's jobs as these are in general paid less well and have less prestige. It is often claimed that a significant increase in the number of women in a job will affect the status of the job. However, Wright and Jacobs (1995) suggest that an integration of women does not necessarily result in a decline of the status of the occupation or in an increasing differentiation within the field. (They refer to law, medicine, management and computer work.)

Before moving on to an overview of some influential efforts to understand gender segregation in work, some words of caution against an uncritical view of the histories and statistics reviewed above are called for. People inspired by poststructuralism or postmodernism in particular think that the use of broad abstract concepts and divisions such as women's jobs, domestic work, the service sector, employment or low prestige are problematic and rely on questionable distinctions in which social dominant meanings are taken for granted. Scott, for example, thinks that

> if we write the history of women's work by gathering data that describes the activities, needs, interests, and culture of 'women workers', we leave in place the naturalized contrast and reify a fixed categorical difference between women and men. We start the story, in other words, too late, by uncritically accepting a gendered category (the 'woman worker') that itself needs investigation because its meaning is relative to history. (1991: 144)

A more common sense critique concerns the notoriousy unreliable nature of statistics. Without going so far as to suggest that it only reflects social norms of classification, it often gives a misleading impression of robustness and precision. The way occupations and industries are divided up is quite arbitrary for example. Are university teachers in one occupation or many –

full professors, instructors, psychologists, nuclear physicists? Behind the seemingly unitary concept of manager, totally different work conditions, tasks and social relations may be found. The health care sector involves activities as diverse as advice-giving about habits, post-mortem examinations and abortions. Terms such as university teacher, manager and health care sector – as other terms – create order and unity out of diversity and ambiguity. Statistics reinforce the former qualities.

Different ways of understanding women's and men's positions in the labour market

How can we understand the pronounced gender division of labour with women and men in different occupations and the low number of women in management, considering that women constitute almost half of the labour force in a number of countries?

We shall briefly refer to and discuss some of the most influential explanations which we have chosen to relate to three different levels, macro, meso and micro. We use these terms for pedagogical reasons mainly, finding them useful as a background for the development of the local cultural approach we develop and advocate in the subsequent chapters of this book. The three terms refer to different types of analysis: macro focuses on general features of society and highly aggregated patterns indicated by statistics, whereas the focus at the meso-level is on organizations and culture and at the micro-level, on the individual/person. At the *macro-level* we deal with Marxist feminist analyses, patriarchy theories and the dual systems theory. At the *meso-level* it is theories at a more concrete social level, for example, workplace structure and dynamics. Here 'middle-level' institutional conditions are in focus. Structural explanations which, for example, address sex ratio and the effects of minority status are of relevance in organizations. At the *micro-level,* role theory, socialization theory and psychoanalytic theory are salient. Of course, far from all theoretical approaches may be easily divided up in this way. As we will see in the next chapters, on masculinities and femininities and culture theory respectively, it is often productive to transgress such divisions. Nevertheless, most work trying to account for gender segregation focuses on one analytical level and therefore we follow this principle in the overview below.

Macro-level

Marxist feminist analyses are interested in investigating the specific nature of the oppression of women under capitalism in the light of the gender relations preceding capitalist production relations. They start with the assumption that capitalism is dependent upon the reproduction of the workforce, on a daily basis and over generations. The unpaid labour of women in the home served as a means to reproduce the (primarily male) labour force and thus the relations of production (and capitalism). Because of this primary role of women, it was possible to pay them less when they had waged work – their labour was (is) valued at a lower price than men's labour. In some periods of history male unions campaigned for family wages, meaning that the male worker's value (price) should be set on the basis of the reproduction costs for himself, his wife and their children. This ideal of a family wage was threatened when women had waged work; it was difficult then for unions to maintain men's need for a family wage. It should be added that it is debatable whether a family wage ever existed for more than a few.

Some Marxist feminists saw (see) capitalism as the root of all social inequalities, and the family as the foundation for women's subordination. Family is believed to serve as a necessary and functional means for the reproduction of labour, ideologically as well as materially and therefore it is in the interest of capitalism to maintain the gender division of labour in the family, women's unpaid work being vital for capitalism. For Marxist feminism the concept of reproduction is central to understanding the gendered division of labour. Following Engels, some claimed (for example, Firestone, 1971) that the capacity for reproduction was the major obstacle to equality between the sexes, and because of this capacity women would not be emancipated before they participated in the labour market on a large scale and abolished the family as an economic unit. The sexual division of labour in the home, where women today also seem to do most of the work, Marxist feminists argue, contributes to women's worse situation in the labour market. The present gendered division of labour is regarded as 'firmly established' in capitalist production relations.

Others (for example, radical feminists) believe(d) in a more universal oppression. Inequality between the sexes cannot be reduced to being an epiphenomenon of capitalism; it is men as a group which dominates (and controls) women as a group. Patriarchy is the concept meant to explain universal and transhistorical oppressions. Patriarchy is a concept much debated, and by many still seen as being of central importance for under-standing gender relations of today. Although there are major controversies most feminists will agree that it refers to 'a system of social structures and practices in which men dominate, oppress and exploit women' (Walby, 1990: 20). Society is seen as a system of social relations between men, who are dependent upon each other and who create solidarity, making it possible to control the labour of women and maintain the original division of labour between the sexes, which is seen as the root of the present divison of labour. Hirdmann (1988) says that there are two principles – one that the female and the male must never be mixed, the other that there is a hierarchy between the male and the female, the former being superior and thus counting as a norm.

There have been many attempts to develop the concept of patriarchy in order to make it less abstract and more historically adequate for understanding the situation of women and men in present-day 'advanced' capitalist countries. Patriarchy is not exclusive to the macro-level. As is well known, radical feminists introduced the slogan, 'The personal is political' to emphasize that the relations between men and women are characterized by men's oppression and domination of women at all levels. Walby differentiates between an abstract level where patriarchy exists as a system of social relations and a more concrete level consisting of six structures: 'the patriarchal mode of production, patriarchal relations in paid work, patriarchal relations in the state, male violence, patriarchal relations in sexuality, and patriarchal relations in cultural institutions' (1990: 20). Walby defines patriarchal relations in paid work as follows: 'A complex of forms of patriarchal closure within waged labour exclude women from the better forms of work and segregate them into the worse jobs which are deemed to be less skilled' (p. 21). Walby distinguishes between a private and a public patriarchy. The former, based on the household, is a possible private place for the expropriation of women's labour. As household production is no longer the dominant structure the private patriarchy has lost importance. Walby regards the public patriarchy as the dominant form today, which implies that in the labour market there is a collective appropriation and strategy to segregate and subordinate women into low-paying industries and occupations and part-time work.[7] Women are thus excluded from certain types of occupation, at the horizontal and vertical levels. Patriarchal threads run through the state and government; women do not have access to equal political representation and the welfare state is believed to support these inequalities.

Finally, the two concepts have been synthesized, the Marxist explaining class differences and the patriarchy concept explaining the maintaining of the original division of labour which is seen as the root of women's present situation in the labour market. The *dual systems* theory was introduced by Hartmann (1979) as an attempt to make a synthesis of Marxist feminism and radical feminism. The main point is not to exclude either of the two theories but to regard them as equally important to the way gender relations are structured. Capitalism and patriarchy are seen as two analytically distinct systems of power relations which meet and interact and empirically work together, encouraging gender antagonisms and systematically oppressing women, respectively. Not just capital (as an abstraction) but also men's actions are believed to reproduce gender segregation. Historically men's struggle for a family wage was a means of keeping the competitive, lower-paid women in the home (and thereby securing the reproduction of the family) and when women had work men used segregation as a means of keeping the best-paid jobs for themselves. The present division of labour is regarded as a result of a long process of interaction between patriarchy and capitalism and is fundamental for the reproduction of patriarchy.

In opposition to Hartmann, who tends to see patriarchy and capitalism as in harmony with each other, Walby sees them more as in conflict. On this basis she refined the dual systems theory further into the more complex form of patriarchy, with the six patriarchal structures mentioned above.

Discussion

Marxist feminism is relevant for understanding the situation of women and the family in the beginning of industrialism – where the dissolution of the family was central and which led to necessary legislation in the interest of capitalists (and the patriarchal families). The family was the necessary 'buffer' between raw capitalism's usurping power and individual labour power. The development of the state has, however, reduced the importance of the family today. Like many other Marxisms, feminist Marxism does not fully acknowledge the importance of the state and its intervention possibilities, for example to minimize conflicts between labour power and capital. Neither does it pay much attention to the 'problem' that the state and women in many cases are allies, primarily because state institutions are the biggest working places for women, secondarily because many women are dependent on the state, for benefits, family allowances etc. As stated earlier, we must not forget that state policies regarding childcare, parental leave possibilities, legislation, and so on, matter, and influence women's lives and possible participation in the labour market.

One of the problems with Marxist feminist theory is that its explanatory power is too narrow for the understanding of women's situation today. It would hardly be possible to reduce the gender relations of today to relations to capital. Neither can subordination and all inequalities be understood as founded in the family. Families and husbands are different, some are even egalitarian (double-career families often have to show more solidarity with each other) and exploitation of women's work in the family is also shown to be dependent on, for example, ethnicity. bell hooks (1984) claims for instance that the family plays a completely different role for black women, as it is the place for resistance and solidarity against racism and it cannot be reduced to the place for subordination of women.

Patriarchy theory is based on conditions which were different from those of today and patriarchy (in the form of men's unions) played a role historically in keeping women out of well-paid work and gendering this work as male work. Like other grand macro-theories, patriarchy theory was supposed to be able once and for all to explain research problems, in this case the gender division of labour and women's subordination. Many authors agree that it is appropriate to talk about a patriarchy in the household production which pre-dated capitalism but there is much disagreement about the usefulness of the concept today. Some choose to confine the concept of patriarchy to pre-industrial societies while capitalist societies are described as 'masculinist' or male-dominated or the like.

It is important to be concerned about the division of labour in the household and how this is contributing to women's unfavourable situation in the labour market. Women's work in the home was not reduced much until the 1960s (although scholars disagree about whether machines in the house 'liberated' wives or just gave them even more work; for instance in the case of washing machines it is claimed that the amount of washing has increased dramatically, that it is more complicated because of many different textiles and on average takes more time, see Cronberg, 1986). Statistics show that it is still women who spend most hours doing housework while men have more paid work. In some countries in continental Europe the dominant ideas still promote women as primarily housewives, dependants and childminders, and men as breadwinners; women face a double day and choose the solution of part-time jobs as long as the children are small. Having said this, it is worth discussing whether it is really possible to speak about gender equality within household life on the basis of exact time measurements and number of tasks done (see Doucet, 1995).

Hartmann's dual systems theory is relevant for understanding the conflicts in the beginning of capitalism where the family (in many countries, like Britain) was threatened as an institution because of married women's paid work and where men's trade unions' exclusion of women meant that they were excluded from better-paid jobs. Men never wanted or fought for equal pay for women whom they never regarded as equal, and also they pictured themselves as breadwinners. The gendered divison of labour was needed to secure, and to justify, differences in pay.

There is some disagreement about unions' roles in the early days of industrialism. Some claim (like Hartmann, 1979) that women historically have been kept away from the job market and certain jobs, because men were interested in getting a family wage and women on the labour market were a threat to this established right, partly because the competition was harder and partly because it was difficult to insist on a family wage when most women worked. Others claim (Carlsson, 1987) that wages were low anyway and that it was in the family interest that both partners worked.

There is a tendency in macro-theories to objectify women (and men). They are regarded as passive reproducers of existing structures. This makes it difficult to conceive of women as actors on the historical scene – and it also makes it difficult to understand variations in women's situations, such as the recent increase of women in positions of power (at middle management at least). Many macro-oriented theories are at a level of abstraction where it is difficult to conceive of differences from the classical pattern and very difficult to understand how anyone could transcend the vertical division of labour. Of course, the very idea of addressing the broad picture is not to see exceptions or consider nuances, as part of the critique mentioned here may be seen as being of questionable relevance. Nevertheless, it is important to be aware of what is neglected in macro-level systems approaches. From a poststructuralist position it could be argued that the use of the concept of subordination as a universal way of grasping the situation of all women is totalizing and creates too rigid a sense of order in a social world characterized by fragmentation, variation, contradictions and disruptions. Macro-approaches easily inscribe regularities and patterns in gender relations.

In particular in the context of organization studies, more specific patterns, variations and ambiguities than are normally captured by macro-approaches are of interest to investigate. Also the actions and processes by which gender segregation and – at least sometimes – integration are accomplished should receive considerable attention. Macro-theories are relevant, as specific observable and experience-near phenomena cannot be understood in a societal and historical vacuum, but the tendency to treat the societal whole as a relatively uniform totality is of little help in understanding the specifics and diversities of organizational life.

Meso-level

At the meso-level the specific institutional sites – corporations, workplaces, occupational groups – in which gender differentiation and inequalities are socially constituted become the objects of investigations. Compared to macro-approaches the more concrete social level is studied. We see three meso-level approaches as significant. *Structural explanations* see the dynamics and effects of positions in organizational hierarchy and the ratio of sex as crucial for understanding career patterns and work orientations connected with gender. *Organizational policy* focuses on how employers and managers through their more or less visible hands create gender division of labour. A third approach is *organization culture theory*, in which shared meanings, symbols and understandings 'inform' people how they should live their gender lives in organizations. We will say very little about culture in this chapter as it will be treated at considerable length in Chapter 4 and, in particular, Chapter 5.

At the meso-level an organizational *structural approach* means that the construction of gender differences is understood as a reflection of the gender's situation in a formal and material organizational context. A seminal work within this tradition is Kanter (1977). One of her main points is that attitudes to work and work behaviour do not have anything to do with a person's sex, but with the person's position in the organization. Behind what is superficially seen as gender-related orientations other forces are operating. She notices three different factors as decisive for how men and women see themselves in the organization and the self-esteem they develop which is important for women's and men's opportunities to make a career. These are (1) the opportunity structure; (2) the structure of power; and (3) the proportional representation of a social category (e.g. of the same sex) in these positions. Kanter thinks that it is decisive for one's career progress to be centrally placed in the opportunity structure, to be on a career track, and not to be in a dead-end job. This sounds self-evident, even tautological, but Kanter's analysis is interesting because it points to structure rather than the actor as being vital for one's chances of getting ahead. The fact that many women are less oriented towards careers could then be explained by their being in subordinate positions in the organization, where they develop an anti-success culture, and not by women's personality traits or the like in some fundamental sense. One's attitude towards work is a function of how one is placed in the organizational structure. The central positions will advance attitudes and values which make it easier for the people (men) holding them to move upwards in the hierarchy. Women are 'late entries' in organizations, where male values (like working late) already prevail, thus making it harder for women. The male-dominated power structures and a tendency to homosocial reproduction, meaning that men seek, enjoy and prefer the company of their own sex, contribute to the gendered division of labour. If women want to get ahead it is important for them to make alliances with others, including men. Finally, people of any social category (e.g. women) who are few compared with others of a different social type (e.g. men) will experience pressures and be caught in social processes which stereotype them into positions which are more in accordance with their social category. The numerical relation between the majority and the minority is believed to influence women's career opportunities, making it easier if their number exceeds a certain critical mass (about 30 per cent).

Kanter emphasizes that gender *per se* does not matter as much as the structural situation of individuals where we find sex differences with regard to engagement in work, career interests, etc. This is supported by other research, for example, Lefkowitz (1994) who found that differences between men and women in relation to their jobs, such as preferences, values and attitudes, were largely spurious effects of other variables. Although 18 significant differences were found which reflected traditional gender stereotypes, almost all these disappeared when sex-related differences in perceived job characteristics, age and tenure, level of education, income and occupational level were controlled for. His conclusion was that 'men and women react similarly to the world of work when one controls the spurious effects of systematic differences in the jobs held and rewards received by women in comparison with men – especially differences in income level' (p. 323).

Ely (1995), in demonstrating how the proportional representation of women in positions of power affects women's gender identity at work, also supports Kanter's ideas about the significance of gender ratios. In a study of US law firms, she found that women in firms with few women in senior positions (in comparison with women in firms with a higher proportion of senior women) characterised men as more masculine and evaluated attributes they associated with women less favourably in relationship to success criteria.

Other studies (Ott, 1987) have raised some doubts about Kanter's claim that the numbers of people in a particular category rather than sex is significant in order to understand what keeps women back from certain jobs and positions. Ott shows in a study of minorities working in jobs where the opposite sex is in the majority, male nurses and female police officers, that the male nurses mostly experience advantages while the male majority within the police group rejected women when they had reached the critical mass. Other studies of males in gender minority positions do suggest a mix of advantages and negative effects, like positive attention and suspicion of being too masculine for the job calling for feminine skills (Williams, 1993).

Also the action patterns of employers and employees may (re)produce gender segregation. One may here talk about *gender policies*, that is, the inclination to make various types of jobs available or unavailable for different sexes. Here, a gender policy does *not* refer mainly to public statements responding to contemporary norms for the sake of legitimacy (at this level all organizations are pro-equal opportunity). It rather refers to regularities in actions, i.e. the level of what is practised rather than espoused, at the organizational level. Such action patterns, to the extent that they emerge from a central source and are systematic in character, count as structural explanations. At the organizational level there is some evidence of male workers' resistance to females joining 'their' field. Some of the reasons for this have already been touched upon. Men's fear of loss of status of the job and the accompanying lower wages is relevant here, although there are different research results which show that predominantly female jobs pay less than predominantly male jobs. Other reasons for wanting to keep women out are given by Astrachan (referred to in Reskin and Padavic, 1994: 72). These are that 'women's performance may make men look bad, that women may not do their share, that women may use their sex to get out of work, that men may have to clean up their language or change their behavior'. More important perhaps than the employee's actions are the actions of the employers, who are often seen as the real gatekeepers, as they recruit new people for the organization, and decide who is to do which job (Reskin and Padavic, 1994). According to the position discussed here, employers and their representatives thus to a significant degree control the gender division of labour. Stereotypes about the genders or about the job are vital in this respect. Hochschild's (1983) study showed that employers held very firm ideas about the attributes which were 'necessary' to carry out a certain job, and that these expectations are connected with the jobs requiring different attitudes that can have gender connotations. For example, there are different expectations about the emotional and relational orientation dependent upon whether one is hired as a flight attendant or as a ticket collector.

A manager's decision to discriminate is sometimes explained on the basis of a psychological theory called the rational bias explanation. This suggests that discrimination is dependent upon whether this decision is viewed positively or negatively by relevant stakeholders and also on the possibility of receiving rewards for discrimination (Larwood et al., cited in Morrison and Von Glinow, 1990).

Another meso-level approach is *organizational culture* theory. It addresses not so much 'objective' positions, numbers and other factors external to the individuals, but the meanings, ideas, values and beliefs shared by a collective of people. While structural theory focuses on what is out there and measurable, culture theory pays attention to the ideational level, on socially shared meanings as expressed in communication and collective symbols. While structural theory gives priority to the 'objective' side of organizations and views behaviour and attitudes as reflections of it, cultural theory sees actions and other externalized phenomena such as formal structures and positions as manifestations of socially shared beliefs, ideas and definitions (see Chapter 5).

Discussion

As we will discuss a cultural approach later on (Chapter 5), our critical discussion here only concerns organizational structure and gender policy. Both express important insights but the neglect of the level of meaning and the subjectivities of men and women creates problems. Cultural inertia and the possibility that people bring with them certain work orientations and preferences are not seriously considered. In addition, the understanding of power is rather mechanical. The verdict is similar in the case of Kanter, due to the emphasis on the effects of numbers.

The idea that organizational structures are believed to affect women's and men's behaviour and attitudes, and that norms and expectations are connected to a specific position in the structure of opportunity, does not leave much room for actions on the part of individuals or groups of men or women. People are seen as appendices to structures. That structures are (re)produced by people and really only 'exist' in actions is not considered. The neglect of the importance of socialization and education preferences is problematic. There is a heavy gender differentiation in the educational system which accounts for a great deal of the location of men and women in different jobs (men become engineers and women nurses, for example). This can hardly be explained by structural factors in Kanter's sense, as in early education, in most schools, there is a numerical gender balance and no gender minority or homosocial reproduction mechanisms contingent upon the gender ratios viewed as so crucial by Kanter. The importance of pre-workplace experiences and orientations is also illustrated by Forsberg (1992) who found that a group of male and female university students expressed rather different visions about their future family and career lives. Males indicated a stronger career orientation and emphasized economic responsibility for the family while females expressed a stronger concern for children and family relations.

Kanter's concept of power tends to become somewhat static; power is regarded as a certain amount of something which one might or might not have a share in. (For a critique of this concept of power as well as a review of the literature on the subject, see, for example, Clegg, 1989.) Arguably, power is better understood in terms of interacting processes between people in the organization, trying to reduce the scope for action of others not only through influencing overt behaviour, but also by ideological, symbolic and disciplinary means. The power structure, rather than static, may be seen in terms of the often ambiguous and unstable social relations between organizational actors and groups, and is a temporary 'result' of complex processes, which may or may not reproduce the status quo. The theory of the importance of numbers is also somewhat mechanical, or rather has been uncritically adapted as a mechanical rule. The expression 'critical mass' is taken from physics, where it has been possible to show that changes happen when the minority increases to more than one third. This statement may be criticized for applying an idea of causality from natural science and adjusting this to relations between humans. People are not atoms. Neither argumentations nor empirical evidence for why things should drastically alter when a minority passes more than 30 per cent are very strong. Kanter's focus is women (and men) as variables and does not contribute to a rethinking or new understanding of the organization, apart from issues related to the location of structural forces behind work orientation which, according to her study, are misleadingly ascribed to sex.

As is the case with structural organizational theory, the gender policies (employer action) approach does not account for the fact that men and women to a high degree follow different education patterns, something which has consequences for the division of labour in organizations. In many cases employers, especially in the public sector, are not merely neutral but actually encourage men to apply for female-dominated jobs and vice versa thus overcoming gender-dominant workplaces. There are, in Scandinavia at least, efforts to get more men into, for example, childcare jobs and to encourage more females to get an engineering education. During periods of shortage of labour, there have also been efforts by employers to get females into jobs which were previously dominated by males, for instance, in industry. On the whole, such efforts are not particularly successful, partly due to the reluctance of people to make untraditional choices. It can, of course, also be questioned how serious employers are about such policies. The point here, however, regards whether employers are the chief agents behind the active creation of gender segregation, as Reskin and Padavic (1994), for example, claim. Indications of efforts to accomplish the opposite, weak or not, seriously go against their claim. Also the recent expansion of women in managerial jobs suggests that employers' motives for 'keeping women in their place' are not particularly strong.

In addition, even if it could be argued that employers often do not have any great interest in promoting equal opportunities, it is in many cases not clear why they should actively resist this ideal and prevent women from getting certain types of jobs. Why should employers be concerned about the sex of a worker? Employers will consider what is profitable and may benefit from employing women as their labour is cheaper, because of the lower recognized social value of their work. What are considered to be female jobs are generally less well-paid than male jobs (Reskin and Padavic, 1994). Realizing that there are sometimes economic motives for a certain gender division of labour – in particular regarding the use of women, as well as other 'weak' groups which could be a source of cheap labour – in many other cases the chance of increasing the potential labour force, rather than excluding half of it, may pay off both in terms of better chances of recruiting good workers and of depressing wages because of a more favourable relationship, from an employer's point of view, between supply and demand of labour. Even though employers seldom have obvious good reasons for denying females access to certain jobs due to their gender, this does not of course mean that conservatism, mixed feelings and stereotypes are not prevalent. An employer may prefer a man to do a certain job based on the belief that the characteristics (or skills) connected to the job are male, accompanied by the belief that only biological men have these characteristics. Then gender has become a polarity, men being associated with masculinity and women with femininity. Often such beliefs are not restricted to employers but are dispersed in the organizational and societal culture, and also embraced by women.[8] We elaborate further on this in the following chapters.

Seeing established organizational structures primarily in terms of gender ratios at different levels and considering how socio-structural situations may account for orientations, as well as emphasizing that employers prevent or discourage females from getting certain jobs, has a certain relevance for understanding gender division of labour. Neither qualifies, however, as being *the* explanation, accounting for the impact of significant parts of these patterns on labour markets and in organizations.

Micro-level

Micro-level approaches take individuals more seriously. This does not necessarily imply a psychological approach. Socialization and role theory are not necessarily psychologically oriented. Micro-studies may also look at interactions rather than individuals. Most micro-level theories on gender are social psychological. They draw attention to expectations and norms and the influence of these on the individual. But also a more psychoanalytical approach within socialization theory has developed ideas about the psychological background underlying differences in the emotional development of children and subsequent consequences for identities.

Roles are normative in the sense that it is expectations to 'ideal' behaviours that are focused. Expectations as to sex (gender) roles are believed to influence who we are, how we behave and how others see us. By accepting the culturally 'agreed upon' rules, as mediated by people we interact with, we internalize the cultural norms and rules, we live up to expectations and thus perhaps constrain ourselves in different ways in the prevailing gender roles. One way of restricting oneself is, for example, to believe that only certain jobs or behaviours are appropriate for one's sex and that others are sex-inconsistent.

Many jobs are characterized by roles which we associate with either females or males or something feminine or masculine. In our part of the world for example it is still unusual to see female police officers and male nurses. They are in minorities within their work groups – and there are different expectations of the two categories. There are strong norms prescribing what is the 'proper' place for men and for women. Historically, we can detect taboos against one sex working in an area which 'belongs' to the other sex. Stereotypes about women and men even make it 'natural' that women and men do different jobs. Women in jobs which are unusual for them sometimes feel that they are regarded as unfeminine. For example it is often said that it is a difficult balance to be a top manager (which is associated with masculinity) and to be female, because we associate the opposite traits with masculine/feminine, thus it will be regarded as a contradiction to combine a top management job with being feminine. To become a manager it is necessary to transcend the normative woman's role because the management role is not compatible with what is stereo-typically associated with women. Men in 'women's' jobs are sometimes regarded as feminine (or possibly gay). The biological dichotomy justifies reducing masculinities and femininities to one dualism. Everything is male or female.

Sex roles are learned through socialization; girls and boys learn what is 'appropriate' and 'natural' for girls and boys. Many investigations have shown different expectations of girls and boys, women and men – for example essays have been judged differently dependent upon the believed sex of the contributor (Nieva and Gutek, 1980). It is culturally communi-cated, in a variety of ways, that girls and boys are supposed to be capable of different things. That women and men are believed to have different psychological characteristics and thereby capabilities is part of the cultural raw material that produces women and men as social beings. Socialization is believed to influence our choice of education and work. A number of investigations have shown that it was (is) important in a career choice for women to reject traditional normative gender roles (Rapoport and Rapoport, 1976). Hennig and Jardim's (1977) study of top women managers showed that they had engaged in traditional masculine activities and identified more with their fathers than their mothers. Accepting the above we can imagine that it is, or at least has been, more helpful for a managerial career to identify with masculine traits than to have a feminine identification (a mother occupying a traditional female position). These studies were carried out at a time when opportunities for women were increasing. One way of explaining the small number of female managers at the top level then is to point to the female socialization process that at least traditionally has meant the development of traits and abilities which are not compatible with top positions.

Sometimes the gendered division of labour today is explained by the fact that women and men simply apply for different jobs because of different interests. This is because women and men are being socialized differently and are 'accepting' different gender roles and positions in life, their jobs and work behaviour reflecting their orientations. Men seldom apply for women's jobs, not only because of their low wages and low prestige but also because they have a 'feminine' label. Women feel that men's jobs are alien to their identities and interests. (Others, such as Reskin and Padavic, 1994, would argue that women take the best they can get and that they are kept out of better-paying jobs.) Role and socialization theory assume that women prefer 'women's' jobs' because they are more in line with what we earlier on called women's original six tasks and are seen as usually female or in other ways more in line with the orientations of women. Behind this is a powerful historical and cultural tradition connecting women to work with children, health care and human relations. Women's jobs may fit in with other role requirements better than men's jobs do, such as family circumstances and part-time job opportunities. Some would argue that men's identity is more connected to and dependent on a paid job while women's identity is more connected to the home and the family.[9] An effect of socialization would be that many women may not be interested in managerial jobs or want a balance between career and family.

While most socialization authors emphasize the entire period of childhood and youth, the psychoanalytical feminist approach focus is on the first few years of a child's life. Chodorow (1978), for example, has developed ideas about gender differences resulting from the mother–child relationship. The most important influence on the perception of male/female by the individual is found to be created through the early experience with the parents.

According to Chodorow (1978) the division of labour between the mother and father in relation to 'mothering' is regarded as important for the development of the child's self-perception. The development process is believed to bring about different sexual identities in the two sexes, boys basing their identity on opposition to all that is feminine and thereby consolidating a male sexual identity, whereas girls' identity is much more based on closeness with the mother, and girls' separation is believed to be incomplete because of the continuing identification of girls with their mothers. As masculinity is being defined through separation and femininity through closeness, male sexual identity will be threatened by intimacy while female identity will be threatened by individuation. According to this theory it is possible to understand girls'/women's greater interest in social relations and social/humanistic education and men's in technical and managerial jobs. There is a basic contradiction between femininity and achievement deriving from socialization. Women are socialized to be passive and ambivalent toward career. Women's and men's different choices of work and careers make allowance for this difference in needs.

Discussion

Role theory has been criticized for many good reasons. The sex or gender role theory finds it difficult to explain what cannot be categorized in one-dimensional categories, the stereotypical (masculine) manager and the stereotypical female role. If people were totally fused with their roles there would be no discussions of gender division of labour; it would be given by nature. But what is on both sides of this dualism is very different and historically specific. Roles are normative and historically changeable, gender roles are culturally and socially constructed. In sex role theory there is a presupposition that the female and the male sex role are complementary and equal, but the fact has been disregarded that the biological category (women/men) has been interpreted in gender terms which have dictated a specific cultural identity, the individual woman being placed in a world of roles, expectations and social fantasies (Benhabib and Cornell, 1987). Her individuality is dissolved in some role definitions of her as a mother, a spouse, a working woman, and so forth. If one calls motherhood a role, Elshtain says, 'the effect is to distort the full meaning of mothering. Mothering is not a role on a par with being a file clerk, a scientist, or a member of the air force. Mothering is a complicated, rich, ambivalent, vexing, joyous activity which is biological, natural, social, symbolic, and emotional' (1981: 140). Not only is the language of roles a problem because it is flattening and homogenizing our social life, but in addition to this it is also oversimplifying what could/should be done to alter things.

Even if early interaction between parent(s) and child has a significant impact on the psychological orientations that a person carries with herself, one may warn against the assumptions of a fixed subjectivity proposed by psychoanalysts, especially in the context of understanding work organization and labour market phenomena. The psychoanalytical approach is over-emphasizing the primary socialization at the cost of the secondary socialization and general life and work history. In an organizational context the latter aspects may be more relevant to consider. A relevant critique of Chodorow is that her subjects are almost predetermined, or over-socialized, leaving no space for the unpredictable in terms of what happens during early childhood and the consequences of it (Elshtain, 1981). A large number of other factors may well influence the child's situation, such as the social context, background, personality, age of parents, the child's position in the family order, important early separations, the constitution of the child, his/her mother working outside the home and her satisfaction with her work. The child's own participation in the process is also significant but undervalued. Just because a parent and a child share the same sex, it does not follow that this is leading to a close identification with far-reaching psychological consequences.

The problem with only dealing with the micro-level is that it disregards other conditions, like the organization, the societal expectations and the structural factors which might help or hinder women; the specific workplace and societal cultural context in which the person lives is also disregarded. Of course, all kinds of theoretical foci lead to neglects and reductions. In organization studies, a micro-approach has too little to say about collective patterns to offer a strong basis of understanding. Although there might be a general pattern, such as the vertical gender division of labour, there is no reason to believe that this outcome needs a single coherent general explanation. A variety of different forces and processes may well contribute to gender division of labour – and certain tendencies to its de-differentation. The problem is the classical one – to interpret the outcome of people's actions without privileging either structures or actions, without defining away either society or individual subjects. This we wish to explore more in the following chapters.

Final reflections

To sum up, it is too simple to regard the present division of labour between the sexes and the inequalities in the labour market and in the home as a simple continuation of the pre-industrial gender division of labour. The gendered division of labour today is the result of a long historical process, with women and men sometimes in reversed roles. Much energy is spent trying to keep whatever balance there is. The general cultural conceptions and expectations of the sexes are influenced by those left over from a time when the 'roles' of men and women were more fixed. We are still influenced by these cultural expectations and conceptions of how to view, judge and treat the two sexes. Larger numbers of women are now being segregated into fields of work that are poorly paid compared to men, and have fewer promotion possibilities.

We have chosen to differentiate between three levels for analysis, macro, meso, and micro. This is of course somewhat superficial, as they overlap. As we have already noticed, the three different feminist perspectives reviewed in Chapter 2 to some extent coincide with these levels. But on the whole, the three perspectives may be combined with a focus on any level. For example, it is possible to locate various streams within liberal feminism at all three levels – the focus of analysis at the micro-level being on sex differences and similarities with regard to motivations, commitments and performances, at the meso-level on inequalities as they show themselves at workplaces and at the macro-level on the sex structuring of society and inequal access to well-paid jobs. Radical feminism's focus is mainly on the macro-level but the gap between the macro and micro is eradicated as all personal problems are believed to be political as well and patriarchal power is believed to be ubiquitous.

Marxist feminism we presented at a macro-level where we focused on inequalities and power differences at a general level; at the meso-level the focus would be 'moved' to concrete sites for the intersection of patriarchy and capitalism (for example dual systems theory could be applied to the meso-level), and patriarchy theory has been applied at an organizational level (for example, Cockburn, 1991).

The reproduction of gender inequalities and differences resulting in different power and pay outcomes has been analysed in a variety of ways. We cannot once and for all provide the final explanation for segregation. What we can say is that the empirical outcome is a high degree of segregation, although there are also trends towards gender integration. Many commentators leave the question of the origin of gender segregation (for example, Hirdmann, 1988) and are more interested in how one can understand its dynamics, effects and how it can be changed. In the context of change, for many feminists it makes more sense to focus on the division of labour in the public economy than to start by trying to change the subjectivities of people or the division of household labour in relation to childrearing:

> [A]lthough in the history of the individual the household division of labour . . . comes first, in the history of society at large and of the culture, which dictates and sustains these systems, what comes first is the division of labour in the economy. In other words, a radical change in the division of labour in society would do much to undermine the division of labour in the household. (Coser, 1989: 205)

We believe that all of the explanations may offer some, although at best partial, illuminations of gender division of labour and, relatedly, other gender phenomena such as particular work values or leadership styles of men and women. The phenomena are over-determined in the sense that a variety of different factors and mechanisms are at work and that there may be different ways of explaining different aspects of segregation and trends to integration – such as an increase over the latest decades of females in jobs such as managers, military persons and police officers and the increasing presence of women in managerial and high-level political positions. In the next chapter we will suggest one line of thinking around the gendering of labour markets and positioning in work organizations. Here explanations – in terms of what causes certain outcomes – are less central than an understanding of what goes on in gendered organizational contexts.

Notes

1 As mentioned earlier we primarily address Western (post-)industrial, late capitalist societies in this book. Unless otherwise stated, we identify tendencies and characteristics in these societies.

2 What Engels called the modern nuclear family he considered to be built upon women's slavery in the house, and because men in most cases were the supporters they were also the rulers of the home. Engels believed that the first condition for women's emancipation is that they have paid work (as opposed to unpaid work, often not regarded as 'real' work), and that the nuclear family should lose its characteristic of being an economic unit of society.

Demographic differences, like a surplus of women in Sweden, are important to investigate in order to understand the difference in numbers of women working as paid labourers. At the beginning of the century (1910), 40 per cent of Swedish women worked, compared with 18 per cent of American women (Sommestad, 1992).

3 The ideology of two spheres was not so pronounced in the Scandinavian countries as in the USA where women were supported by their husbands.

4 In Denmark where day-care opportunities are more favourable the labour force activity of Danish mothers of young children (0–10) is significantly higher than in other EC countries and the labour force activity is highest of all among men in couples where the youngest child is

0–6 or 7–12 years old (Stenvig et al., 1993). In Denmark only four per cent of the women with children under six are housewives (1991). This could partly be explained as a consequence of the gender ideology of today; presumably this behaviour also reinforces the ideology. Intertwined with this ideology is a high tax level – public childcare and the welfare state is costly – which also makes it necessary for women to work. In the UK the increase in women's paid work in the post-war period has been almost entirely in part-time work (Itzin, 1995).

5 This statement is, however, open to dispute, as the meaning of 'higher level' is ambiguous. Even though jobs such as nurse, social worker or kindergarten teacher do not represent career tracks, they do not lack opportunities for promotion. Many male occupations, e.g. policeman or electrician, do not involve many career options for the average job-holder – at least not in terms of promotion to a superior position.

6 Of course, there is no simple causal explanation for the phenomenon. The amount of public childcare is partly the outcome of a high employment rate for women, leading to strong pressure to expand this service.

7 An extraordinary and interesting attempt to get away from the central notion of work is to focus on the power of love instead, which Jonasdottir (1991) does. She criticizes the focus on work (by Marxist feminists) as the decisive reason for women's subordinate position. She argues that women and men as sexual human beings are the main characters in a special exploitation relationship in which men tend to exploit women's capacity for love and care and transform this to individual and collective power where women lose control. She regards the (socially constructed) institution of marriage as the central link between state and society and as the institution which keeps the process going.

8 For example, it seems as if many women are hostile or antipathetical to female managers who sometimes say that they find it easier to lead male subordinates. At least, interview statements pointing in this direction sometimes occur (e.g. Lindvert, 1997; Sundin, 1993).

9 That there still are more men than women in the labour market in most countries and more women than men working part-time may be an outcome of different identities *vis-à-vis* paid labour. Of course, one could also reverse the logic and say that this fact brings about different degrees of identification with work. As always, pointing at such mass data and overall tendencies obscures enormous variations, including those contingent upon class.

Also authors mainly emphasizing more social explanations conclude that work identity is still often more significant for men than women (Leidner, 1991; Morgan, 1992).

4

Masculinities, Femininities and Work

A way to avoid focusing too strongly upon a particular analytical level is to use a social constructivist approach to masculinity and femininity to understand gender patterns (as well as deviations from clear patterns), e.g. segregated labour markets and division of labour in work organizations.[1] These concepts make it possible to connect on the one hand to the overall societal culture and on the other hand to the feelings, thoughts, self-understandings and values – in short subjectivities – that characterize individuals. Expressed slightly differently, the concepts refer to how broad domains of life are culturally gendered as well as to how people conform to or transgress the social standards and guidelines for living suggested by what are culturally defined as masculine and feminine. In other words, masculinity and femininity have the advantage of making possible connections to macro as well as micro. They offer an alternative to the variable-oriented fixation on 'men' and 'women' using the bodies as a firm criterion for classification as well as being an alternative to standpoint researchers' tendency to use the female sex as a robust point of departure for ascribing experiences and interests to a unitary and unique half of humanity.

Apart from being able to throw some light on gender segregation in labour markets and work organizations, the social constructivist use of masculinity and femininity as an interpretive framework is useful for exploring a wide range of aspects of organizations, including organizational culture and leadership. This chapter thus offers some additional illumination to some of the broader gender work patterns covered in Chapter 3 – while we still do not attempt to offer *the* grand explanation – and provides some ideas of value for the further study of culture and leadership in organizations (Chapters 5–7).

We will to some extent say more about masculinity than femininity in this chapter – although the terms presuppose each other. One reason for this is that more work has been done on the former than the latter concept within the field of gender and organization. (There are many more books and articles including the words masculinity and masculinities than femininity and femininities.) The large majority of all gender research has emphasized women, either in variable terms or through an interest in women's perspectives, interests, values or experiences, typically in the light of male domination (patriarchy). The personal experiences of men have not been seen as very interesting, or perhaps as too unreliable or dubious to serve as a point of departure; instead the somewhat more distanced and problematizing concept of masculinity has served as a point of entry for studies of men, perhaps more seldom of 'men as men' but as privileged carriers of a dominating form of masculinity (or patriarchy).[2] Only recently have a few researchers started discussing men more specifically (for example, Williams, 1993). The norms and values by which women's and men's actions have been assessed have been defined in a 'male' way and it has not been necessary for men to reflect upon or problematize social conditions in relation to their sex in the same way that women have done. These norms and values have been and are increasingly being questioned and the former unquestionable and 'natural' masculinity is attacked. This has encouraged (some) men to take another stance and be occupied with themselves as a relational category, as a sex which is one part of gender relations (e.g. Kimmel, 1993; Meuser, 1996). Although to some extent we concentrate on masculinity in this chapter we are still interested in gender relations and are not focusing on men *per se*. Another reason for the emphasis on masculinity in this chapter is that some of the other chapters of this book are more women-centred, reflecting a massive body of research of such a nature, especially Chapters 3 and 6 and part of Chapter 7, which makes it reasonable to devote some space to men and masculinity.

Some views on masculinity and femininity

Organizational and occupational structures, processes and practices may be viewed as culturally masculine and, perhaps often less salient when it comes to dominating patterns, as feminine. Masculinity and femininity are thus not essential categories but should be seen as 'products' of, or themes in, different discourses. Gendering organizations usually means paying attention to how organizational structures and processes are dominated by culturally defined masculine meanings. (Feminine meanings dominate less frequently although they may be central in some organizations.) Masculinity is a vague concept, but can be defined as values, experiences and meanings that are culturally interpreted as masculine and typically feel 'natural' to or are ascribed to men more than women in the particular cultural context. It makes sense here to recognize the variety of masculinities, avoid single masculine–feminine scales (Connell, 1987) and talk about 'multiple masculinities'. Collinson and Hearn (1994) identify five such versions in the context of organizations: authoritarianism, paternalism, entrepreneurialism, careerism and informalism (men building networks on the basis of shared masculine interests and excluding women).[3] Variations between differerent classes, nations, occupations, ages, organizations and ethnic groups are sometimes pronounced when talking about masculinity and femininity. Some forms of working-class masculinity may, for example, be quite antagonistic to management and white-collar work, which is perceived as non-masculine (Collinson, 1988). Morgan, while recognizing the diversity of masculinities, suggests that they are not 'like a well-stocked supermarket', but 'are linked to each other, hierarchically, in terms of power' (1992: 45). He does not say very much about how. One should not neglect the possibility of various subcultures developing different forms of masculinity also in the absence of an overall hierarchy or well-connected pattern.

A typical description of masculinity stresses features such as '. . . hard, dry, impersonal, objective, explicit, outer-focused, action-oriented, analytic, dualistic, quantitative, linear, rationalist, reductionist and materialist' (Hines, 1992: 328). The concept of masculinity overlaps with what Marshall (1993: 124) views as male values or the male principle: self-assertion, separation, independence, control, competition, focused perception, rationality and analysis. While recognizing the multiplicity of masculinity, Kerfoot and Knights view as its core, at least in managerial and organizational work, 'a preoccupation with a particular instrumental form of "rational control"' (1996: 79). Femininity is defined in complementing and corresponding terms. For Hines (1992: 314), femininity is a matter of 'the prioritizing of feelings . . . the importance of the imaginative and creative . . .'. Female values or the female principle are characterized by interdependence, cooperation, receptivity, merging, acceptance, awareness of patterns, wholes and contexts, emotional tone, personalistic perception, being, intuition, and synthesizing (Marshall, 1993: 124). Grant (1988) talks about 'nurturance, compassion, sensitivity, empathy'.

The concepts of masculinity and femininity cannot be understood in isolation. According to Kimmel (1994: 126) masculinity is viewed as the antithesis of femininity: 'This notion of anti-femininity lies at the heart of contemporary and historical conceptions of manhood, so that masculinity is defined more by what one is not rather than what one is.' In a similar vein Hollway (1996: 28) argues that the idea of 'woman' has been produced 'as the negative of the masculine'.

There are considerable problems when talking about and identifying masculinity(ies) as well as femininity(ies).[4] One issue concerns the ontological status of the mentioned ideas. Do they reflect social reality in some way or are they used for analytic purposes by the researchers? Are ideas on masculinity/femininity open to empirical impressions or are they purely in the hands of the researcher to define and use accordingly? Are the definitions cited above valid across culture and history or do they reflect contemporary Western, or only contemporary gender researchers', ideas on what is masculine and feminine? A second issue concerns how the concepts should be related to physical males/females. Are masculinity and femininity tightly connected to men and women, respectively, or can they be used also to illuminate 'non-human' phenomena such as artefacts and techniques? We start with the last question and later address the empirical vs. analytic character of the subject matter.

Some authors believe that the concept of masculinity 'may be thought of as representing the discourses and practices which indicate that someone is a man, a member of a category' (Collinson and Hearn, 1994: 6), and that it means 'individual signs and institutional indications that this is a male' (Hearn, 1993: 151).[5] A problem with this understanding is that masculinity is associated with males, and femininity with females, defined according to biological criteria. Also men rejecting traditional masculinist orientations are defined in terms of 'other forms of masculine identity, such as that of 'the new man', the male feminist or the various forms of homosexual male identity' (Bradley, 1993: 22). Linking masculinity tightly with males and femininity with females is unfortunate as it gives priority to biological sex, that is, the chromosomes and genitals of people. As pointed out earlier in this book, this is not necessarily the best point of departure for gender research. We just remind the reader of the heavy critique of the variable approach. Even if the social constructions of gender proceed from genitals and other body signs, the enormous variation in these constructions – leading to outcomes for women as varied as striptease dancer, grandmother and businesswoman – means that care should accompany the researcher before stating that masculinity is definitively related to biological sex. Such a body focus is implied in the statement that 'this is a man' – in contrast to 'this is a masculine woman' (style, value, etc.).

Another version is to relate the concepts of masculinities and femininities more loosely to physical gender (sex) and apply them to both sexes and also to 'non-sexual' phenomena – for example, nuclear power may be seen as a masculine technology irrespective of the number of females working with it or politically supporting it. When Collinson and Hearn (1994: 4) talk about the 'highly masculine values of individualism, aggression, competition, sport and drinking' they are clearly referring to values on which males today have no monopoly, unless one defines a male as someone who scores high on these values. Defining a male through specific values would imply that one disregards anatomy; a person may value individualism, sport and drinking, irrespective of genitals. A person may actually score high on all these dimensions, but still be seen as feminine according to some other dimensions (looks, mothering, for instance).

One way of using the concepts of masculinities and femininities without tying them essentialistically to the bodies of men and women is to treat them as traits or forms of subjectivities (orientations in thinking, feeling and valuing) that are present in all persons, men as well as women, although to different degrees. Women, biologically defined, are thus typically seen as more characterized by femininities than masculinities, even though there is great variation in terms of the composition of the two (sets of) qualities. This could be called the *cocktail view on gender*. In the average male version, there is typically a lot of gin and not much vermouth while the female prototype includes primarily the latter with just a few drops of the stronger stuff. (End of irony.)

We believe that it is acceptable and important to use the concepts of masculinities and femininities to describe cultural beliefs without connecting these very closely to men and women. Masculine meaning may therefore be traced also in language, acts and artefacts loosely coupled to sex/human bodies. To explore how people think, feel and make sense in relation to these categories is vital for understanding gender relations and gender identities. Ideas about what is masculine/feminine and what is natural/ normal for men and women in relation to these qualities guide, constrain and trap people in all respects from occupational choice to acceptance/ rejection of tasks in everyday working life, although people may be more or less independent in relation to these guidelines and constraints. (Facilitating such independence may be defined as one purpose of gender studies.)

A second topic concerns the extent to which the researcher proceeds from an analytic/theoretical definition to an empirically grounded, historically and culturally oriented understanding of masculinities and femininities. The first alternative means that the researcher him- or herself decides what is to be defined as masculinity/femininity or follows certain research authorities. The latter version calls for a sensitive listening to and reading of when and how people in a community ascribe a masculine or a feminine meaning to a phenomenon. Empirical grounding is necessary before labelling/interpreting something as masculine/feminine. Recognizing historical variation is important here. When masculinities and femininities are used as analytical concepts, the researcher analyses the deeper gendered meaning of social phenomena irrespective of what surfaces in terms of explicit, socially recognized cultural meanings. One may interpret something as masculine even in the absence of empirical indications that natives (the people being studied) view a phenomenon in such a way. Authorities such as Jung may for example offer ideas of what it is to be understood as masculine or feminine. (Jung views these qualities as depth-psychological qualities, a part of human nature.) Masculine and feminine then refer to 'essences', basically independent of cultural and historical variation, even though manifestations may vary cross-culturally.

The researcher must be clear about the use of the concept analytically and with little or no grounding in the cultural meanings of the natives. Often researchers choose a middle way, having some feeling for cultural ideas among people in the area studied without carefully investigating how they ascribe a gendered meaning to phenomena. Caution is, however, called for before departing too far from, or speculating too wildly about, the level of meaning. A basic problem is that the terms easily incorporate commonsensical notions held by the researcher, who may be as strong a victim of prejudices as other natives. She or he can simply read in mascu- linities whenever she or he feels like it. Talk about masculinities easily becomes a bit arbitrary. Let us give some illustrations of this problem.

Connell (1995) claims that the hegemonic ideal of masculinity is a man who is independent, risk-taking, aggressive, heterosexual and rational. But why are these characteristics singled out? Why not reliable, mentally balanced breadwinner, sexually attractive, physically strong, placed in a high-status position, wealthy or something else? And are not rational on the one hand, and risk-taking and aggressive on the other, rather contradictory ideals? If one of these ideals is hegemonic (culturally dominating), may the other not be? Ideals like independence and aggressiveness may look good on movies for adolescents, but are not necessarily embraced in social life. In US corporate life, for example, it is rather the socially sensitive team player that is appreciated (Jackall, 1988). Connell is aware of the discrepancy between ideals and the possibility of living up to these, but this does not prevent the claim about the hegemonic masculinity from being debatable.

Another example of problems with interpretations of masculinity we found in Tewksbury who says, in a study of male strippers, that they restructure their work roles 'to emphasize the traditionally masculine ideals of success, admiration, and respect' (1993: 168). We feel uncertain whether these ideals are best understood as masculine. Would many people experience it as unfeminine to strive for these ideals? Ferguson also seems to talk about femininity in an arbitrary way when she writes: 'Women are not powerless because they are feminine; rather they are feminine because they are powerless, because it is a way of dealing with the requirements of subordination' (1984: 95). This equation between femininity and power-lessness fixes a particular view on the feminine that is of uncertain relevance for understanding contemporary cultural meanings of femininities – which do not necessarily include powerlessness. It may freeze the interpretive orientation not only by being culturally insensitive, but also analytically too narrow. Powerlessness (like power) can take many forms, some of which may be seen as feminine, for instance a participatory people-oriented soft 'leadership' style may also be seen as feminine (see Chapter 6), sexual attractiveness may be a significant source of power, as may parenthood. One obvious counter-example to understanding subordinates as feminine would be private soldiers in an authoritarian army, operating in a very strict hierarchy and forced to obey. Despite their subordination, they are normally seen as highly masculine. Arguably, there may thus be masculine as well as feminine kinds of subordination, as there may be corresponding forms of superiority and power, although in the feminine case they may be less clearly recognized. There may, of course, be forms of power/subordination that are not easily or productively interpreted in gender terms. Stivers, like Ferguson, thinks that there is a 'prototypical femininity' involved when men in organizations must cater to their superiors and become sensitive to their idiosyncracies (1993: 22), but that their interest in being seen as 'real men' works to prevent them from acknowledging this feminine quality. That subordinates obey their bosses may, however, be recognized without necessarily calling for labelling in gender terms. Our comments do not, of course, contradict the idea that masculinities often rank higher – in relation to monetary rewards, social status and symbolic power – than femininities, although there may be changes underway (see Chapters 5 and 6). It should be noted, however, that in organizational contexts, both past and present, the majority of all men have been subordinates. That subordination in an organizational context should universally have a strong feminine quality is therefore a questionable assumption.

A particular problem with the concepts of masculinities and femininities is that they easily draw upon, as well as (re)produce, cultural stereotypes. We cannot take for granted how the values mentioned above by Collinson and Hearn (1994) relate to men and women – even if they, as we tend to do in this book, restrict the discussion to contemporary Western societies. Many women (biologically defined) practise sport, appreciate whisky and may be described as equally individualistic, aggressive and competitive as many men. Many men may be described as social, relaxed, friendly and team-players. Studies of all-female shopfloors suggest that women often swear and participate in aggressive and sexualized forms of behaviour (Collinson and Hearn, 1994 themselves refer to such research). One may, of course, say that they are 'masculine' or express 'masculine' behaviour, but the point of using this concept is presumably that it is, in a particular cultural context, more typical for and appealing to men than women. Otherwise, these concepts become too one-sidedly researcher-driven and too insensitive to cultural context, given the criteria that the cultural meanings of masculinity and femininity should be balanced in the way the researcher uses the terms.

One way of avoiding the premature imposition by the researcher of his or her understanding on social phenomena would be to adopt a more local, emerging approach in which the people in the area being studied may define what is masculine or feminine for them. In a specific organizational context, for example, one may investigate to what extent a particular vocabulary or behaviour is seen by the natives as masculine or feminine or gender-neutral. Such interpretive research tries to avoid imposing pre-structured categories and follows carefully the meanings of the natives. This may be a painstaking enterprise – at least if one wants considerable depth in the meanings being studied. The interpretive powers of the concepts masculine/feminine may be weakened or even lost. It is likely that there is some variety in what people see as masculine/feminine or as neutral in these terms. For most gender researchers the entire area of management may be seen as fused with masculine meanings, but for many blue-collar workers, the polite, tidy and physically safe area of management and white-collar work may appear as feminine or as perhaps rather ungendered. Such confrontations between perspectives are valuable as a counterforce to elitist/a priori researcher ideas,[6] but interesting interpretations often call for the use by the researcher of some core concepts as an aid and not just letting these float and vary with the meanings of various groups and individuals.

As in many other cases, finding a balance between the theoretical/analytical use of the core concepts for the sake of direction and interpretive depth, and being empirical/sensitive to cultural meanings of people in the context of the study is important. Such a balance is never contradiction-free, as a critical reading of any research on the subject matter will make obvious. We here come close to the poststructuralist (postmodern) critique of dominant research that assumes and – consequently finds – fixed and coherent meanings. Any attempt to freeze a specific masculine or feminine meaning may be an easy target for a deconstruction, in which the fragile nature of the ascribed meaning is exposed. We will not here go so far, but briefly illustrate problems with using ideas on masculinity/femininity.

Stivers (1993) uses these concepts with respect to US public administration. She argues that its self-understanding, 'as reflected in its images of leadership, expertise and virtue, is culturally masculine (although its masculinity is as yet unacknowledged), but that it also reflects a significant element of femininity (although consciousness of its femininity has yet to dawn)' (p. 122). The approach taken may be said to be rather elitist, in the sense that the voices of the people in the field do not seem to have been considered. (The reader does not encounter any in the entire book text.) People in the area are viewed as ignorant about the cultural meanings gendering their organizational world (within as well as outside US public administration). It is likely that there is great variation among different groups about its masculine or feminine characteristics. If one continues Stivers', questionable treatment of US public administration as a unitary whole, its masculinity/femininity varies with the yardstick or object of comparison. From a traditional working-class horizon, much of it presumably appears as rather unmasculine. Compared with business life, often seen as more competitive and powerful, the public sector is generally also understood as unmasculine. Trying to adopt business management rhetoric may strengthen a superficial aura of masculinity, or may do the opposite – for some groups exposing its hollow character in terms of masculinity. From the viewpoint of a feminist (or an anti-masculinist, i.e. a critical student of masculinities), wanting to promote radical transformation, masculine domination emerges almost routinely as the most appropriate interpretation. If one considers the enormous variation within not just US public administration but also most specific organizations, it is likely that one may find many examples of culturally masculine as well as feminine meanings, not just contingent upon how one frames and positions the object being studied but also as a result of the enormous empirical variation.

Consequently, given the problems with the concepts of masculinities and femininities we think that particular caution is required when using them. To repeat, they are appealing as a response to the critique of essentialism – discussed in Chapter 2 – and the narrow variable focus on 'men' and 'women', but they are certainly not unproblematic. In particular, the risk of reproducing stereotypes and of arbitrarily imposing masculinity or femininity must be considered. It seems that (almost) all jobs may be constructed as male or female, depending on which dimensions one emphasizes, the language used and how one chooses to reason (Leidner, 1991). This is the case not only for people being studied but also for researchers. Researchers may construct jobs and other phenomena quite freely according to what they choose to emphasize. Rather than feeling free to label all sorts of phenomena one believes appeal to men or are more typical for men than women in thinking, acting and valuing 'masculine', great care and restraint should be exercised. What is masculine for one group or person may not be for another. Many phenomena are not necessarily best interpreted as masculine or feminine. In addition, the general recommendation emphasized in Chapter 2, that writing should be marked by irony in Rorty's (1989) sense, that is, doubting the appropriateness of one's framework and way of reasoning and awareness about alternative ways of framing discussions and interpreting phenomena, is particularly valid in the use of the concepts of masculinities and femininities. Nevertheless, these concepts are valuable interpretive tools and gender studies could not do without them. A cautious, ironic approach is therefore to be recommended. One should be careful in sorting out analytical use of the terms and empirical descriptions of cultural meanings among people being studied, and seek a balance between analytical definitions and theoretical reasoning on the one hand and sensitivity for cultural context on the other. When combined with careful listening to the meanings ascribed by the subjects being addressed and followed by cautious interpretative work and careful grounding, an interest in masculinities and femininities as aspects of workplace cultures, social practices and identities may be productive in gender studies.

Division of labour, sex typing and gender symbolism

In society there exist more or less profound ideas that certain types of education, career choices, work and certain positions are connected with a particular gender. As we saw in Chapter 3, labour markets as well as work organizations are divided up according to gender. One can say that most jobs are sex-typed. They are defined as feminine or masculine and thus seen as natural for women or men, respectively, to occupy. One could also say that a job has a certain gender symbolism (Billing and Alvesson, 1994). Symbolism refers to objects – words, physical things and acts – which are seen as carrying a broader meaning than they 'objectively' do. A symbol is rich in meaning and evokes a subjective response, shared by people who are part of the same culture. The concept of gender symbolism goes a bit deeper than sex-typing, meaning not only that a particular job is openly viewed as women's or men's work, but that it refers also to non-explicit meanings, unconscious fantasies and associations. While sex-typing only means that some jobs are defined as suitable (only) for men or women respectively, gender symbolism refers to the cultural logic behind such typing. Most work does not exist as gender-neutral but is attributed some form of masculinity or femininity, either vaguely or in the shape of more specific ideas about what the work involves and the kind of qualities typically possessed by a 'man' or a 'woman'. Examples of occupations with a strong masculine gender symbolism are fireman, post-mortem examiner and army officer, while secretary, seamstress, fashion creator, hairdresser and nurse are as a rule connected with different versions of femininity.[7] (Such appears to be the case at least in the part of the world in which we live.) Jobs perceived as including affirming, beautifying, enhancing and celebrating the well-being and status of others are typically seen as feminine, while jobs requiring the jobholder to be stern, impassive or cool – such as policing or bank management – are seen more as masculine (Cockburn, 1991). Many technical jobs are constructed as masculine, and thereby as antithetical to women (Burris, 1996).

Many socially important jobs have traditionally been given a masculine flavour. Management and leadership are regularly viewed as socially constructed in masculine terms, making it difficult for a female manager to strike a balance between being seen as a competent manager/leader and as sufficiently feminine not to be viewed as breaking with gender expectations. According to Stivers (1993), professional expertise is often described in masculine terms, inconsistent with dominating understandings of woman-hood. Professions are often successful in promoting an aura of objectivity, an assertion of autonomy, hierarchicalism and the norm of brotherhood among the members. As we mentioned above, the masculinity of these work areas is not self-evident. In addition, there is variation between the professions.

The social construction of education and jobs in terms of masculinity and femininity is crucial for how men and women become located in the labour market and in organizations. Most people conform up to a point to social norms and expectations of engaging in sex-consistent behaviour, for example, for men to exhibit signs of masculinity and avoid too much feminine behaviour. They also identify with and feel natural about choosing an education, forms of employment, job tasks and career moves that are in line with cultural conventions or at least do not break radically with these. The emphasis on masculinities and femininities draws attention to a connected set of social and psychological levels and acknowledges life history as well as the power of social forces contingent upon established cultural notions of masculinities and femininities. This approach is quite different from viewing gender segregation as an outcome of abstract macro-patterns, as if Mr Patriarchy, himself or in the shape of a prolonged arm in the form of an employer, moved in and ordered men and, in particular, women around. It also differs from psychoanalytic understanding, in which the glint in the mother's eye during the first few years of living determines that men should do engineering work and women become nurses some decades later.

This approach argues against the reductionism involved in most explana-tory efforts. As we saw in Chapter 3, such reductionism is common, in which researchers focus either on external social structures or on levels of psychology. Reskin and Padavic (1994: 77) reject socialization explana-tions, arguing that 'far more influential than the messages we picked up 20 years earlier as children are the opportunities, rewards, and punishments we encounter as adults'. They suggest that women, like men, 'choose among the best opportunities open to them', according to criteria such as good pay, autonomy and prestige. They substantiate their argument by referring to several cases indicating that when jobs such as coal mining were opened up for women a large number applied. While it makes sense to argue that gendered socialization does not fully determine occupational choices, it is still of relevance for educational and job choices. Although these choices are not fully free it would be equally problematic to see an objective opportunity structure, mastered by employers and to some extent male workers, as a sole determinant of women's heavily circumscribed choices. The 'best' job is, of course, evaluated according to subjective and inter-subjective criteria. Gender may be highly significant here for the values behind the criteria. Even if high pay has an appeal for most people, other aspects certainly matter, including what is viewed as interesting work and, relatedly, what is meaningful given one's (gender) self-image and identity. Identity is not fixed through early socialization, but is certainly not independent of it. It is best seen in the light of early as well as later life history. How we are constituted by, and relate to, cultural masculinities and femininities must then be related to early and late socialization but also to the present life context and the cultural meanings that permeate it.

We would emphasize the combination of two elements: the wish to confirm one's gender identity, and the historical and contemporary social processes constructing various areas, tasks and positions in gendered terms, with the operation of power in which people are, if not directly punished, then at least deprived of the valuable support of cultural guidelines for doing what is defined as appropriate and natural, leading to insecurity and (self-)doubt.[8] This combination of subjective, cultural and power aspects may account for the gender-conservative orientation of many people in some respects and the ideological and social support by various institutions and powerful actors for this orientation. The complex interplay between external pressure and internalized, subjective orientations must then be considered in order to understand gender division of labour. Explanations then call for manoeuvring between determinism and voluntarism. Determinism is not just about external forces preventing people from fulfilling their wishes, but also about the forces of power producing certain wants, for example to appear masculine or feminine – or, for that matter, to earn a lot of money.

The strong tendency for cultural definitions of masculinities and fem-ininities to guide perceptions and structure the way people live their lives as men and women is not a matter simply of men doing men's work and women doing women's work, but goes much deeper. This is shown by some case study research on the social construction of work.

Hall shows that within a particular occupation there may be different expectations and self-understandings for males and females meaning that the gender symbolism is created in different versions. In the case of waiters and waitresses, there are common ways of doing the job at the same time as there are gender-specific patterns:

> . . . restaurants do gender by defining the smiling, deferring, and flirting scripts in gender terms and by demanding appropriate behaviour, whereas male and female

servers do gender by differentially enacting gendered scripts of good service. (1993: 458)

Female servers, for example, see themselves as friendlier than male servers and are also perceived by customers and managers in this way, Hall says.

Adkins (1992) also mentions examples of different expectations of women and men regarding appearance. At a hotel and a leisure park, regardless of which jobs women applied for, they had to be attractive; for men there were no parallel requirements (although all had to be well-groomed). Gender segregation meant that at the hotel men constituted the majority of the bar staff and women the majority of the waiting staff. The task content was similar, and one could imagine that similar worker qualities were required. This was the case to some extent, but in addition bar staff 'were required to be "strong", "smart", and to have "good communication skills",' whereas waiting staff 'were required to be "attractive" and "caring"' (p. 215). The specifications were not related to occupational requirements but to the gender of the occupants, says Adkins. 'The conditions and controls operating in relation to women workers' appearance and dress acted together to produce a sexually commodified female workforce' (p. 218). Besides being attractive to get the job women also had to maintain this attractive appearance in order to keep the job.

> . . . Examples of such forms of control included warnings about looking tired, having chipped nail varnish, wearing 'weird' make up, and looking 'sloppy'. In all these cases management reported they had 'no option' but to intervene to attempt to get the women to correct their appearance problems, and if, as was the case for some of the women, they did not respond to the warnings, the managers had 'no choice' but to dismiss them. (Adkins, 1992: 216)

According to Adkins, the requirement for men was to wear their uniforms, but their appearance was never subject to intervention.

An important observation is that it is seldom the inherent character of a particular job that determines its femaleness or maleness. When one gender comprises most or all of the jobholders, people tend to believe that this gender is particular well suited to do the job and that the one-genderedness is a natural – rather than a cultural/socially constructed – phenomenon. Many jobs have over the years been redefined in terms of gender. We mentioned clerks in the previous chapter. As Leidner (1991) shows, almost any job may be constructed as either male or female, through emphasizing some dimensions and labelling them in a particular way. (The exception is mainly jobs calling for physical strength.) Leidner has studied insurance salesmen. These people had the task of visiting potential customers at their homes, establishing contact ('warming up the prospects'), going through the basic sales presentation to counter any objections raised by the prospects and to persuade them to buy as much life insurance as possible. Most people they contacted tried to prevent this sequence from being fully implemented, making the work difficult. Despite the fact that this kind of job is interactive and may equally well be said to call for 'feminine' qualities, almost all the sales staff in the company were men. The male persons Leidner interviewed felt strongly that women would be unlikely to succeed in the job. The manager said that he 'would never hire a woman' for the job. Leidner notes that this kind of job is done primarily by women in Japan and, also in a US context, requires skills that are not generally viewed as 'manly'. Sales staff must swallow insults, treat people with deference and keep smiling. Of interest therefore is how the salesmen construct their jobs through reinterpreting some features and de-emphasizing others. According to Leidner the company's trainers and agents 'assigned a heroic character to the job, framing interactions with customers as contests of will. To succeed, they emphasized, required determination, aggressiveness, persistence, and stoicism' (p. 166). Through stressing toughness as a key quality the job was constructed as manly. Women were felt to be too sensitive, too unaggressive and not able to withstand repeated rejection in sales calls, according to some salesmen. In other sales organizations employing mainly women, qualities such as nurturance, helpfulness and service were viewed as crucial. These qualities were not absent in accounts of work in the insurance company, but they were clearly less pronounced. The conceptualization of work as an arena for enacting masculinity has several consequences. The salesmen become more inclined to accept conditions that otherwise may have been seen as unacceptably frustrating and demeaning. The definition of the work makes the men employed unprepared to accept women jobholders.

In the area of advertising, in Sweden, the job of project assistant is at present regarded as being 'feminine' (Alvesson, 1997). It is seen as a typical women's job. Some decades ago this was not the case. Then project assistants were typically men. It was considered to be a natural start for people who eventually became project managers. Nevertheless, this gradually changed and at present it is looked upon as a little extraordinary for a man to have this job. A woman interviewed mentioned that at one of her previous workplaces there was 'actually' a male project assistant! According to her he himself wanted to work as such: 'He had a humble personality and wanted to start somewhere to learn the advertising trade. Many were sceptical towards a male project assistant, but it worked out very well.'

It can be noted that an extraordinary – and perhaps for a male rather atypical – personality trait explains this successful outcome of a deviant case, according to the (female) person interviewed. Closely associated with the conceptions that it is 'natural' for women and not for men to be project assistants is the hierarchy regarding positions. In society as a whole men are greatly over-represented in higher posts while women to a larger extent are found in the lower posts. It is interesting to note the changes in the meaning of the genderedness of this work. Earlier project assistant work was seen as apprenticeship – a temporary position on the road upward. An assistant was understood to be a future project manager. The job was then viewed as typically and properly male. At present the job as assistant is viewed as a more stable position, not necessarily leading anywhere (a dead-end job) and as typical for women.

Gender symbolism is not restricted to the work or occupation but also to the social field and organization in question as well as to specific activities. Also social positions are sometimes loaded with gender symbolism. Generally, masculinity is associated with higher positions, while assisting work is not just subordinate but also regarded as feminine. One should note the spatial metaphors used for describing hierarchical social relations: high and low. (More about metaphors in the next chapter.) By seeing these relations in such terms, the particular image of the subject matter is illustrated. That height and position are unconsciously seen as related is illustrated by a study in which a person from England visiting Australia was introduced in various ways for different audiences. Some were led to believe that he was a student, others a laboratory assistant, again others a lecturer, and a fourth group was told that he was a professor. People were asked to estimate his physical height. Perceptions of height were neatly correlated with academic standing, and the 'professor' was seen as being two-and-a-half inches taller than the 'student' (Wilson, cited in Johns, 1983). Given that height symbolizes authority – we talk of high positions, senior officers in organizations are typically located on the top floors and, as the experiment shows, we even perceive 'higher' graded persons as physically taller than others – and that men typically are taller than women, we can see how gender becomes trapped in the spatial metaphors of height. The idea of higher/lower position has a masculine/feminine bearing and the relative height of men seems to reinforce notions of authority and high positions/ranks. This phenomenon is reflected in various situations, from the norm that males should be taller than their female partners to the observation, made by Rosen (1988), that at a corporate party males danced with junior females and females danced with their senior males and colleagues at the same level, but the combination of higher-ranking female and lower-ranking male never materialized on the dance floor. More generally, the norm appears to be that the husband should not have a lower position or lower pay than the wife.

These cases show the deep-seated nature of masculine and feminine meanings governing gendered life. To understand these dynamics, the interaction between various levels must be considered: the macro-level of cultural definitions relating masculinity and femininity to certain sectors in life, the meso-level in which social interactions bring about constructions which cannot simply be predicted or understood from a macro-level (illustrated by Leidner's and Alvesson's studies above) and the subjective orientations of people in which established clues for sex-consistent and, thereby, identity-confirming actions and orientations are embraced and reproduced. Without stressing the level of psychology too much, it is vital to appreciate the significance of identity for understanding the role of cultural masculinity and femininity. We will therefore develop this particular aspect at some length.

Masculinities, femininities and identity

Understanding masculinities and femininities thus calls for an interest in identity. Identity marks the consistency and distinctiveness of a person. It answers the questions, 'Who am I?' and, when identity is ascribed to someone else, 'Who is he/she?' Identity is also a matter of continuity, coherence and distinctiveness. Identity is, of course, heavily gendered as perhaps nothing is so crucial as gender for one's self-definition and others' inclination to fix a person in a social category. There are, however, situations where other aspects of identity (race, nationality, occupation, ethnicity, age, group membership, corporate belonging) or personal identity (aggressive, sport-freak, shy, having-been-brought-up-by-unloving-parents) may be more salient. Identities must be constructed: they do not exist as an objective set of characteristics, but involve the creation of meaning on the part of the individual persons and others contributing to the definition of identity. Answers to questions, 'Who am I?' and, 'What kind of person am I?' are thus not answered once and for all, but call for continuing struggles as social interactions and experiences change not only over time, but also during the work day as one encounters a variety of people and situations in a complex, ambiguous and often fragmented social world. It is important to stress that this fluidity – the processual nature of identity – is contingent upon social relations and language use. One does not develop and maintain identity in splendid isolation, but in close interaction with other people, who confirm, support or disrupt different identity claims. Language is vital as there are a variety of ways of answering identity questions.

People in their lives, inside as well as outside organizations, routinely engage in identity work – aiming to achieve a feeling of a coherent and strong self, necessary for coping with the ambiguities of existence, work tasks and social relations. Identities are multiple and contextual. A person may see herself as a result-oriented manager as well as a loving mother and a politically conservative voter. Fragmentation and diversity are then counteracted through links showing some mediation and continuity. A high income associated with making a career and being a manager may be seen as securing a materially good home. Pressures from work as well as family can come together in an attitude of 'effectiveness': being well organized, using working time effectively, being impatient with 'nonsense' and red tape, balancing work and home life. Family values and conservatism may be seen as supporting each other.

Identities are crucial in the regulation of self-esteem and self-perception as well as social interaction and work behaviour. Identities are associated with values, meanings and logics of action. They govern deeper forms of subjectivities – feelings and thinking – and are thus a highly significant aspect of work organizations.

Identities may be individual or social. A social identity refers to answers to the question, 'Who am I?' that are of a social nature. The person defines herself (is defined by others) as a member of a group or a social category.

A woman, an engineer, a Canadian, an IBM employee are all examples of social identities. Sometimes it is said that men more often are identified as autonomous persons, with an individual identity, while women are identified as a part of a collective (Sahlin-Andersson, 1994). In a study of nurses and doctors, this tendency was clear. Of course, the (male) doctors were defined in terms of a group identity, with clear boundaries between the occupational group and other groups, but also the individual differences in style, preference, and so on, were clearly considered at the workplace. The nurses were treated more as members of a collective:

> The nurses as a collective responded to the needs and wants of the individual doctors. The nurses seldom go to just any doctor for information; nearly always they need to give or get information from a specific doctor, and they know how to adjust their own work to the individual doctors. (1994: 139)

The gender point should not be overstressed; it presumably overlaps heavily with location in the organizational hierarchy (class). The hierarchy overlaps to some extent with sex distribution, but there are female managers and professionals as well as a lot of male low-level employees so the sex/hierarchy correlation is far from perfect. The higher the position, the more likely that group qualities are weakened and individual features are emphasized in defining a person. Nevertheless, there may still be a tendency for women to be seen in terms of social category irrespective of hierarchical position. At least it is worth considering whether sex-belonging may be seen as more crucial than individuality for women than men in many organizational situations.[9]

Identities are, at least partly, developed in the context of power relations (Foucault 1980, 1982; Knights and Willmott 1985, 1989). The exercise of power depends on the development of subjects tied to particular identities regarding how one should feel, think and act. This aspect of power/subjectivity is crucial for understanding gender identities.[10] In comparison with role theory, this understanding of identity in the context of masculinities/femininities emphasizes how power works through constraining feelings, thoughts and actions. This is accomplished through offering standards for being and discouraging 'abnormal' ways of thinking, feeling and acting. Power here operates through normalization, through defining what is normal, natural and acceptable, and through invoking fear and uncertainty about deviating from this ideal – not through knocking people on the head or preventing them from doing anything.[11]

The trend in modern society is that the material practices – crucial for the identity of the traditional peasant or blacksmith (whose identity was never at stake or even emerged as a meaningful category as the question, 'Who am I?' was hardly ever raised) – are less significant today. Social–discursive interaction, including talk and narratives, becomes particularly vital for identity (Alvesson, 1994; Giddens, 1991; Shotter and Gergen, 1989). Through describing oneself in a particular way, one expresses and reinforces a particular identity. The contemporary age tends to produce highly precarious identities as a consequence of rapid changes, a wide set of options and the presence of a broad set of models, not least in terms of gender. This situation triggers intense efforts at securing identities, including finding a balance between continuity and flexibility.

This means both opportunities and vulnerabilities. In the context of gender, it is clear that modern forms of gender identities are more multi-faceted and varied than they were a couple of decades ago. Domesticity and sexuality as images of women still exist and facilitate some self-understandings and behaviours and make others, including those that facilitate careers, less viable. But in large sectors of contemporary society they do not dominate any longer. The modern, professional, career-oriented woman is certainly a legitimate social identity – although potentially a problematic one for women to adopt if it breaks too strongly with traditional ideas of femininities associated with sexual attractiveness and family orientation. There is also an increased openness and accept-ability of homosexuality and of living single. In the mass media we encounter a broad set of male and female types: from those one-dimensionally and stereotypically emphasizing looks and appearance through female detectives and other heroines on television and on film to journalists, managers and politicians. In the Nordic countries there are, or have recently been, one female president (Iceland), one female prime minister (Norway), two female foreign ministers (Sweden) and even a female defence minister (Finland), plus several female leaders of political parties represented in parliament. The person of today, at least in the Western world, encounters many females in high-status public positions, although still considerably fewer than males. At the same time, the influence of role models (in the media), ideals and options coexist with opposite features such as the continuing gender division of labour, in and outside work. There are more successful females in the mass media than in the average corporate workplace. There are clashes between ideals and realities; the continuing presence of traditional and patriarchal under-standings of gender, and conflicts between espoused, progressive and unconscious, conservative understandings of the meaning of being a man or a woman, mean that gender identities are precarious and vulnerable. The fight between opening up and broadening the space for acceptable potential gendered – and perhaps non-gendered – identities and securing an identity not exposed to social sanctions and self-doubts is ongoing and very much felt by many younger persons in the more progressive sections of society in modern countries. For older persons such changes towards redefinitions of gender identities may offer less opportunities and more confusion and irritation. For older women, it may signal lost opportunities and arouse grief, triggering defensive reactions such as hostility to gender equality.

There are contradictions between, on the one hand, values, expectations and identities encouraging openness and a broad set of possibilities and, on the other hand, the strains and sanctions associated with breaking with established notions of what is appropriate or not to being a man or a woman. In addition, there is the psychologically internalized rather than externally imposed anxiety concerning being insufficiently masculine or feminine. This creates a messy situation and considerable uncertainty and identity strain for those following paths that are still seen as gender-inconsistent or atypical. To choose highly gender-traditional routes is not always fully satisfactory in contemporary society. There is an increasing pressure to avoid falling into sex roles and also to avoid gender-stereotypical behaviour. In Sweden, statistics indicating that men do not do their share of the housework and care of the children receive critical attention in the mass media and this situation is seen as unsatisfactory among an increasing number of people. The position of the housewife is almost stigmatized by younger people. It is broadly viewed as old-fashioned and a trap for women.

Even though people breaking with established gender patterns are encouraged, sometimes seen as pioneers and valued as individualistic and progressive, at the same time they often face scepticism. Male elementary teachers, for example, are sometimes stereotyped as feminine because of their work; sometimes they are suspected of being 'too masculine' for this kind of work and not sensitive enough to the needs of the children (Allan, 1993).[12] More generally, men in non-traditional occupations are sometimes suspected of being homosexual. In the Danish trade union for kindergarten personnel 15 per cent of the members are men, but they hold all posts on the board and are in a majority as trade union workers. There are no simple explanations for this unexpected pattern. It appears, however, that men are more interested than women in having these 'male' positions in order to escape from being stereotyped as above and to sustain a male identity (Billing, 1995). Similarly, most of the employees in the sectors of cleaning and childcare who started their own companies (when the Swedish public sector opened up for privatization) were men, despite the fact that they only formed a small minority of all the employees in the sector. This may partly be explained by the masculine appeal of being an entrepreneur (Sundin, 1997).

Summary

In this chapter we have argued that a focus on the social construction of masculinities and femininities may be a productive approach to under-standing gender division of labour and other organizational phenomena. One advantage is a broad interpretive range – that is, if one is not tying the concepts too closely to what are viewed as characteristics of men and women – capable of interpreting a large number of organizational aspects. Another is that it transcends the reductionism associated with either a macro- or micro-focus. It avoids 'sociologism' as well as 'psychologism' (it may, however, be accused of 'culturalism' and of missing economic and structural as well as 'deep' psychological dimensions). Through looking at how we construct, conform to or transcend notions of masculinities and femininities we can connect to subjectivities, experiences and intentions as well as to cultural wholes, broader patterns and social constraints.

The weaknesses and problems are, on the other hand, profound. Stivers's remark about the dangers of using dichotomies is relevant for researchers to consider as much as people 'out there' in everyday life:

> The dichotomous nature of our thinking, the conviction that masculinity and femininity are mutually exclusive, sometimes leads us to leap to one extreme in an effort to avoid or deny the other. (1993: 123)

It is also too easy to read masculinities or femininities into everything. Arbitrary ascriptions are common. Researchers often rely on commonsensical or vague impressionistic understandings, sometimes expressing rather than just 'correctly' illuminating stereotypical ideas. Sometimes what is seen as masculine may reflect the view of white middle-class feminists rather than the cultural meanings of other groups. Feminists sometimes seem to have rather 'weak' criteria for seeing something as masculine, while 'higher' standards may be employed by blue-collar workers as well as by people in business life. This of course does not prevent interpreting masculine meanings in settings where these are not socially recognized by one group or another from being potentially productive (for example, Fondas, 1997). But care should guide such enterprises so that they do not get caught up in arbitrary interpretation or cultural and theoretical relativism: where what is masculine for one person or group is not so for another and any opinion is as good or bad as the other. The ambition must be to go beyond what is viewed as 'masculine' only by an individual or even a group of feminists and 'masculinists' and ground this ascription/interpretation in more broadly shared cultural meanings. One should always raise the question, 'For whom does something appear as a form of masculinity or femininity?'

An important aspect of masculinities or femininities is identity. Historical determinations and restrictions as well as tendencies to transcend these must be considered. Contemporary forms of identities offer a broad set of possible ways of being for men and women, at least in parts of the Western countries. Many of these identities are, however, far from contradiction-free. Choosing unconventional tracks often leads to difficulties in securing stable self-identities. These difficulties follow from explicit social sanctions or lack of support as well as internalized conventional ideas about attaining sufficient signs of masculinity if one is a 'man', or of femininity if one is a 'woman'. These cultural standards still constrain people in terms of options that work well, socially and psychologically. Contemporary possibilities and life history, including early identifications, such as with parents or mass media models, do not necessarily go hand in hand, thus making identities vulnerable.

The social origin and relational character of identities mean that a focus on identity goes beyond the psychological level. But drawing attention to the multi-level character of masculine and feminine meanings, to the need for personal reflection and self-transformation as a part of gender changes, is emphasized. It is not only or mainly structures 'out there' that matter. Most people – including professional students of gender – are at least in some respects stubborn carriers of conservative gender patterns and reproduce these in everyday life as well as in important choices, such as in education. Arguably, the interplay between culture – at various levels from the societal level to the workplace level – and subjectivities suggested by the concepts of masculinities and femininities is a fruitful way of avoiding sociological as well as psychological reductionism. In the next chapter we continue this line of inquiry and address organizational culture and gender.

Notes

1 Social constructivism refers to a rather broad set of orientations. Some of these tend to focus so strongly on the social that psychological consideration is excluded. Here we adopt a looser approach, in which the study of subjectivities and identities, while seen in the context of social processes and constructions, also includes an individual element that is not best translated into social terms. Some versions emphasize the constructedness of everything, giving analysis a relativistic orientation, social constructions being impossible to evaluate in terms of 'true' or 'false'. At the risk of being eclectic or indecisive, we push the constructivist line of thinking less far and view social ideas as more or less well founded – for example, beliefs about female managers may be compared with studies of the behaviour of female managers – even though the major focus is to investigate how people create their social reality, which is something else than testing this reality.

2 In this sense, it may be argued that the voices of men belong to those neglected by dominating trends in gender studies. The critique of mainstream management studies for being male-centred does not seem to consider the difference between men as managers and/or as oppressors of women, and men voicing more personal experiences.

3 The list gives the impression of being rather unsystematic and the empirical grounding of the five forms is not clear. The terms seem to refer to partly disparate, partly overlapping phenomena.

4 For matters of convenience we sometimes talk about masculinity/ femininity, which should not obscure our awareness of there being a variety of versions of these.

5 Some authors distinguish between masculinity as a set of traits, i.e. a part of personality, and masculinity as an ideology, i.e. beliefs that a man should have these attributes (Pleck et al., 1993). The view adhered to by us is a third one, in which masculinity stands for an ascribed meaning to a phenomenon. One may think of a phenomenon in terms of masculinity without necessarily endorsing or rejecting it.

6 An elitist/a priori approach means that the researcher decides in advance, and without listening to the voice of the field, about central categories, theoretical concepts and/or hypotheses (Deetz, 1996).

7 These jobs are, of course, also sex-typed. The fact that the jobs are sex-typed according to a male/female dichotomy co-exists with a much more varied gender symbolism. The masculinities typically ascribed to the work of a fireman and a post-mortem examiner, respectively, have little in common.

8 The 'rewards and punishments' accounting for gender behaviour are thus not just, or even mainly, a matter of receiving money or negative sanctions, as Reskin and Padavic (1994) seem to be suggesting, but also a matter of confirming or frustrating one's self-image and self-esteem. While sometimes cruder forms of rewards and punishments may be involved, the most significant ways in which modern power operates in the area of gender are in terms of encouraging and discouraging certain gender standards and the production of emotions of

uncertainty and anxiety when we and/or people around us feel that those standards are not being met.

9 A (possible) tendency in this direction is not simply conservative and anti-women, although it may in particular situations work in that way. Feminists too emphasize the social identity of women, for example, when they talk about women's experiences and encourage solidarity. To stress belongingness to a social category rather than individuality and individual variation is part of the political project of feminism. Of course, men too – when considered – are seen in terms of a social category, so feminism does not reproduce the tendency to ascribe to men an individual identity and to women a social one.

10 There is a tendency among some Foucault-inspired authors to connect power and identity (subjectivity) very tightly. We have some problems with an all-embracing view on power as something lurking behind any expression or sign of subjectivity. As with all concepts and ideas, hampering the inclination to use the concept of power everywhere and saving it for especially productive interpretations may be a good, albeit an imprecise, rule.

11 The reader may recall the critique of role theory for neglecting issues of power, reviewed in Chapter 3, and ask why a connection between role and power cannot be made. We would not rule out the possibility of using role concepts in a more power-conscious way, although most uses of role theory and the associations of roles do not seem to encourage such a move.

12 Minority status was a mixed blessing for male kindergarten teachers, according to a Finnish study (Kauppinen-Toropainen and Lammi, 1993). They were often treated as favourites by the children and their parents, while their female colleagues sometimes felt envy and frustration, as they saw this as an effect of maleness and greater visibility rather than professional superiority.

5

Gender, Organizational Culture and Sexuality

In this chapter we continue the investigation of workplace relations from a cultural point of view. It is organizational level cultures and related issues, such as occupational cultures, that are of interest. In particular, the chapter examines cultural meanings associated with masculinities and femininities and discusses some problems and advantages with the idea of studying organizations and other gendered institutions through this framework. The meaning of, and norms regulating, the expression of sexuality in workplaces is an important element of organizational culture. The chapter shows some of the complexities and unexpected patterns and contradictions of gender in a case study of the openly 'sexualized' workplace culture of an advertising agency.

On organizational culture

Interest in organizational culture existed long before the 'corporate culture boom' of the early 1980s, but since this time a broader and more consistent interest in this area has emerged. There is enormous variation in the definitions and even more so in the use of the term 'culture' in organization theory, particularly among practitioners. Culture certainly has no fixed or broadly agreed-upon meaning in anthropology (Ortner, 1984) – a discipline that many organizational culture authors draw upon – but the variation within the latter group is probably greater than within anthropology and most other cultural disciplines. This has partly to do with the fact that organizational culture literature varies substantially in terms of both purpose and depth. Many studies are narrowly management-oriented and pragmatic while others are interested in broader, more reflective forms of understanding which include more complex aspects of culture which cannot be 'managed' or controlled. A lot of these views of culture are pretty vague. Many who talk about culture refer to everything, and thus nothing.

We use the concept of culture to characterize a set of meanings, ideas and symbols that are shared by the members of a collective and that have evolved over time. Talking about culture then means 'talking about the importance for people of symbolism – of rituals, myths, stories, and legends – and about the interpretation of events, ideas, and experiences that are influenced and shaped by the groups within which they live' (Frost et al., 1985: 17). Culture then directs attention to (1) what is shared by a group and departs from highly individualized ideas and circumstances; (2) the ideational level, that is what is on people's minds, their ideas and beliefs rather than how they behave or something else tangible (although the meaning of behaviour or material is a cultural phenomenon); and (3) the non-rational aspects, the value-laden, partly non-conscious dimensions of social life, including emotional aspects. Culture is thus not measurable, at least not in any simple sense. To understand cultural meanings calls for interpretation – unpacking the deeper aspect of a phenomenon. What surfaces in vocabulary, behaviour, practices and material artefacts must be deciphered. The more interesting cultural meanings are non-conscious and call for considerable depth, including imagination, creativity and tolerance of uncertainty, in interpretative work (Ehn and Löfgren, 1982; Geertz, 1973).

Culture may refer to an entire society or any collective within it, such as a class, a region or a social movement. It may also refer to other entities, for example an organization, a part of it or an occupation. In the present case, organization-related cultural phenomena are not restricted to issues considered to be unitary and unique for a specific organization, but may refer to much broader cultural phenomena, such as industrial-level or Western management culture ideas and meanings, or narrower cultural objects of study, such as group or workplace-level cultural issues. In gender studies it is apparent that the shared orientations of men and women in an organization may differ, despite a possible existence of a set of common values, beliefs and understandings among those working there, i.e. an organizational culture. But men and women-specific orientations may be reinforced, weakened or even almost disappear as gendered meanings and values overlap or are crossed by cultural formations associated with age, occupations, classes, work groups and so on. In one organization there may be male engineers and female secretaries with highly different orientations. In a Finnish study it was found that dominant cultural values of initiative and boldness hardly included the female, low-level employees (Aaltio-Marjasola, 1994). In another organization, young female professionals expressed other orientations than somewhat older low-level female staff and in many respects showed more cultural similarities with the male pro-fessionals (Sundin, 1993).

A qualified cultural study thus calls for attention to a variety of cultural configurations in an organization. Sometimes a unique and unitary organ-izational culture may be of interest to focus on, sometimes a variety of subcultures will be central in the study. Before making crucial choices in terms of level and adequate conceptualization of interesting cultural groups a number of different possibilities must be considered (Alvesson, 1993). Sometimes conventional organizational divisions may mislead rather than sensitize cultural analysis.

The cultural approach in organization studies proceeds from the assump-tion that the ideas, the definitions of reality and the meanings which are shared in common by a collective (a company, a work group, for example) are a central – perhaps even the central – feature of organizations. This approach draws attention to the question 'How is organization accomplished and what does it mean to be organized?' (Smircich, 1983: 353). More or less integrated patterns of common ideas and meanings constitute the core of structures which denote relative stability in an organization. They have their roots in, and are influenced by, various social and material practices. They do not persist unchanged, but are recreated and reinforced (and sometimes weakened or changed) in a multitude of different situations, in everyday language, in actions and in material structures – and in a multifaceted network of symbols, meanings and significations (Alvesson and Berg, 1992; Frost et al., 1985, 1991; Martin, 1992; Smircich, 1983, etc.).

Culture is the framework that guides action and social relations, 'the medium of life' (Czarniawska-Joerges, 1991). It facilitates social life, but also includes elements of constraints and conservatism as it tends to freeze social reality: to subordinate people to dominating ideas, beliefs and taken-for-granted assumptions. Even though there are also cultural meanings and values in organizations that are pro-equality, in gender studies critical aspects of the gendered subtext of organizational life are often of the greatest interest.

As we have said, culture involves assumptions and ideas that are taken for granted. This quality means that questioning, or at any rate serious questioning, of existing social conditions is not pronounced. Basic social conditions tend to be taken for granted and the social world will be regarded as natural, neutral and legitimate (Deetz and Kersten, 1983; Frost, 1987). There is often limited awareness that social reality can be experienced and understood in radically different ways, and that an infinite number of approaches are possible. An acceptance of this calls for selectivity in the view of experienced social conditions, and 'complementary' selectivity in interpreting and assessing what is heard and seen. Culture closes minds. Behaviour assumed to be feminine is for example seen as natural and self-evident when performed by females, but surprising, odd and unnatural when characterizing a man and vice versa.

The creation and recreation of meaning is not primarily located in the heads of people, although something must happen there too for culture to 'work'. Rather it comes in the form of a traffic in significant symbols, which guides thinking, feeling and social interaction. Meaning, from a cultural point of view, is social and public. Its natural habitat is the market place and the town square, according to Geertz (1973: 45), and, one could add, meetings and other social actions and events in a company. But also stories, vocabularies and artefacts – physical objects such as buildings, equipment and office arrangements embodying meaning – may be seen as cultural expressions. Through investigating such phenomena we can study how selectivity and control in the construction of meaning is accomplished.

As we have stated, our sympathies in this book imply that we do not strongly link a gender perspective specifically to 'men' and 'women' as fixed objects to be counted in organizations. Instead it is conceptions and discourses about men and women, the masculine and the feminine, that are focused upon. As important social phenomena, gender relations thus influence the fundamental functioning of organizations and our general way of thinking about aims, rationality, values, leadership and so on (Calás and Smircich, 1992a, 1992b). This kind of thinking works well with a cultural approach. One may talk of a gendered-organizations perspective rather than a gender-in-organizations approach (Hall, 1993) as a way of illuminating the gendered nature of organizational and occupational cultures. This means that 'gender is not simply imported into the workplace: gender itself is constructed in part through work' (Leidner, 1991: 170). Gender is thus partly seen as an organizational accomplishment – and not something that is fixed and ready and then the object for certain arrangements and mechanisms in organizations. Workplace culture thus is seen as constructing beliefs about and self-understandings of men and women, what is masculine and feminine, thus shaping gender identities.

Gender can function as a perspective or as an inspiration for a set of metaphors for the understanding of organizations (Billing and Alvesson, 1994; Gherardi, 1995). Gender dimensions can thus be observed also on a more abstract level than simply in relation to the concrete circumstances and relations of men and women.

Gendering organizational culture theory thus provides an approach for an exploration of cultural meanings of physical objects, actions and verbal expressions loosely coupled to the specific mix of sexes – or even lack of a mix (in one-sex only contexts) – directly involved. All kinds of organizational structures and processes are seen as carriers of cultural meaning, drawing upon and producing gendered ideas, values and assumptions. This does not mean that everything is treated in terms of gender, but that everything is carefully *considered* in these terms before one finally decides if and how to treat subject matter. Business language and practices, such as corporate strategy, campaign, conquests of markets, raiders or take-overs, may, for example, be conceptualized in terms of dominating masculinities (Knights and Morgan, 1991), but the origin of, for example, strategy in the military is not in itself sufficient to say that all corporate strategy talk and practice express masculinity.

The cultural patterns of organizations may be of particular interest to investigate in the following ways: (1) how cultural meanings interact with gender division of labour – both in terms of how organizational structure brings about certain meanings (Kanter, 1977) and how these cultural meanings contribute to a certain sex distribution in the organizational structure; (2) how dominating values and beliefs are culturally defined as, or associated with, maleness or – but probably more rarely – femaleness, and thus in different ways guide everyday organizational life and social interaction; (3) how organizations play a part in the socializing processes in which people acquire, mould, change, broaden or constrain gender identities; and (4) how organizational goals, structures and social relations lead to 'external' consequences, for example, for social life outside the core organization, or for the environment, due to their gendered nature. Investigating masculine domination in certain types of organizations may, for example, throw light on control and exploitation of customers and nature.

As mentioned in earlier chapters, the cultural meaning of jobs is highly significant for the division of labour. Many ideas on gender are culturally shared well beyond the individual organization or occupation. Images and self-understandings of women associating them with subordination, domesticity and sexuality are, for example, an integrated part of Western culture and account for the distribution of women in certain types of service jobs. The cultural meaning of a 'woman' may thus include the more or less explicit and conscious element of a service-provider. (The meaning may well be partly non-conscious.) But there is an enormous variation in this respect between different contexts, associated with wide although uneven and often contradictory changes taking place. The images and self-understandings may be more or less embraced by different groups – of men as well as women – and thus be noticeable to different extents and in various ways in different organizational contexts. Also within a specific industry there may be clear variation between different organizations in the same field in terms of gender meanings, as Blomqvist (1994) shows in a study of 17 Swedish knowledge-intensive companies. Organization culture studies are thus interested in local variation and uniqueness as well as broader cultural phenomena in the context of organizations. Specific organizational cultures form fine-tuned nets of meaning that subtly inform and encourage people to play out gender in certain ways and discourage them from doing so in ways that are not socially sanctioned.

Pressure for homogeneity and culturally competent behaviour

As we have said, culture is about shared meanings. The concept implies a certain degree of homogeneity in the ways of relating to reality. Even in a 'liberal culture' in which individualism and variety are celebrated there are shared expectations and understandings of what is identified as 'individualism' and not social incompetence, deviance or psychiatric problems. The moral pressure for being 'individualistic' may include an expectation that people adopt one of ten or so prefabricated lifestyles and consumption patterns designed and marketed for 'individualists'. The celebration of 'individualism' may be accompanied by intolerance of a person who does not appear to be a 'true' individualist. There are thus shared, conformist ideas defining and prescribing 'individualism'.

In an organizational context, the level of tolerance for deviations is often rather low. Corporate culture stands for ideas, meanings and norms bringing about homogeneity and predictability in understanding, thinking and valuing among people. This is vital for the efficient functioning of complex large-scale organizations. The need for smooth communication and the reduction of uncertainty and, relatedly, the importance attached to knowing the rules of the game, means a strong pressure toward conformity (Kanter, 1977). Especially in the context of management work in large companies, where the level of ambiguity is high and the importance of nurturing one's image, appearing successful and going upward is vital, the social rules are in favour of 'team playing'. The expectations and norms in this respect are sharply explored by Jackall (1988: 56):

> . . . a team player is alert to the social cues that he receives from his bosses, his peers, and the intricate pattern of social networks, coteries, and cliques that crisscross the organization . . . a team player 'fits in'. He is a role player who plays his part without complaint. He does not threaten others by appearing brilliant, or with his personality, his ability, or his personal values. He masks his ambition and his aggressiveness with blandness. He recognizes trouble and stays clear of it. He protects his boss and his associates from blunders . . . In short, he makes other managers feel comfortable, the crucial virtue in an uncertain world, and establishes with others the easy predictable familiarity that comes from sharing taken for granted frameworks about how the world works.

More generally, having the correct, well-targeted cultural competence and skills to master symbolism in appearance and language use is crucial for success in many areas (Bourdieu, 1979; Swidler, 1986). This pressure for similarity in understandings and style acts against outsiders – those people whose characteristics deviate from the established groups. Women may experience feelings of uncertainty, if all or a large majority of the other group and especially senior managers are men. Even when negative expectations do not prevail, the mastery of the cues for operating and the skilful mastery of the 'team player' role may be more difficult for women. The word 'team' in itself – originating in the sports world – may be seen as more alien for many women than for men, even though the social and cooperative connotations of the term may also be seen as including feminine meanings. Even if a specific female has no problems, the surroundings may give the impression that it is a world which one more easily associates with men than women. More generally, talk, appearance and actions of women may appear as more ambiguous and difficult to read for an established community of men. Women may thus sometimes be in an unfavourable situation in terms of assuring seniors and colleagues of the reliability and predictability so much valued in complex organizational settings.

Of course, it is hardly so that women are the only group which may encounter this level of difficulty in relationship to the world of white, male, middle- and upper-class corporate management. Other, or overlapping, social characteristics may also create problems. Colour, ethnicity, sexual orientation, education, class background also matter. In Western countries, a white woman with an upper-class background and an MBA from a prestigious university may act symbolically more smoothly in the upper levels of many companies than a black, muslim, homosexual engineer with a lower-class background. In fact, the upper-class MBA woman is not unlikely to reach a relatively high position, although probably lower than her male peer, while the black muslim engineer probably would not go very far. All this varies, of course. In some companies, where senior managers have worked themselves up from below and a large part of the labour force does not have higher education, an upper-class background may not facilitate integration and skilful symbolic behaviour. Even though many other social factors than gender matter for cultural adaptation and a career in management, the female sex still represents a source of uncertainty in many contexts and women may thus be more inclined to face unease, scepticism and even resistance and hostility or at least some difficulties in smooth interaction and manoeuvring (Gherardi, 1995).

Illustrating culture: rituals, artefacts and metaphors

Culture is often seen as expressed and reproduced in three basic forms: through actions and orchestrated events, material objects and verbal expressions rich in cultural meaning (Alvesson and Berg, 1992; Pondy et al., 1983). Many actions, events, physical objects and language in organizations do not say very much about culture, as they are more technical than rich in symbolism and meaning, but some others do. Some such actions and sets of actions are called rituals, while physical objects are referred to as cultural artefacts. After briefly addressing rituals and artefacts, we will at some length deal with culturally rich verbal expressions, or metaphors.

Rituals

A ritual is an activity including certain repetitive patterns which contain symbolic and expressive elements. A ritual has a specific form guiding behaviour. In organizations, meetings often function as rituals. Instrumental outcomes – decisions, information sharing, problem solving – are less significant than symbolic outcomes, such as sentiments, attitudes, values (Pfeffer, 1981). Meetings are seldom efficiently carried out or lead to rational outcomes, but reflect the messy, ambiguous nature of complex organizations (Schwartzman, 1987). In meetings the right values and norms are learned and reproduced. Hierarchical relations may, for example, be expressed and segmented, for example, when a senior manager's authority is underscored by his or her domination of a meeting (Alvesson, 1996a).

A ritual among the top marketing people in Pepsi-Cola described by the former vice-president John Sculley illustrates how a ritual may work:

> Like other meetings, this one was a ceremonial event. We marked it on our calenders many weeks in advance. Everyone wore the unofficial corporate uniform: a blue pin-striped suit, white shirt, and a sincere red tie. None of us would ever remove the jacket. We dressed and acted as if we were at a meeting of the board of directors. (1987: 2)

People entered the room in hierarchical order. First came people from the marketing investigation consultancy company, then junior and subsequently senior managers arrived in order corresponding to their ranks. Corporate formality dictated where people sat. The company's top officers gravitated to the front of the table, the junior executives toward the back. The core of the meetings was the monitoring results. These were often harsh:

> These sessions weren't always euphoric. Often the tension in the room was suffocating. Eyes would fix on Kendall (the chairman) to capture his response at every gain or drop in every tenth of a market share . . . An executive whose share was down had to stand and explain – fully – what he was going to do to fix it fast. Clearly in the dock, he knew that the next time he returned to that room, it had better be fixed . . . Always, there was another executive in the room, ready to take your place. (pp. 4–5)

This example may be contrasted with a ritual in a Swedish industrial company (Alvesson and Björkman, 1992). This organization is also primarily populated by men, most of them engineers or marketing people with an engineering background.

Every third month there is an information meeting for the 40 or so managers in the division. (All are men, with the exception of the female personnel manager and the secretary.) Gustaf, the divisional manager, stands in the door and welcomes all the participants. During the introductory speech he gives a 'soft' impression; his jacket is unbuttoned. The agenda is characterized by several speakers and the divisional manager has a low profile. The manager could have held some of the presentations himself, but chooses to let someone else take the centre stage. The atmosphere is informal and friendly. Sometimes the manager is joking with people and sometimes he is the object of their jokes. During his presentation of results, the controller uses the manager's picture aimed at showing changes in results on different markets in a pedagogical manner: 'Now we go over to Gustaf's own picture, the quantum physics diagram [everybody laughs].' After some comments, Gustaf asks the audience: 'Everybody laughs at me and this diagram. Do you find it unclear? I think it is rather revealing.' Some people reply: 'At first glance it looks quite difficult [laughter] but when you have looked at it some time . . .' 'It is easier for me as I'm colour blind [more laughter].'

During the break, the divisional manager serves coffee together with his secretary and the personnel manager. The overall impression from the meeting is one of community rather than formalism and hierarchy.

Judging from the reactions of Swedish MBA students and managers, who have read the excerpt of Sculley's book as case material in their education, male as well as female evaluations tend to be strongly negative to Pepsi's corporate culture as it appears in the text. According to Sculley (1987), the people in the company accepted the conditions without complaints. We have few indications of how outsiders feel about the other case. A couple of (male) managers during a seminar felt that the manager may have problems with his authority if his subordinates joked about him. People in the organization, including two interviewed women, were on the whole positive to the social and easygoing style of the divisional manager. Even though there may not necessarily be strong gendered reactions in the sense that men appreciate a 'hard' style and women prefer a 'soft' workplace climate and managerial style, it is not unlikely that more women than men would have problems in adapting to – or being fully accepted in – the top management group of Pepsi and that the Swedish industrial company, at least as visible in the observed situation, represents a more gender-neutral, or at least less gender-biased, cultural environment irrespective of the heavy domination of men in terms of numbers.

Rituals may contribute to the construction and reproduction of cultural patterns in a variety of ways. Lindgren (1996) observes in a case study that men engaged in rituals confirming their superiority and women their subordinancy. Often rituals express a rich variety of meanings, some of them heavily gendered, others less so. Consequences in terms of equality or gender segregation may be contradictory, for example when a female manager heads a meeting in an authoritarian way or, as in the case with Gustaf above, a male manager deviates from conventional masculine leadership models.

Cultural artefacts

Cultural artefacts include buildings, offices, furniture, corporate logos, dress and other material objects. In the context of gender, dress is of particular significance. In the case of Pepsi Cola, dress for senior managers is strictly prescribed and appears as a corporate uniform expressing socially shared meanings. Different norms guiding men and women are pronounced in organizational contexts, especially in workplaces and positions where appearance is seen as vital and/or the level of discipline is high, meaning that people are clearly restrained (for example top-level jobs and low-level jobs in which people interact with customers). Managers of both sexes are often strongly constrained. Female managers – as well as many other women in organizations – should neither appear too feminine, nor too masculine. Gherardi (1995) notes that female managers, in Italy at least, typically have medium-length hair. Those asked about it indicated a preference for it, but from the outside it seems clear that they respond to a social norm prescribing avoidance of the impression of excessive masculinity signalled by cropped hair and of the sexiness of long hair that clashes with the role and authority of the female manager, a norm which they may have gradually internalized.

Cockburn (1991: 151) notes in a study of a large retail company the strong distinction signalled by the dress and behaviour of the men and the women employed there:

> To sit in the staff canteen at head office and observe the employees deliver their lunch trays before returning to their offices is to witness a kind of ritualized daily

ballet in which gender is the organizing principle. The men move together, a solid mass of grey, conversing in deep tones. The women by contrast tap-tap along, chatting and laughing, colourful as a bunch of flowers.

Eriksson (1997) also noted the impact of dress in recruiting interviews. The applicants for a trainee programme met, during the final phase of the selection process, eight men in dark suits. The selection outcome was perfect in terms of equality – half of those employed were men, half women – but one may note the symbolism involved in facing this all-men group of senior representatives in their strongly masculine-coloured dress. An indication of the masculine character, in certain respects, of the upper echelons probably makes different impacts on the male and the female trainees and forms different expectations. It may, however, be premature to say that the dress code appeals to (all) men and feels alien to (all) women. In general, many men do not feel comfortable with this style. It could be said that the dress code signals a masculinization for all the trainees, which clearly calls for a higher degree of adaptation for women than for most men.

Buildings and office interiors also carry cultural meanings. Some offices give a strict, impersonal impression. They signal neutrality, objectivity, concentration and the suppression of feelings and personal relations as values – themes often seen as masculine. Most people would probably think that this tends to alienate women more than men. Other organizational buildings and workplace interiors are more colourful and appeal to the senses. They signal a broader subjective involvement in the workplace environment and give it a more personal touch. In a computer consultancy company management put much energy and imagination into a new corporate building to express corporate values emphasizing personal involvement, fantasy and creativity (Alvesson, 1995a). Straight lines and corridors were avoided. On the walls, floors and some interiors there were colourful paintings, for example, picturing a sky and clouds. This is highly different from what is common in corporate contexts and expresses 'non-masculine' values. (We will return to this company.) As far as we know, there is still relatively little knowledge about this aspect of organizational life. Gagliardi (1990) has edited a useful collection of articles on corporate artefacts, but it does not treat gender.

Gendered organizational metaphors

One interesting feature of organizational cultures is the vocabulary used to make sense of what is going on. Vocabularies facilitate and guide interpretations. They also inform action and shape organizational practices and relations. A specifically powerful kind of vocabulary is metaphors (Lakoff and Johnson, 1980; Morgan, 1980, 1986). Metaphors are verbal symbols: rich in meaning and expressiveness. They appeal to the entire person – intellect as well as feeling and imagination – and are therefore important. We discussed one above: the organizational member as a team player. A metaphor works through invoking a concept originating from another field or level than the one that is to be understood. The former modifies the latter and forms a specific image or gestalt. Through the interaction between the issue to be understood and the alien element, fantasy and imagination are played upon and a particular image is produced. One may for example view a boxer as a tiger in the ring or the female teacher as a mother for her class. Many workplaces are pervaded by game and military metaphors. Riley (1983: 427) for example studied a professional organization, a 'trouble-shooter development and training firm', where the interviewees talked about games and players, wars, teams, battles, armies, pugilistics, and wounds. 'Game (with a particular emphasis on sports) and military (with a vicarious interest in espionage) scenarios repeatedly emerged along with a discerning sense of their use'.

Another type of common metaphor is of a completely different type: it portrays workplace reality in terms of friends, family and home. The owners and managers in the computer consultancy company mentioned above tried hard to create this vocabulary and thus encourage particular types of social relations and emotions to permeate the organization – with a high degree of success. Not only vocabulary, but also social activities and a corporate building (mentioned in the previous section) indicating a relaxed, comfortable, partly home-like atmosphere – including a piano-bar, a bubble-pool, sauna and other recreation facilities located on the top floor – aimed to support this image of the company (Alvesson, 1995a).

It may be tempting to see the game and war metaphors as masculine and the family and home metaphors as feminine, thereby supporting the employment, everyday work life and promotion of men in the first case and women in the second. It may even be said that it is self-evident that the first organization discriminates against women, as sport games and, in particular, wars are activities which are strongly dominated by men and supposedly feel more 'natural' and comfortable for men. We don't learn anything directly about the sex composition of the organization or the sex of the people interviewed in Riley's study. One may expect that many more men than women work in the company, at least in senior positions. However, even though the above mentioned vocabulary should be seen as an indication of male domination and as something that may work against the presence, comfort and acceptance of those women – as well as those men – who find military and sport images alien or boring, this is a topic for investigation and *not* something that one should take for granted. There is no indexical or mechanical gender meaning following from the vocabulary used. We think that one should (1) avoid glib and simplistic ideas about what expresses and reinforces male domination without having a deeper knowledge of the local context and how different people think, feel and react, but (2) be prepared to raise the warning flag and thus encourage further critical exploration of the issue. In the case of the sport and military metaphors the masculine meanings are rather obvious, but one should be somewhat cautious in drawing firm conclusions on their gender-discriminating effects without having listened to the people in the organization.

The second case is less clear-cut in its gendered meaning. Even though home and family are typically culturally seen as feminine images it is not likely that they are strongly linked to the orientations of women and less appreciated by men in an organizational context. In the computer company about three quarters of the workforce and all senior managers were men. This probably reflected gender division of education and career choices more than organizational practices discriminating against women, although the management team consisted of only men and was characterized by a spirit of social cohesiveness that probably made the introduction of a single woman difficult. Generally in Sweden the field of computing has traditionally attracted more men than women.[1] The company had a reputation for having developed a personnel-oriented 'corporate culture' and being skilled in dealing with the personnel. Men and women appeared to be equally satisfied with the workplace. It is possible that the strong social orientation of the company (owners, managers), in which the social (communication, team work, project management) rather than technical components of the work were emphasized, discouraged some people, perhaps more men than women, from joining the company. It may also have increased the attractiveness of the company for women. On the other hand, extensive travelling and calls for long working hours during certain periods may have had a stronger negative effect for females. On the whole, however, it appears as if the home-and-family metaphors had a broad appeal and were considered positive for both sexes.

It should be added that the metaphors mentioned are not exhaustive in telling the cultural stories of the two organizations. Even 'masculinistic' organizations are more than games and wars and also include friendly cooperation just as organizations emphasizing friendship and community harbour politics, conflicts and suffering. The home-and-family vocabulary sometimes corresponds to other vocabularies and social practices and sometimes contradicts them in the organization concerned. A heavy emphasis on international corporate growth in the computer consultancy company is, for example, somewhat inconsistent with the value of close community (Alvesson, 1995a). Nevertheless, the metaphors give interesting clues about these organizations. All organizations exhibit a mix of ideas and language use that may be seen as culturally masculine or feminine. But masculine or, although less commonly, feminine coloured metaphors and vocabularies may dominate in a specific organization – or a unit within it.[2]

One-gendered workplaces

Workplaces occupied by one gender only are of interest in themselves, as significant empirical objects. They are also, however, useful for the illumination of some forms of femininities and masculinities which characterize organizations in general, but which are far from always clearly visible in complex, culturally multifaceted organizations. These patterns may come through more transparently in one-gendered workplaces.

All-women work groups exhibit a tendency to celebrate private life at work (Reskin and Padavic, 1994). In many workplaces female workers hold parties for birthdays, engagements, pregnancies, weddings and retirements. Although such activities take time off from work, they also create a community and bridge gaps between different social groups (ages, ethnicities) through emphasizing common experiences. How should we evaluate such practices in terms of accommodation or resistance? Celebrating domesticity may be conservative, encouraging escapes from unsatisfying work situations to the benefit of family life. It may also, however, strengthen social relations and a sense of identity through group support and belongingness which increase self-esteem and provide a basis for resisting domination both at work and at home (Reskin and Padavic, 1994).

In a study of British women in a sewing industry, Young (1989) found similar patterns of collective orientation, including regular meeting in the leisure time. Pronounced values of solidarity informed the workforce. This also included the relationship with the company, employees regularly noting their long-standing ties with it. A closer look, however, led to the identification of two broad camps, contingent upon different jobs, different employment situations (some were exposed to fluctuation in work demand and to temporary unemployment) and length of time with the company. Each of these two groups engaged in claim and counter-claim regarding their mutual superiority, and depicting the social distance between one another. Symbols celebrating shop-floor distinctiveness and unity at an overall level expressed these qualities, but there were also elements indicating separate groups. For example on one day every year everybody wore a red rose during the work day. Money for the purchase was collected and the purchase made collectively. But the two groups did their collecting of money separately. The entire event thus underscored unity and separateness simultaneously. Such differentiations are common not only within organizations – where a complex mix of subcultures associated with class, occupation, age, level and unit, occurs – but also within what many people believe to be broadly shared shop-floor cultures.

When evaluating these studies – and other research on all-women work cultures – it must be emphasized that they concern (Anglo-Saxon) blue-collar workers. There is every reason to be careful about generalizing across classes. (Whether one should emphasize ethnic/racial differences on this account seems more uncertain.) Professional women are probably less inclined to put a strong emphasis on family issues and other 'private' parts of life at work. Lindgren (1992) found that female nursing aides expressed such orientation but that female nurses and physicians did not. While nursing aides build their relationship on a shared sense of subordination and equality and an absence of competition, nurses have a position in the middle, try to improve their conditions, differ in terms of social background and create community more based on individuality and in relation to specific issues than on a broader basis. Class and position – not just gender – are consequently crucial for understanding how different groups of women develop work cultures and form their relations.

One all-female type of organization is the feminist organization – a type of organization created by women to promote the interests of women, such as health clinics (e.g. Brown, 1992; Morgen, 1994). This kind of organization has its foundations in ideas about a specific feminist standpoint (Chapter 2). The purpose is not only to achieve pro-female goals, but also to work according to certain principles and values, seen as feminine: workplace democracy, minimum hierarchy, including rotating people in positions of management, openness for feelings, supportive social relations and the integration of private and work life – both in the sense of balancing the demands of the two spheres and in being open about private life in talk at the workplace. Life in this kind of organization is often characterized by efforts to realize these goals and a high level of commitment, but tensions and conflicts also appear to be common. Financial problems and the existence of an often less than positive external environment partly account for that. Involvement of the entire person and close personal relationships also make a lot of issues highly sensitive and emotionally charged. The absence of bureaucracy and hierarchy as a 'protective shield' reducing the personal involvement in sensitive issues – such as bad performance, the need to fire persons due to incompetence or financial reasons – make these issues often highly emotionally charged and the risk of destructive social processes great (Morgen, 1994). This organization is special in terms of goals, styles of working and high degree of selectivity in recruitment, making it difficult to draw any conclusions valid for more conventional workplaces.

In all-men work groups gender is active in the creation of their own workplace culture. Beer-drinking and talk about women in sexual terms underscore the shared masculinity (for a review of such studies, see Reskin and Padavic, 1994: 138–41). Rough joking between men, for example giving each other insulting nicknames, also fulfils this function. 'Real men' can take a hard conversational tone, it is assumed (Collinson, 1988). Sometimes gender displays highlight masculinity through a show of physical strength, toughness and daring – safety rules may be neglected for example.

When an all-men workplace faces the employment of women workers, reactions of a more or less negative character are reported as common (Reskin and Padavic, 1994: 72–4). Crude sexual jokes or more or less indirect statements that this is not a job/workplace suitable for women may face the female workers. Sometimes even threats of violence intended to drive a female 'intruder' away occur. Possible explanations for such behaviour are, as mentioned in Chapter 3, that men think that women may not do their share, that men think they have to clean up their language, that wages may be cut or that the presence of women may diminish the prestige of the job or undermine its status as 'real men's' work (Astrachan, cited in Reskin and Padavic, 1994: 72). We find the last point of greatest interest. Apparently workers in certain sites often construct their work as highly masculine and the presence of women, especially if they show themselves capable of doing the job, may threaten this self-understanding. In particular, persons and groups with a precarious identity and self-esteem associated with social status and repetitive, dirty, boring or dangerous jobs – often compensated for by engaging in hyper-masculine activities, talk and relations – may feel threatened by the weakening of the 'manly' character of the job and workplace by the presence of female workers. In many cases, this negative feeling only extends to some unease, which presumably is reduced over time if the female worker continues and the men get used to having a two-gender workplace, but in other cases the woman faces overtly hostile reactions and will then often depart.

As with all social phenomena, there is considerable variation in how formerly one-gendered workplaces encounter a representative of the other sex. Gherardi (1995) illustrates this well through six cases of women entering all-men workplaces. In one case, of forest workers, the men are antipathetical, indeed directly hostile, but in most of the other cases they have no problem in accepting a woman. One woman, just graduated from a school of graphic design, joined a group of 15 technicians, all men, many of them over 50, of whom all but two had moved up from the bottom and had no diploma. She reports that 'I was welcomed with such enthusiasm; everyone was friendly, ready to teach me and help me. I didn't have any difficulties with the job, or with combining the job and looking after the family' (p. 110). This does not mean that the minority status was totally unproblematic, but the overall impression from this and most of Gherardi's cases is that an all-male group may be quite open to receiving a woman. Gender may, however, similar to differences in age, education and social background lead to some uncertainties or difficulties in interaction and in fully fitting in. Gherardi's material also includes an illustration of a strongly anti-female orientation: the case of a woman starting as 'the first, and perhaps the last, forestry worker' (p. 120) and who faced a very hostile environment, where the men strongly felt that this was not a job for a woman and reacted very primitively.

Reskin and Padavic (1994) note that much of the behaviour intended to drive out women is initiated by individuals and not, as in the female forestry worker case, from the whole group of male workers. It probably varies if the active individual man is a social deviant, hostile to women and/ or so uncertain about his own gender identity that the presence of women forms a threat to the defence of the workplace symbolizing masculinity, or if the active person is supported by workplace norms – norms that he may be seen to push to the limit but still without being perceived as an oddball by his fellow workers. From a cultural point of view the meanings, interpretations and (re)actions of the fellow workers to a specific person's efforts to drive out women is of greatest interest. In certain contexts, the group would raise sanctions against the person, presumably stopping him or hampering his behaviour; in others active or passive support or no clear opinions on the matter may prevail.[3]

While reactions of the women-do-not-really-belong-here type probably appear in many types of all-men workplaces, they are probably most common in workplaces that have a strong masculine image, such as the police, the military and certain kinds of blue-collar work. It is likely that those occupations and workplaces attract men very eager to prove their manliness to themselves and others. Anxiety related to pre- or unconscious fantasies about homosexuality (homophobia) may sometimes account for this orientation. Cultural phenomena cannot be reduced to simple off-springs of psychological processes, but the level of the unconscious may still be significant for the understanding of the logic of excessive masculinities. Psychological processes may fuel certain collective constructions of meaning, for example stereotypical and pejorative views on women or rigid distinctions between the worlds of men and women. In other cases, a heavy emphasis on masculinity may be more related to the material options of constructing work in terms consistent with the broadly shared values of physical strength and courage – values associated with masculinity. These constructions are challenged by the presence of women. The inclination to construct work in terms of masculinity may also be seen in terms of class conditions. Blue-collar workers, poorly paid, having physically demanding jobs, working in physically unattractive, perhaps noisy and dirty physical environments and having low social status face considerable strains on their self-esteem. To construct the job and workplace as highly masculine – and emphasizing the non-masculine nature of the upper classes, for example managers and white-collar workers – is a way of gaining self-respect.

> The uncompromising banter of the shop-floor, which was permeated by unin-hibited swearing, mutual ridicule, displays of sexuality and 'pranks', was contrasted, exaggerated and elevated above the middle class politeness, cleanliness and more restrained demeanour of the offices. (Collinson 1988: 186)

This kind of workplace culture, documented in studies of British and US factories, may also facilitate resistance against management power and thus increase worker autonomy and solidarity. It may, however, also lock the workers in a fixed subordinate position, where positive participation and influence are absent (Collinson, 1994). An anti-feminine orientation may be provoked and made visible through the presence of women in this kind of workplace, but the cultural orientation is perhaps better understood as a matter of stressing masculinity (including devaluing non-masculine work and groups irrespective of sex) rather than anti-women *per se*. This does not, however, mean the absence of sexism, only that it is understood in a broader class and status context than as just males devaluing women. The consequences in terms of fixing gender-stereotypical thinking and preventing women from entering or feeling comfortable in this setting may, however, still be strong.[4] Research on military officers shows that expressions of anti-women sexism to support the construction of oneself as masculine goes beyond resistance to management and class society (for example, Barrett, 1996).

It appears as if the workplaces consisting only of men or women often develop values and practices that are in harmony with gender stereotypes – which actually makes one wonder about the border between a stereotype and something that is a roughly fair picture of a group of people. The emphasis on family issues in all-female work groups and the 'manly' behaviour of all-men factory workers and military officers are strongly supportive of gender stereotypes. A comparison between groups of male and female strippers indicated interesting differences in their social orientations (Tewksbury, 1993). While female strippers, according to available (US) studies carried out in the late 1960s (the results are not necessarily valid 25 years later, nor in other contexts), often developed strong friendship relationships within their work groups and were sexually involved with other strippers, this was not the case for their male colleagues. Male gay strippers typically had no relationship with other strippers and male strippers were, in general, friendly yet very competitive with their colleagues, according to Tewksbury.

Having reviewed these studies, some words of caution are called for, mentioned in Chapter 2 but worth repeating to help the reader maintain her/his awareness. As with all research in social science, the results in gender studies are more uncertain than they appear. There may be elements in the workplaces studied, less easily incorporated into conventional ideas of masculinities and femininities, that are not discovered or emphasized by the researchers. As stressed earlier in this book, the researcher cannot avoid being guided by her or his own stereotypes and taken-for-granted ideas. Conventional ideas about what are examples of masculinities and femininities often appear a priori to define many of the results of empirical studies. Apart from selectivity in paying attention to and interpreting much empirical material, lack of space and the wish to stress a clear point, for example, often means a high degree of selectivity in what is reported. The results cannot be generalized throughout cultural, class and historical context. It is also important to bear in mind that what is exhibited in one-sex workplace group culture does not necessarily tell us much about what is characterizing individual persons. That all-female workplaces often express a lot of family-oriented values and orientations does not necessarily mean that all or even most women at workplaces have such a strong orientation. That all-male workplaces often exhibit behaviour, talk and relations characterized by excessive masculine symbolism does not automatically mean that all or even most men are eager to prove or strengthen pronounced masculine identities in all work contexts. Group-level phenomena may follow their own dynamics, including norms and expectations about how women and men should interact with each other. As Gherardi (1995: 144) writes, one may ask 'how many women and men only superficially profess the traditional values of femaleness and maleness, and how many forms of resistance are raised in covert and private form'.

Sometimes one has the impression that men and women act and function in different ways depending on whether it is a one-gendered or a mixed group. Often informants communicate this impression (for example, Billing and Alvesson, 1994). This would underscore the idea that one does not possess a fixed orientation, but different kinds of social interactions and situations may trigger different kinds of subjectivities (ideas, values, feelings).

Often it is claimed that work groups composed of a mix of men and women are more satisfying for those involved and even more productive or effective (Blomqvist, 1994). One may argue that learning is facilitated through diversity in a group. It is probably difficult to say something universal on these topics. Sex composition does not involve any mechanics but may mean different things and lead to any outcomes. Satisfaction, productivity and learning may be accomplished in different ways. The same factors may sometimes facilitate, sometimes obstruct the attainment of a certain value. If a single-sex work group has developed a workplace culture around gender-stereotypical habits – beer drinking and sex joking or celebrating family matters and sewing – they may find this satisfying. It is probably easier to evaluate the level of satisfaction rather than the productivity/effectiveness associated with mixed groups. Issues of effectiveness are often hard to investigate. As with all other gender issues, results of specific studies should not lead to broad generalizations across time, space, class or ethnicity.

Sexuality in organizations

A crucial gender aspect of organizational culture is sexuality. Sexuality is thus not viewed as simple biological drives or individual psychological phenomena, but constituted – expressed/repressed and interpreted in accordance with social norms. Sexuality affects social relations, is a source of pain and pleasure for organizational members and is a vital part of the job in many cases, in particular in interactive service jobs. Sexuality in organizations as a research field has attracted a certain amount of attention in recent years; earlier complaints about its neglect (Burrell, 1984) are hardly valid today as there is a rapidly growing literature on the subject (for example, Brewis and Grey, 1994; Burrell, 1992; Gherardi, 1995; Hall, 1993; Hearn and Parkin, 1987; Hearn et al., 1989).

To define sexuality – which comprises a lot more than specific sexual actions – is not easy. Hearn and Parkin (1987: 58) arrive at the following view: '[S]exuality . . . is the social expression of, and relations to bodily desires, real or imagined, by or for others or for oneself, together with the related bodily states and experiences.' Hearn and Parkin thus say that sexuality in workplaces in this sense is not a marginal phenomenon, but is central, at least in certain kinds of organizations.

Some authors prefer to talk about sexuality in a wider sense, including broader, more vague aspects signalled by labels such as eroticism or desire (e.g. Burrell, 1992; Calás and Smircich, 1991). Recognizing the potential value in breaking up conventional meanings and unfixing terms that risk freezing understanding in established ways, such an enterprise is not without drawbacks as what one chooses to define as 'sexuality' easily becomes a bit arbitrary. A high level of discretion also characterizes authors discussing the 'deeper' meanings of sexuality. In other words, the argumentation appears a bit too idiosyncratic, far-fetched and immune to checking, even counter-argumentation. See, for example, some of the authors reviewed in Brewis and Grey (1994). We will focus on sexuality in a relatively narrow and empirically accessible sense.

Some research deals with the repressive attitude in organizations towards sexuality in workplaces, which has been looked upon as an element in the general disciplining of the workforce (Burrell, 1984). Dominant bureau-cratic–rational principles for organizations are antithetical to erotization and sexuality and thus give little leeway for such impulses, ideas and talk to materialize. Many authors, however, broaden the definition of sexuality and, consequently, think that there are a number of sexual elements in organizations – which do not have to be a question of manifest sexual actions but can also be a question of the undertone in workplace climate, acting and language (Calás and Smircich, 1991; Hearn and Parkin, 1987; Martin, 1990). Sexuality is, according to this view, almost everywhere and permeates workplace culture. Pringle (1989: 159), for example, claims that 'gender and sexuality are central . . . in all workplace relations'. Hearn and Parkin (1987: 3) say that 'enter most organizations and you enter a world of sexuality'. Perhaps this increasingly popular view reflects the inclination of contemporary people to define themselves and others in relation to dis-courses of sexuality – sexuality offers standards for normality against which the modern person assesses herself – more than it mirrors the workplace relations 'out there' (cf. Foucault, 1976). Dominant discourses 'force' us to talk about sexuality, indeed to use it as a basis for the definition of self and identity, Foucault claims. Even though people in general certainly are affected by the popularity of the sexuality discourses, and the talk has its effect of acting as self-fulfilling prophecy, those sensitive to trends in poststructuralism, feminism and psychology may push the interest in sexuality rather far. Discourses on the topic may affect social scientists, interested in the subject matter more than conventional organizational participants. Any kind of emotional work or attractiveness is seen in terms of sexuality. A certain amount of agnosticism about the general interest in sexuality and a tendency to see it everywhere would not prevent us from confirming the relevance of the claim by Pringle and other sexuality-in-organization specialists for understanding some workplaces, in particular certain service companies in which the attractiveness of the personnel is seen as vital for business. Below we will examine one organization in which sexuality appears to be central for workplace relations.

Generally, in terms of sexuality there are four areas which are of particular interest to address: (1) sexual harrasment; (2) sexuality as a source of pleasure in organizations; (3) sexual attractiveness affecting employment chances and placement and as a vital part of the job; and (4) sexuality in relation to identity, for example, sexual jokes as a way of showing one's identity. Of course, the four themes sometimes overlap, as when (3) or (4) may lead to (1) or when a particular act (harassment) is experienced as a source of pleasure for one person and pain for another.

A great body of research has dealt with sexual harassment at work.[5] This term entered the language in the middle of the 1970s and has had a major impact. It is normally defined as an offence, as unwelcome sexual advances, requests for sexual favours, and other verbal or physical conduct experienced as negative. Sometimes sexual harassment may be seen as the work of individual persons, sometimes it is better understood as related to broader collective patterns of sexism and to workplace cultures. In the first instance organizational norms may be more or less restrictive or tolerant to acts of harassment, which are often said to be contingent upon as well as to produce asymmetrical relations of power. A superior position increases the likelihood of harassing behaviour (at least for men, but one should also be open to the possibility of women in senior positions sometimes acting in a similar way). But the act of humiliation also marks and reinforces inequality: the victim learns her or – more seldom – his subordination. Survey studies typically show that sexual harassment is frequent at workplaces. In US public administration, for example, almost half of all women felt that they had been exposed to sexual harassment (according to statistics referred to by Stivers, 1993). British surveys produce similar figures (Thomas and Kitzinger, 1994). We are sceptical about the possibility of producing surveys mapping this kind of often elusive and ambiguous phenomenon. There are problems including the difficulty of defining the phenomenon, memory is often unreliable, different people may interpret a specific definition in different ways and the inclination to answer questions about sexual harassment probably varies according to what one feels about the subject matter. Social norms provide clues for sense-making and labelling.[6] As Gherardi (1995: 37) notes, 'when sexuality is involved, the distinctions between what is acceptable and what is offensive are very subtle'. She mentions that she has carried out research in settings which she judged to be excessively sexualized, but which were deemed 'fair' by those who worked there and vice versa. All this should not prevent an acknowledgement that sexual harassment – irrespective of how it is defined – is far from infrequent. This does not, of course, mean that harassers are equally frequent. It is possible that a minority of men repeatedly harass women. Still workplace norms and meanings are important for understanding when and how individual sexualized acts of a harassing character are initiated, accepted or punished by fellow workers or managers. Workplace cultures may be more or less discouraging of acts that may be seen as harassing and be more or less inclined to define acts as harassing (meaning unacceptable).

Sexual harassment may take many forms from subtle to very harsh, from verbal comments to physical assaults. It may also take the form of obscene graffiti. Reskin and Padavic (1994) report one case where the name of a female coal miner appeared in obscene bathroom graffiti at the workplace – a signal that her presence was not wanted.

Case studies provide a more selective but a more lively, rich and precise picture of the specific phenomena, even though the methodological problems should also be borne in mind in this kind of study. The actions are seldom observed by others than the villain and the victim – if these positions are accepted as good representations – and the former's story is seldom heard. Even though the victim is normally much more trustworthy, one should not underestimate the methodological problems involved and no accounts can be taken at face value in social science (Silverman, 1993). Victims may also censor themselves in reports. As emphasized in Chapter 2, the difficulties of drawing conclusions are even more pronounced in questionnaires.

Sometimes sexuality in workplaces is one-sidedly associated with power, seduction, sexism and oppression. This is, of course, the case if and when the focus is on sexual harassment, but this focus may well be rather too one-sided and narrow. Sexuality in organizations is not only a matter of sexual harassment or of other issues related to male domination. On the positive side, an 'open' or 'affirmative' attitude to sexuality may mean a less impersonal, boring or bureaucratic workplace culture. Gherardi (1995) notes that some suggestions for minimizing sexual harassment involve excessive rules and constraints that reinforce bureaucratic and management control often experienced as impoverishing working life. A confirmation of sexuality as something legitimate and potentially positive in organizations may create positive, pleasurable, more spontaneous and emotionally liberated workplace climates and counteract the dull and bloodless features of bureaucracies (Brewis and Grey, 1994; Burrell, 1992). This would in vital respects be in line with feminist criticism of bureaucracies, even though such critique seldom addresses the issue of, or possible consequences in terms of, sexuality (Ferguson, 1984; Savage and Witz, 1992). Arguably, for the virtues to be realized for both genders radical changes involving the reduction in gender-based power relationships are needed. Otherwise some may feel open and unconstrained while others may experience negative effects as strict norms for proper conduct and 'neutral' social relations are abandoned. The general impression is that males may be overrepresented among the first orientation while females may encounter less constraints on harassment if the repression against sexual impulses is weakened in organizations. Still, acknowledging that work and pleasure are, or at least can be, intertwined, and that we all may seek erotic gratification in our work and organizations, is important (Gherardi, 1995). Research needs to address not only problems but also possibilities associated with gender and sexuality at work. Pringle (1989: 167) suggests that rather than seeing women as 'pathetic victims of sexual harassment it might be possible to consider the power and pleasure they currently get in their interactions and raise the question how they can get what they want on their own terms'.

When looking at sexuality, as with all issues, the enormous variety of 'men' and 'women' must be taken into account. Individual and most forms of social diversity cannot be treated here, for reasons of complexity, space and shortage of studies on the subject. In terms of class, significant variation must be considered. Gherardi, who for five years had regular meetings with (Italian) female factory and office workers, observed that the two groups very often found it difficult to understand each other: 'At moments of tension, the office-workers accused the shop-floor workers of colluding with the sexism of their male workmates, and were in turn accused of being bourgeois hypocrites who considered sex to be "dirty"' (1995: 52).

One may interpret this as the view and practice of males on sexuality being taken over by the female factory workers, who are then seen as victims of patriarchy reproducing a cultural style that constrains them and, indirectly, women in general. Alternatively, one may understand this phenomenon in terms of working-class culture, in which a workplace characterized by physical labour in which a more explicit approach to sexuality is preferred, partly in opposition to the genteel, middle-class and prudish office and managerial middle-class culture (also shared by most students of gender). A third, perhaps more plausible, interpretation is to combine the two. Sexualized expressions of female workers' culture may, as in the case of men, be seen as ways of reducing boredom and resisting the control of superiors and the middle class through the engagement in counter-symbolism (cf. Gherardi, 1995). The form it takes is not independent of male norms and practices, but bear some imprints of these. As with almost all gender issues, other dimensions – of which here we only touch upon class and occupation – must be considered; there are no pure gender patterns in organizations – gender is always fused with other social, individual and material circumstances. Gender can never be treated as discrete from other issues.

Behind patterns of sexual behaviour, seemingly voluntary, there may be non-obvious social structures and dynamics associated with a non-favourable position of women. Ely (1995) found that compared with women in sex-integrated law firms (that is, with a comparatively large number of senior women) women in male-dominated firms (with very few women in top positions) rated themselves and women in general as more flirtatious at work, and they also rated themselves as more attractively dressed. This indicates that 'the feminine attributes that distinguished women in male-dominated firms from those in sex-integrated firms may reflect the sexualized gender role their firms prescribed' (1995: 627).

In a different way to factory work, sexuality is visible in organizational contexts not least in occupations where physical attractiveness is important, for example receptionists, waitresses, air hostesses, guides, a large part of the sales personnel etc. Here sexuality, although less directly addressed and perhaps more accurately labelled attractiveness or appealing appearance, is a matter for management and a topic of systematic control. Sexuality/

attractiveness is an essential part of business and work (see, for example, Hall, 1993). Service work is 'personality intensive' (Normann, 1983) and may be seen as emotional labour (Hochschild, 1983), which means that the personal image of the service worker and the contact between him/her and the customer is important. In modern society, where so much of the success of organizations depends on the ability to produce the right image, the visual impression that is given means a great deal. Gender symbolism, including sexuality, is vital here.

Attractive (subordinated) female staff can symbolize power, prestige and success both for the superior person who employs and heads the staff as well as for the organization as a whole. Looks and appearance are vital for the employment prospects of women – and men – in many jobs. Evaluations are often coloured by sexual appearance. Gherardi (1995) reports a case of an Italian university department where the female students felt that if they dressed up before examinations this had a positive effect on the grades they were given by a male professor. In a reply to male students complaining about this injustice, the females countered with the example of good-looking male students getting higher grades from a female lecturer. (It is difficult to comment on the 'truth' of the example; what is of interest is the ideas and beliefs it expresses.) In the next section we shall report a case study at some length illustrating some features of sexuality in a workplace culture.

Workplace culture and sexuality at Ludvig's Advertising Agency

Ludvig's Advertising Agency, LAA, is a small Swedish company, employing 20 people: 10 women, all in assisting positions, and 10 men, all but one in professional positions, that is, working as project managers, art directors and copy writers. The women are below or around 30, on average 10 years younger than the men. Both groups seem to be interested in fashion and appearance. The agency has been the target of a depth study, more fully reported in Alvesson and Köping (1993) and Alvesson (1997).

The advertising agency appears to be a comparably sexualized environment, in the sense that it is inhabited by people who care about their attractiveness, where the gender role patterns are clear and where the room for expressed emotions and sexual allusions is rather large. In the organization sexual attractiveness and desire are legitimately shown off and sexual impulses are allowed to be verbally expressed. From the following observation we get an example of this type of environment.

One Friday afternoon the female co-researcher was sitting talking to Boris, one of the male employees. Ludvig, the founder, who had a question for Boris popped in and sat down for a while. It was about five p.m., and Marcia came in to say that she was leaving and wished them a nice weekend. Her lips were painted bright red and she wore a miniskirt. When Marcia had left, Ludvig looked at Boris with a twinkle in his eye, and said: 'That one! With butter on!' Boris laughed. It can be noted that in spite of the presence of the female co-researcher, the two 'gentlemen' have a 'relaxed' attitude to their impulses. (Possibly it can also be seen as a provocation aimed at the female researcher.)

Sexually explicit jokes seem to be very common in advertising agencies. It is not only men who joke with or about women, but jokes on behalf of men also occur. This issue has not been studied in detail and it is not clear as to whether the joking can also be (productively) interpreted in terms of power. Some researchers see the power aspect as crucial in sexual joking in organizations (Cockburn, 1991). There may be hidden meanings behind the jokes which go beyond the good-natured. The jokes of women may be seen as women's defence against men's crude joking. Of course, the male organizational members are in positions where it is easier to set the norms, but it can hardly be assumed that sexual jokes are alien to females or that masculine domination produces subjectivities that accept and perpetuate this kind of joking behaviour. A claim that men exclusively set the norm, and that two-way sexual joking necessarily reflects male domination, appears a bit gender stereotyped if not backed up with careful observation, although, more generally, females may sometimes feel pressure to tell dirty jokes in order to respond to male workplace norms (Reskin and Padavic, 1994). However, some of the boldest sexual jokes one of the authors ever heard were told unprovoked by some of the women at a party for a class finishing their business studies course.

'Friendly' sexual humour seems in any case to dominate at LAA. There were no signs of discontent with the atmosphere at LAA amongst the females. Both these characteristics – openness in sexual relations and, at least as far as we could detect, a positive attitude among female employees – appear to be typical for many agencies in Scandinavia. Three Danish female advertising professionals, commenting in a Danish professional journal on the Swedish book in which this study was presented (Alvesson and Köping, 1993), reported that they only felt positive about the sexualized environment. They claim that 'it is wonderfully liberating to walk around and pinch the guys' bottoms (and to get pinched oneself) and refer to them as "mother's little baby". It is just another way of saying that "I like you and our cooperation"' (*Orienteering*, no. 7, 1994: 10). This may sound like irony but the overall impression of the text is that the female authors celebrate the sexualized work environment. A study of another advertising agency included the observation of a female assistant pinching male workers' bottoms, seemingly without any immediate earlier provocation. The jokes may also contribute to the conception that sexuality and sexual attractiveness are important, in the workplace. This contributes to the projection of men and women as sexual beings and constructs sexuality as significant for their identities, traditionally with the strongest constraints for females. As the (hetero)sexual factor brings gender differences and gender dynamics to their extreme – here gender differences are highlighted – it contributes to the gender structuring of the organization. Through indicating that men and women are different, different work roles and routes appear to be natural.

Organizational values and practices thus influence the importance of sexual attractiveness for gender relations at the agency, among other things by giving priority to women's appearance in recruitment and selection. Here, male power is explicit. Control at the point of entry to the organization means that certain personal styles and norms are incorporated into and signalled in the organization. But also self-selection is important. Those women and men who are comparatively uninterested in dress and appearance are probably less inclined to apply for work or carry on working at the agency (or in the industry). The organization and the entire industry – the individuals, groups, relations and cultural patterns of which it is composed – thus reinforce a feminine orientation of the female staff and a certain form of feminine gender identity in which looks are central. This phenomenon, and the partly corresponding one of males who are also strongly oriented towards dress and physical appearance, reflects the task of advertising: the creation of desire.

LAA is an organization led by men, while the women manage routine jobs and the 'domestic chores'. As reviewed in Chapter 3, gender division of labour is common in working life, but in LAA it is extreme, at least in the context of the non-technical professional service sector in Scandinavia. If you add to that the appearance, age and general image of the female staff coupled with jokes with sexual allusions, you could perhaps draw the conclusion, based on conventional wisdom in gender studies, that this must be an extraordinarily male-chauvinistic organization, where 'masculine values' are predominant and gender oppression pronounced.

But such an image is misleading at least if masculinity is defined in the ways it usually is in the gender literature. The organization is much more inconsistent. It is very 'soft' in many regards. Social relations are emphasized. People talk a lot about personal chemistry. According to the interviewees, the female employees are satisfied with their workplace. The atmosphere – in contrast to the practices associated with the division of labour – is hardly chauvinistic, with the possible exception of some jokes of a sexual nature, but even these are two-way, rather than being simply a question of the men alluding to women's sexuality.

It is hard to find examples of people constructing their work in masculine terms. The art directors regard themselves as being the 'feelings' in advertising production. They 'feel' whether an advertising product or idea is 'right' or 'wrong'. They say that they do not work analytically and/or rationally but emotionally.

> Advertising people are normally very outgoing and they are emotionally loaded. Because feelings and things like that are the basis of creativity, so to speak. They are often very rich in ideas and associative, they can quickly associate with various phenomena. They are normally rather difficult to steer and jump for joy when they become happy or hit the roof when they become mad. The breadth of their reactions is much greater than for example people in companies' accounting departments. Advertising people are seldom very systematic or structured . . . (male advertising worker)

On the whole LAA may be said to have a 'feminine' orientation with regard to self-understanding, the method of working and customer relations. At least on an overall and cliché-like level it corresponds with the ideals of many feminists around the importance of emotion for thinking, work and organization (Jaggar, 1989; Mumby and Putnam, 1992). Correspondingly, males are conventionally seen as non-emotional (Hearn, 1993). Hollway (1984: 253) writes that 'in our society, the judgement is a sexist one: expressing feelings is weak, feminine and in contradistinction to men's rationality'.

Without saying that most features of LAA – and the advertising industry in Sweden – are clear-cut examples of femininity it is very hard to see that it matches a typical description of masculinity as '. . . hard, dry, impersonal, objective, explicit, outer-focused, action-oriented, analytic, dualistic, quantitative, linear, rationalist, reductionist and materialist' (Hines 1992: 328). Not all of these qualities are, of course, totally absent. When one male interviewee stresses that 'we are not just freely floating artists, but work a lot with analysis', one may interpret it as an attempt to construct a masculine element in work, but in order to see this as an expression of dominating 'masculinity' the qualities mentioned must be much more pronounced. Arguably, elements of analysis are part of even the most extremely 'feminine' activity. The agency shows very little endurance of the five types of masculinity that Collinson and Hearn (1994) view as typical in an organizational context: authoritarianism, paternalism, entrepreneurialism, careerism and informalism. Some elements of entrepreneurialism characterized the company in the beginning, but this was not salient during the time of the study. Of course, the agency is not completely devoid of interaction within gender groups, but a certain amount of this, some based on gender, age, ethnicity, ideology, etc., is presumably a characteristic of every workplace. It is far easier to pick out feminine elements when characterizing LAA, for example, 'the prioritizing of feelings . . . the importance of the imaginative and creative . . .' (Hines, 1992: 314). The feminine is typically understood as marginalized in organizations by students of gender, but in LAA masculinities come closer to risking this fate. More broadly, some new organizations and principles for management – stressing flat hierarchies, team work, open communication and skills in dealing with other people – reject the principles of masculinities associated with bureaucracies and may be seen to be 'women-friendly' (Blomqvist, 1994; see next chapter). Of course a great deal of work and organizational conditions and constructions are not best understood in gender terms.

A key feature of the work and – we believe – a crucial aspect behind the almost caricatured gendered division of labour is the high level of ambiguity involved in advertising work and the scepticism among clients as well as the public directed at the advertising profession (Alvesson, 1994; Tunstall, 1964). '. . . everybody has the right to express opinions in this business and everybody's opinion is equally important. Sometimes a client rejects a proposal that you have made because the wife of the manager did not like it' (male advertising worker).

Advertising is seen as arbitrary and workers face considerable difficulties in developing stable work identities. Conventional resources such as formal education, socially sanctioned authority, high social status and substantive work results in which competence is proved are, on the whole, not available or are of minor significance. In relation to clients, the agency is typically weak. The relationship means that the agency adopts a low position in terms of masculinity. The contributions are constructed in pro-feminine terms: to the bureaucratic–rational client the agency offers feeling, imagination, group work, intuition and playfulness.

Another problem for people in the field concerns the broadly shared view that advertising people should be young. There is an expectation in the field that one should be fashion-minded and sensitive to trends – qualities that may be seen as inconsistent with ageing. As Tunstall (1964: 17) writes, 'this is a business in which youth has a special kind of moral advantage'. It is no coincidence that the men at LAA want to be called the 'lads' (guys) and that they dress in a youthful style. Gender relations may also be helpful here. One female interviewee thinks that the recruitment policy within the agency is largely a matter of the dominating group being on its way into middle age:

Q: Most of the art directors here are men; why do you think that is? And all assistants are women!
A: They would never take on a lad as assistant, never.
Q: Why not? Is it more fun with girls?
A: They are striving to be 21 again. It must be in order to make them feel younger.

The wish of the men to stay young may be facilitated by the presence of young, good-looking women. One could here add that being fashion-oriented and negative about ageing characterizes our time in general, but these values also have a feminine undertone and are thus not entirely gender-neutral.

Constructing the work and the agency through a specific set of meanings facilitates identity work, that is, the establishment and sustaining of an identity, as the difference to clients is highlighted and the distinctiveness of advertising people is underscored, but the identity is not without problems for male workers as it lacks the assurance of masculinity. This is the case because the set of meanings are generally culturally seen as feminine/low-masculine – even if the constructions are not specifically recognized by the people involved in gender terms.[7] Given the client's as well as the public's doubts of the intrinsic value of the work and the vulnerability of work results to the client's arbitrary evaluations, there are considerable strains on the identity and self-esteem of advertising workers.

The structuring of the gender relations at the agency can thus be seen as a way of strengthening identity and compensating for the insecurities regarding identity which lie in the cultural nature of the business. Clear-cut gender relations can be of help here. They compensate for the strains contingent upon the construction of work in non-male terms. While the femininities at the agency are a question of sexual attractiveness, youth, service functions and subordinated positions, masculinities are character-ized by earning money, high status, creative and leading posts and, above all, the stress on gender difference in internal social relations. The emphasizing of explicit femininity – when employing, joking and socially interacting in different forms – thus becomes a way for the men to handle the existential and psychological difficulties which characterize the modern person in general but which is greatly added to by the material work situation which distinguishes advertising work. This accounts for the fact that the men at LAA seek gender interaction, not gender isolation, which is sometimes said to be a form of masculinity (Collinson and Hearn, 1994). Being a 'man amongst men' may not be reassuring in a work context weak on (other) signs of masculinity. It would probably reinforce tendencies to homophobia, even though this anxiety may in certain respects be more intense in contexts appealing to men very eager to prove their maleness. (Such men may be more inclined to join the army than an advertising agency.) Unconscious fantasies – crucial for gender identity according to psychoanalytic feminists (for example, Butler, 1990) – may be fuelled by the constructions of the nature of the work, the client relationships, and so on. Engaging in gender interaction of a seemingly marked heterosexual character, including sexual joking, may be the safest route to achieve feelings and reassurances of masculinity. While the construction of work means the absence of masculinity, the construction of social relations in strongly gendered terms may compensate for that.

Final comments about the case

This case is of interest as it shows that male domination in organizations is not just a matter of cultures penetrated with masculine values and meanings, but indicates more complex interplay between different types of femininities and, much less obvious, masculinities. In a working life to some extent moving from being dominated by employment in industry and bureaucracies to service industries and more flexible, organic organizational forms, it is vital to be prepared to rethink old conceptions and understand gender dynamics in novel ways. Gherardi (1995: 130–1) views new forms of production as different from those following the masculinistic Fordist logic and believes that ideas on quality, service, flat organizations reducing hierarchical career patterns speak a less masculine language and that this model 'increasingly assumes values that belong to the symbolic universe of the female but cannot be valorized as such as long as the female constitutes the second sex'. A similar point is made by Fondas (1997), observing that recent management literature advocates ideas similar to what are generally seen as feminine qualities, but without using this label or being explicit about the connection. We should be careful about exaggerating trends in this direction. The interesting point is that the organizational landscape is not solely populated by pyramid-like machine bureacracies but also by more dynamic and network-like forms of organizing. Some studies show better career options for women in the latter (Blomqvist, 1994; Kvande and Rasmussen, 1994), although there is no simple or automatic relation between organizational form and possibilities for female employees, as the present case illustrates, as does one of the computer consultancies referred to above. What is important, however, is to look carefully at other examples than the highly masculinistic cultures portrayed mostly in older studies (Ferguson, 1984; Kanter, 1977) and also at organizations in which feminine cultural meanings and values are not marginalized, without necessarily assuming an easy symmetry between such meanings and values and a high promotion rate for women. As suggested by this case, gender is sometimes trickier than that.

Without wanting to generalize too much from the case, it may illustrate some of the complexities of contemporary and future gender dynamics in the context of organizational cultures. There may be subtle tendencies towards de-femininization of certain values, principles and forms earlier explicitly constructed in female terms, changing cultural ideas about what is masculine and feminine and reducing the constraints and prescriptions involved. As the case suggests, this does not mean that simple and unproblematic gender patterns will automatically emerge.

Summary

The very idea of a cultural understanding of organizations is to investigate meanings and symbolism at the local, workplace level. This should be done without neglecting the broader context of local phenomena, such as societal, class and other cultural patterns putting their imprints on groups in organizations. The focus on the subtleties of shared meanings, ideas and symbolism means that models, combinations of abstract dimensions and theoretical generalizations are hardly possible, or at least not very interesting. Careful studies of workplaces and occupations indicate the variation of meanings attributed to gender, the construction, combinations and interactions of a variety of forms of masculinities and femininities, even though there also are similar patterns across workplaces. In this sense cultural studies contradict variable thinking. Neither does a feminist standpoint position receive full support. There is certainly no lack of studies showing cultural bias and discrimination in ideas and social practices regarding women (e.g. Cockburn, 1991; Reskin and Padavic, 1994), but there are also others indicating considerable variety in the cultural expressions of different groups of women as well as the view of men towards women entering and being present in different work contexts. In addition, the experiences and values of women differ. Given variation in the valuation of various forms of masculinities and femininities, and meanings ascribed to and reception of women in different organizational contexts (Billing and Alvesson, 1994; Blomqvist, 1994; Gherardi, 1995; Kvande and Rasmussen, 1994), the case for a specific feminist standpoint with universal aspirations or even to achieve broad generalization is not very strong. A poststructuralist reading would carry themes further, and try to open up the patterns found in, for example, studies of organizations with homogeneous cultural ideas and symbolic practices, showing the fragmented and ambiguous meanings of what is fixed through labels such as 'masculinities' and 'femininities'. We are satisfied here with indicating this possibility, rather than – following the spirit of poststructuralism – demolishing the more or less shaky theoretical and empirical constructions that researchers have built on gendered cultural phenomena in organizations.

Having looked at how certain aspects of organizational cultures may be productively understood in gender terms, and the dangers and traps involved, and having provided some empirically based glimpses into the gendered organizational world and argued for, and illustrated, some patterns in the context of variation, we temporarily rest our case for a cultural approach to gender and organization. Instead we move on to the theme of leadership.

Notes

1 The situation may be a bit different in the USA for example, where 32 per cent of men and 43 per cent women in the labour force use a computer at work (Wright and Jacobs, 1995). In Sweden, in leisure activities, statistics report that women on average spend one minute and men fourteen minutes on computers per day (SCB, 1995).

2 In many sectors, masculine cultural values and expressions dominate, but in much of the personnel-based service sector for example, feminine language, metaphors and principles may be significant, e.g. in nursing, elementary schools, childcare centres. As we will address in Chapter 6, in many modern, progressive companies a 'de-masculinization' of organizational practices may be said to take place (Blomqvist, 1994; Gherardi, 1995). There are presumably also other trends. According to Stivers, there is a strong tendency in the USA to try 'to make public administration masculine by making it "muscular" and businesslike' (1993: 8).

3 For the sake of clarity, we remind the reader that culture refers to meanings, ideas and symbols, not to overt behaviour. The interesting thing about this issue in terms of culture is not the actual behaviour taking place, but the meanings of the work, the workplace and gender and the deeper identity themes in the light of the 'non-masculine' character of the workplace and the unease and perhaps unconscious fantasies triggered by this. Cultural processes, however, lead to actions which are also to be treated in cultural analysis.

4 A study by Pleck et al. (1993) indicates that the adherence to a masculinist ideology, i.e. beliefs in the value of being masculine, is independent of attitudes to women. The efforts to construct oneself in masculine terms may lead to a wish to maintain a male-only environment which does not necessarily have anything to do with a negative attitude to women.

5 For example Cockburn (1991); Gutek and Cohen (1992); Hearn and Parkin (1987); Sheppard (1992); Thomas and Kitzinger (1994).

6 A social constructivist position would say that social and discursive processes – rather than objective behaviours or genuine experiences – account for what is constructed as sexual harassment and what is not.

7 Masculine meanings are implicit here, as often is the case. Thus, even if, for example, intuition and emotion in general are viewed as 'feminine', it does not necessarily mean that they are directly associated with femininity in a specific context. A man may well be ascribed these qualities without being seen as feminine. We recognize that we are vulnerable to critique for being elitists in the absence of clear indications that the people in the case study share the kind of general culturally feminine meaning that we ascribe to notions such as emotional, intuitive, etc. (We have already discussed this problem in Chapter 4.) On the other hand, dominant ideas on these issues seem to have a very clear feminine connotation – according to all the gender literature we have come across – which would make it most likely that the feminine nature of the work in some way – perhaps unconsciously and indirectly – affects the advertising workers.

6
Women and Management I:
A Review of Research Results

Women and management is a subject of popular interest. Sometimes one even gets the impression that the representation and functioning of women in senior managerial jobs is believed to be *the* crucial issue in gender equality, at least in the context of management/organization studies. Women in management is a large and expanding topic. Given that only a very small percentage of the top jobs in business and public administration are held by women in most countries, the lack of equality is especially striking in this part of the labour market. The following are some of the questions that are being asked. Why are there so few female managers, especially at senior levels? Do men and women differ in terms of leadership abilities and style of managing? Is there perhaps a specific female form of leadership which, if not actually practised, is preferred by a majority of women? Are prejudices and other obstacles preventing women from attaining and/or occupying managerial positions? Or do females often express other values and orientations than to exercise authority over others?

The interest in raising and answering these questions seems to be part of an international trend which started in the USA, where the theme has been a popular one for at least the last 25 years. The past and present situation in the USA can perhaps be illustrated by quoting the titles of some of the books and articles in this field. Early titles included for example *Breakthrough: Women into Management* (Loring and Wells, 1972); *Bringing Women into Management* (Gordon and Strober, 1975); and *Men and Women of the Corporation* (Kanter, 1977). Later books included titles such as *Management Strategies for Women, or Now That I'm the Boss, How Do I Run This Place?* (Thompson and Wood, 1981); *Women Managers: Travellers in a Male World* (Marshall, 1984); *Feminine Leadership, or How to Succeed in Business Without Being One of the Boys* (Loden, 1986); and *The Female Advantage* (Helgesen, 1990).

There is a wide variety of social science and more popular, practitioner-oriented writings on the topic. They range from careful, measurement-oriented studies in which sex is added as a variable – often without much inspiration or originality in comparison with older, non-gender leadership research – to normative writings, based on the convictions, impressions and/or empirical studies of the author, on ways in which women lead or organize. Within these writings, the gender-as-a-variable perspective is the most common, even though there are also a number of feminist standpoint position texts on gender and management. Many of these, however, maintain a rather weak version of the standpoint position, putting forward the idea of women's unitary and – in relation to men – different ways of being/relating to others, but embracing a positive rather than critical view on male/female compatibility.

This chapter will provide an overview and discussion of empirical research in the field. At first contemporary changes in leadership and management will be briefly addressed. We will then review the state of the art of empirical and other work on the most common themes concerning women and leadership: explanations for the limited number of women in managerial jobs, including family matters; discrimination and processes of selection; style of leadership of women compared to men; difficulties facing women managers, including stress level and the facing of negative stereotypes. In Chapter 7, we will continue looking at women and leadership, but then focus on the basic positions taken and different ways of making sense of women and leadership against different assumptions about similarity/difference between men and women and different agendas in terms of an interest in effectiveness or political–ethical concerns.

Changing ideas on leadership

As mentioned in Chapter 4, it is generally believed that leadership is constructed with a masculine subtext. Dominant views on leadership are seen as difficult to integrate with femininity (Lipman-Blumen, 1992). There may be changes under way, though, as mentioned in Chapter 5. An interest in moving away from more bureaucratic–technocratic modes of management to more personal–ideological forms means that issues of a more social, subjective and involving nature are increasingly being seen as crucial. It is quite likely that changes in management and organizational practices are grossly exaggerated in many accounts of the 'postmodern world', the 'knowledge-society', 'post-fordism', etc. (Alvesson, 1995b; Thompson, 1993) as not only journalists and consultants but also many researchers want to concentrate on what may appear as novel or radically changing – and not pay serious attention to all the stuff that remains pretty much the same. Nevertheless, some changes in social practices take place and even more so at the 'meta-level' of mass media, books, conferences, debates and public opinion. At present, rational forms of control are 'out' and normative forms are 'in' (Barley and Kunda, 1992). Here, the popularity of adhocracies, corporate culture, flexible forms, decentralization, service management, quality, innovation, empowerment, networks, etc. provide space for constructions of management and leadership partly in less masculine ways than has traditionally been the case (Gherardi, 1995). Machine bureaucracy may be seen as the extreme example of a masculine organization that has lost some appeal – even though it still dominates (think of airline companies and McDonald's for example). Emotions are increasingly seen as significant in organizational practice as meaning, involvement and action to some extent replace rationality, cold calculation and separation of decision and execution (Alvesson and Berg, 1992). Themes like identity, cohesion, teams and social integration also often point in a 'non-masculine' direction. Of course, not only many of the themes which are unchanged, but also some new ones do not necessarily lend themselves very easily to an exploitation in 'pro-feminine' terms. Charismatic leadership is one example of a concept that has attracted considerable interest during the last decade (Bryman, 1993). Most of the public figures who fit into this category are men, often with a clear masculine, even heroic aura.

This general interest in new ideas on leadership appears to have accompanied the interest in feminine leadership and/or women in management. The two streams partly overlap. The issue of changing forms of management/ leadership provides a vehicle (one of many) for considering and facilitating career opportunities for women. If a more participatory, non-hierarchical, flexible and group-oriented style of management is viewed as increasingly appropriate and this is formulated in feminine terms (or androgynous – combining characteristics of the two genders), then women can be marketed as carriers of suitable orientations for occupying positions as managers – network orientation, a preference for participation, and so on. Lipman-Blumen (1992: 183), for example, believes that female leadership 'contains the seeds of connective leadership, a new integrative model of leadership more suited to the dramatically changing workplace of the twenty-first century'. Fondas (1997) also notes that contemporary writings on management prescribe qualities that are culturally associated with women – even though this linkage is seldom explicitly made. Alternatively, and minimally, the new criteria for management would at least open up the opportunity for females to have better access to senior positions in organizations. The strong 'masculine' nature of traditional management/leadership would then lose some of its appeal and the work field would form a more open terrain in terms of the genderedness of those moving into and within it. This last version does not say anything about women in general being specifically suitable – either in terms of having a specific 'essence' or a common set of traits, or that having these is the critical prerequisite for being a competent manager – but only that a crucial gender obstacle for equal access to such jobs may be removed/ weakened.

There are reasons to be sceptical with regard to much of the talk about radical changes taking place in organizations leading to a substantial requirement for 'female skills' or female managers (Calás and Smircich, 1993). Behind the rhetoric are perhaps only superficial changes, which does not prevent some speeding-up of the increase of females in low-level and middle-level managerial jobs.

Explanations for the limited number of women in managerial jobs

As already mentioned, females are strongly underrepresented in managerial jobs, especially at higher levels. Given the limited reliability of statistics –

as we have said, they often conceal ambiguities and norms for classification and give a misleading impression of exactness and objectivity – we see little purpose presenting detailed numbers from different countries, industries, times or organizations. However, even those most sceptical of the value of statistics can hardly deny that females are strongly outnumbered by males in positions of formal power and authority, high status and high incomes. Depending on where one draws the line for 'above-supervisory jobs' and starts counting managers, the proportions vary. In the airline company SAS, at a conference for the top 156 managers some years ago, six of these were women, i.e. four per cent (Billing and Alvesson, 1994). Forty per cent of the total number of employees were female. In the US federal administration, half of the employees and seven per cent of those in the three top grades are women (Stivers, 1993). More broadly in Western countries, perhaps 10 to 20 per cent or so of middle-level managers are females, and less than five per cent of top-level managers are females (Morrison and Von Glinow, 1990). In the USA there are more female managers than in other countries; according to Northcraft and Gutek (1993), 42 per cent of women are managers but hold less than one per cent of top positions.

Efforts to provide explanations for the small numbers of women have pointed at a number of different factors or dimensions, similar to those accounting for the segregated labour market (Chapter 3). One may distinguish between those emphasizing differences between men and women in terms of psychological traits and/or socialization background, work orientations or educational/career choices (or constraints) and those pointing at more sociological, structural explanations for the relative absence of women in managerial positions (for reviews, see Billing and Alvesson, 1994; Morrison and Von Glinow, 1990).

Conventionally, managerial jobs, at least in business and at senior levels, have been defined as very much a matter of instrumentality, autonomy and result-orientation, something which is not much in line with what is assumed to be typical for females, according to psychologically oriented theorists such as Chodorow (reviewed in Chapter 3). That identification with parents is of significance is supported by a US study by Hennig and Jardim (1977) of 25 senior female managers, all of whom identified with their father rather than their mother. In a questionnaire by Carlsen and Toft (1986) of Danish managers at various levels, more women (18 per cent) than men (four per cent) reported a strong attachment to their father, indicating that women identifying with the father may be more inclined to become managers.

Studies of psychological characteristics have had mixed results, but on the whole showed no differences, or only minor ones, between males and females, leading most commentators to suggest that psychological attributes do not account for the variation between men and women in managerial jobs (Maccoby and Jacklin, 1975; Morrison and Von Glinow, 1990). Many authors stress that there is considerable evidence that women and men in management roles have similar aspirations, values and other personality traits as well as job-related skills and behaviours (Dobbins and Platz, 1986; Marshall, 1984). Some other authors do, however, suggest that women differ from men in terms of some orientations, including being less selfish (Lipman-Blumen, 1992). As we will see below, some recent and more popular literature also emphasizes differences in terms of leadership style, which presumably is grounded in personalities or other more stable ways of relating to the world.

One type of individually oriented but non-psychological explanation is called human capital theory. Investments in education, training and other forms of qualifiying experiences are seen as the key factor behind careers. Women's disadvantaged position is attributed to a lower or less relevant kind of education, and the lack of qualified work experiences associated with working in different places, including working abroad. Although it is generally evaluated that women have invested less in managerially relevant qualifications it is a common judgement that such investments lead to a lower pay-off for women, as well as for minority groups, than for white males (Reskin and Padavic, 1994; Simpson, 1996). A more sociological version of the emphasis on education and training would be not to take gender differences for granted, but to examine the social and cultural aspects of educational choices and experiences. Education of relevance for a managerial career such as an MBA may, at least in some places, be said to include a bias against women in terms of the topics and aspects which are given priority in the curriculum as well as the way courses are taught. Sinclair (1995) documents deep frustrations regarding content as well as social interaction by female students in an Australian MBA programme. Swedish data, however, indicate that women are satisfied with their business education (Bergvall and Lundqvist, 1995; Wahl, 1992). Other studies point at differentiated treatment of male and female employees in terms of qualifying assignments as a crucial factor in the processes disadvantaging women – as well as minority groups (Billing and Alvesson, 1994: chapter 9; Reskin and Padavic, 1994).

Such ideas overlap with explanations that point at cultural themes and social practices working against women. Management and leadership are broadly constructed in masculine terms, at least according to somewhat dated US empirical research (Schein 1973, 1975).

> A 'masculine ethic' can be identified as part of the early image of managers. This 'masculine ethic' elevates the traits assumed to belong to some men to necessities for effective management: a tough-minded approach to problems; analytic abilities to abstract and plan; a capacity to set aside personal, emotional considerations in the interests of task accomplishment; and a cognitive superiority in problem-solving and decision-making . . . when women tried to enter management jobs, the 'masculine ethic' was invoked as an exclusionary principle. (Kanter, 1977: 22)

Such constructions, although increasingly perceived as old-fashioned, still prevail (Lipman-Blumen, 1992). It is possible that this tendency is weaker in some other countries and that social changes, including new ideas of modern leadership, will involve a de-masculinization of leadership so that leadership is not any longer constructed in masculine ways. The proportion of female managers is, however, much higher in the USA than in any other country, raising some doubts about how strong and dispersed the 'masculine ethic' is in the USA, compared to other countries. Still, there is a historical tradition and deep cultural ideas that give leadership a masculine image in most countries (Collinson and Hearn, 1996; Hearn and Parkin, 1986/7). It works against women and may prevent women from actively trying to get such jobs as well as provoking scepticism and/or biased evaluations of superiors, colleagues and subordinates. As Reskin and Padavic (1994: 96) say, 'most cultures share the social value, often rooted in religious beliefs, that women should not exercise authority over men'. There are studies indicating that women are unfavourably evaluated compared to men (Nieva and Gutek, 1980), although according to Eagly et al. (1992) in terms of leadership this is only the case under certain conditions (see below). Some research focuses on procedures for recruitment, assessment and selection of managers (but also other jobs). For example, job advertisements are sometimes believed to disadvantage females, as they often call for more qualifications than are necessary, which women often seem to take more seriously than men, and thus do not even apply for the job (Billing and Alvesson, 1994). Some research shows gender bias in assessment and selection (Forisha, 1981; Nieva and Gutek, 1980), but the evidence is, as is often the case, inconclusive, not to say contradictory. A recent US study of applications for senior executive (highest grade) positions in the US federal government shows that female applicants were better evaluated and were offered positions in significantly higher numbers than male applicants (Powell and Butterfield, 1994) – a finding that throws some doubt on the popular idea of a glass ceiling effect.[1]

It is, however, possible that women are more sensitive than men to experiences in the workplace which affect their long-term career orientations. A Dutch study concluded that women employees in one organization perceived lower self-efficacy and, related to that, were less inclined to apply for a managerial job (Van Vianen and Keizer, 1996). This was, the authors argue, a consequence of the women having less experience with managerial tasks and receiving less verbal support in the organization. In another organization studied there were no differences between men and women either in terms of managerial intention or in the dimensions seen as affecting this. The authors conclude that organizations are influential in the ambitions of their female employees to get managerial jobs. A similar conclusion was reached in Billing and Alvesson (1994). Society in general is more supportive of men in those roles and they may therefore have a stronger work and career orientation prior to entry into a particular organization, making them somewhat less sensitive to degrees of encouragement/ discouragement by colleagues and superiors. In a study of an airline company, we often found female managers who said that their appointment to managerial positions was more an outcome of chance and encouragement from others to apply than long-term intention. The interplay between the background, the non-organizational life situation of females and their experiences in organizations should be considered in order to understand their prospects in terms of managerial careers (Billing and Alvesson, 1994).

Another kind of explanation is sociological–structural. As mentioned in Chapter 3, macro-level and structural explanations refer neither to individual traits nor to the level of meaning and intention, but to social forces at the macro-level operating behind the back of individual subjects or micro processes. Some authors, referring to patriarchy and/or the brotherhood of men, believe that the interests of males in preventing women from competing for privileged positions make them reluctant to accept females as managers (Cockburn, 1991; Lindgren, 1996). In a patriarchal society, the subordination of women to men forms a basic rule. The rule is that men command, women obey. The interests of men dominate and positions of power fall into this category, according to this line of interpretation. Another kind of structural explanation (examined in Chapter 3) emphasizes the ratio of men to women and the problems minorities experience in being fully recognized, feeling comfortable and being promoted (Kanter, 1977; Martin, 1985). A critical mass – Kanter says 30 per cent – is necessary for an underrepresented sex to have equal opportunities along with members of a dominating social category.

Finally, researchers have pointed at the significance of the work–family connection as disadvantaging women. Women are often less mobile, as family priorities make them unwilling to take a position meaning longer work days, more travel or moving geographically to a new site of employment. Sometimes the conflict between home and family obligations and male-normative managerial jobs – where the job holders are expected to be able to spend most of their time and energy on the job – is seen as the major problem preventing women from advancing (Martin, 1993).

> As long as it is women who are the ones to step off the fast track to meet family responsibilities, they will be at a competitive disadvantage in career advancement as it is presently structured; the years during which women who want children must bear and raise them are the key years in the struggle for career success. (Rix and Stone, 1984)

In a questionnaire study of Swedish female civil engineers and MBAs there were more respondents who indicated that they did not want to become a manager 'at the present time' than respondents who wanted to (Wahl, 1992). (About 30 per cent of the sample already had a managerial position while 30 per cent indicated that they did not want to have one.) Many respondents emphasized that children are the most important thing in life. Lack of time is a major problem for many career and working women, because they tend to take on a double burden or double work (Nieva and Gutek, 1980; Valdez and Gutek, 1987). Even wage-earning women still take care of most of the housework. In middle- and upper-class families women carry out most housework as well, but they are able to pay other people to do some of the work, at least in some countries. A Danish study showed that all the female managers in the sample but only a few of the male managers had paid housekeepers. Male managers were married to women who were either in part-time jobs or had no paid work, while the female managers typically were either in double-career families or they were single (Billing, 1991).

It is relatively common that female managers are single and childless. English, American and Scandinavian studies showed that male managers are more often married than female managers (Bayes, 1987; Billing, 1991; Carlsen and Toft, 1986; Frankenhaeuser, 1992; Nicholson and West, 1988). According to the above investigations most male managers have children, while on average less than half of the married female managers have children. Forty per cent of the women and only a few of the men among the highest paid officers and directors of Fortune 500 companies were childless (Reskin and Padavic, 1994; UCLA/Korn-Ferry International, 1993).

Like many men, some women put their careers first. They are ready to make the same trade-offs traditionally made by the men who seek leadership positions. They make a career decision to put in extra hours, to make sacrifices in their personal lives, to make the most of every opportunity for professional development. For women, of course, this decision also requires that they remain single or at least childless or, if they do have children, that they be satisfied to have others raise them. Some 90% of executive men but only 35% of executive women have children by the age of 40. The automatic association of all women with babies is clearly unjustified. (Schwartz, 1989: 69)

The above research indicates that family issues work against women making a career. Given that many women in senior positions do not have children, it follows that the underrepresentation of women with children in these jobs is much higher than is indicated by the statistics counting only men and women. On the other hand, it is possible that women without children are not that seriously underrepresented in managerial positions. This is an interesting issue worth exploring: perhaps it is the combination of woman plus children rather than woman *per se* that accounts for many of women's difficulties in getting access to senior managerial and other career jobs? Of course, pointing at this aspect in no way offers a final explanation as the interesting issues concerning why having (small) children is such a strong, career disadvantage only for women.

The deeply culturally ingrained assumptions and expectations that women have a primary responsibility for family, in particular for small children, affect men and women in apparent as well as subtle ways. The relationship between career and family might in different ways influence women's attitudes and interests in careers: they might prioritize children above career (or vice versa), or they might feel ambivalence and insecurity in relation to a managerial job – or the family situation might become a stress factor in relation to a career job. Research on stress shows that female managers react with more stress symptoms than male managers (see the discussion later). Even though the increase in the number of female managers, at least up to the middle level, indicates changes, and even though most women today are less tightly coupled to family work while men are increasingly, though slowly, taking more responsibility for children and housework, family concerns are still a significant obstacle to women getting managerial jobs.

A related issue is that, even if women do not have or plan to have children, or if they have full support from their husbands, women may nevertheless be ascribed this family orientation by employers, which means that in some cases their actual situation and priorities matter less than the expectations or stereotypical ideas of senior members of the organization. These may then influence selection processes, disadvantaging female candidates (Billing and Alvesson, 1994). As with most stereotypes, these contain some 'truth', but they also exaggerate and thus sometimes distort, prevent nuances and lead to misleading generalizations.

Of course, all these explanations are, at best, partial and must be understood in relation to other issues. They never stand on their own. For example, if women have other work orientations or interpersonal styles than men, making some of them less inclined to give priority to, and make sacrifices for holding, a managerial job, these differences in orientations cannot be taken for granted or seen as the final explanation, but call for further exploration. The masculine constructions of managerial jobs, including the norm of very long work days, need to be critically assessed. Similarly, family matters are not to be taken for granted. Inequality in terms of men being less inclined than women to take responsiblity for children and a historical as well as contemporary insensitivity of decision makers in organizations to consider the entire life situation of employees should be treated as the starting points for questions and inquiries, not final explanations for the limited numbers of women in managerial positions. In our opinion, the explanation for the low number of women in managerial jobs lies in the interplay between cultural traditions, relations of power and the subjectivities (work orientations, values) of men and women. The latter are clearly affected by organizational experiences, but experiences prior to and outside work must also be considered. Focusing solely on structure or seeing psychological traits or attitudes as self-contained and static appears to us to be somewhat narrow-minded and reductionistic.

As with all issues, those discussed here may very well be radically rethought. We must avoid taking for granted conservative, constraining questions. Instead of trying to explain the limited number of female managers one might ask why there are so many (male) managers. This question includes two elements. One concerns the 'naturalness' of males to be managers. Why do they so often aspire to positions of superiority and why are they favoured in this kind of job? The other element concerns the number of managers and the cultural significance of this kind of work/ function. It may be interesting to counter common sense and view it in

terms of an ideology of managerialism – glorifying control, technocratiza-
tion of social and work life, heroization of 'leaders' and devaluation of
'followers' – rather than as a neutral function in the service of the common
good (Alvesson and Willmott, 1996; Laurent, 1978; Smircich, 1985; Stivers,
1993). This may throw a different light on the sex ratios in management –
and perhaps reduce the interest in number-counting.

Style of leadership – women compared to men

The extensive research on women and leadership can be divided into two
groups. One is the no-difference camp. Here it is commonly concluded that
'in general, comparative research indicates that there are few differences in
the leadership style of female and male designated leaders' (Bartol and
Martin, cited in Eagly and Johnson, 1990). The other is the gender-
stereotypical camp.[2] Here, some crucial differences are believed to exist.
Feminine leadership is characterized by cooperativeness, collaboration
between managers and subordinates and problem solving based on
intuition and empathy (e.g. Helgesen, 1990; Loden, 1986). The first camp is
typically academic, heavily measurement-oriented and thus adhering to the
variable perspective. The second is more strongly made up of practitioner-
oriented authors, often journalists or consultants, typically relying on
qualitative work and often of an anecdotal character. Some are more
academic and derive ideas about women's way of managing from readings
of literature on the psychology of women (e.g. Fletcher, 1994; Grant, 1988).

   We start with a few examples of studies and reviews by authors
emphasizing similarity. Bayes (1987) has studied female and male managers
in public administration. While some women exhibited a management style
which was open and participatory, other women favoured control in their
management style. Men, too, varied in their management style in the
degree of openness and participation they showed. The only area where
some male and female respondents agreed that women were different from
men was in the area of their dedication to work. Women were perceived to
work harder, to take their work more seriously, or even too seriously, and
to be less concerned with monetary rewards than with recognition when a
good job was done. Bayes concluded that women in public bureaucracies
do not manage by using a different leadership style, nor is any different
leadership style reflected in the attitudes they express regarding organizational structure. Kovalainen (1990) also found no significant differences
in a study of male and female Finnish bank managers.

   Comprehensive research by others has come to the same conclusion.
Bartol (1978: 806) summarizes her examination of different organizations
as follows: 'In most cases, there are either no differences or relatively minor
differences between male and female leaders on leadership style, whether
the leaders are describing themselves or being described by their subordinates'. Powell (1988: 165) reaches the conclusion that female and male

managers 'differ in some ways and at some times, but, for the most part, they do not differ'.

As opposed to the above mentioned studies, a number of other writers maintain that there are clear differences between women and men in their management style. As a rule, this thesis is based on theoretical considerations and has been derived from assumptions about the character and the importance of gender socialization (see, for example, Grant, 1988; Lipman-Blumen, 1992). Some authors, such as Loden (1986) and Helgesen (1990), present empirical examples in support of their ideas about a distinct female style. Their studies do, however, express a journalistic rather than scientific ethos, and are methodologically weak.

While these authors promote a specific female style, Marshall (1984: 13) has another point, namely to refute the thesis that 'women are different from men, therefore they will not become good managers'. On the basis of various investigations she concludes that women are very similar to men in their style of management. Marshall points out that the most frequently reported difference is that female managers score higher than men on the supportive side of management. Marshall concludes that the differences between women and men are very slight and that female qualities may be more in demand in the future in management positions. Women might perhaps become better managers than men, she thinks.

Eagly and Johnson (1990), in a review of the research, find that available (positivistic) academic studies show another picture than the 'no-difference' one that almost all other (academic) commentators have favoured. They refer to research findings indicating that women as a group can be described as friendly, pleasant, interested in other people, expressive and socially sensitive. Even though socialization and selection in organizations may mean that gender differences in managerial jobs are reduced or even non-existent, they believe that some level of sex difference in leadership style may follow from 'gender–role spillover'. In a meta-analysis of other studies they find that laboratory studies – mostly with students as research objects – typically show sex differences in leadership style, while studies of leadership in organizations do so to a lower degree. The explanation of the former may be that in laboratory settings, the rules about how one should behave are unclear, which means that people fall back on gender roles to provide guidance and therefore behave more gender-stereotypically than in other situations, or that the subjects are students rather than managers. In organizational settings, that is, studies of 'real' managers, those occupying these positions are selectively recruited and have typically adapted norms for appropriate behaviour. In addition, structural positions influence attitudes and behaviour (Kanter, 1977). Still, however, Eagly and Johnson (1990) found that women had a slightly more democratic leadership style than men.

In a research review of gender and leadership effectiveness Eagly et al. (1995) found that on an aggregate level there were no differences in the effectiveness of female and male leaders. Scrutinizing the findings, however, they found conditions under which men fared better than women and vice versa: 'leadership roles defined in relatively masculine terms favoured male leaders and leadership roles defined in relatively feminine terms favoured female leaders' (p. 137).[3] They found that sex differences were significantly correlated with the congeniality of these roles for men and women. There were tendencies, albeit weak, for women to be more effective than men in business, education, and government or social service and for men, significantly, to be favoured leaders in military organizations. Or to put it differently, 'women fared poorly in settings in which leadership was defined in highly masculine terms, especially in military settings. Men fared slightly worse than women in settings in which leadership was defined in less masculine terms' (p. 140).

There is thus a trend also in some academic work to bring forward difference/gender-stereotypical explanations. Earlier there was a strong consensus for the no-difference camp. Butterfield and Powell (1981: 130), for example, concluded that 'it is now commonly believed that actual (leader sex) differences in the behaviour of real leaders are virtually non-existent'. Recently, authors summarizing the field have been more inclined to favour the idea that there are differences. Fagenson's (1993: 5) summary of the research is that there is evidence suggesting that women managers 'have a transformational, democratic, and/or "web" rather than hierarchical style of leadership and more satisfied subordinates than men managers'. Still, the majority of the academic empirical work supports the no-or-little-difference thesis (see references above). As we have stressed earlier in this book, positivistic studies are much less reliable than they appear. It is very likely that measurements of leadership styles or behaviours do not catch the nuances and subtleties of processes and relations of leadership very well (Alvesson, 1996b; Smirchich and Morgan, 1982).

The change of emphasis in the literature on women and leadership to embrace the different, supposedly superior qualities of women as leaders may reflect certain 'actual' changes in 'objective' reality. Changes may follow from an increase in the number of female managers and a reduction of constraints in terms of expressing their own 'genuine' style – in case people should have a fixed orientation, installed early in life, independent of work experiences, situational conditions and learning. A trend involving de-masculinization of the construction of management may also be significant here. Helgesen (1990) finds examples of an interest in feminine leadership also among the US armed forces. But the changing ideas about women and leadership may also reflect the spirit of the time in broader and less obvious respects, affecting research respondents as well as researchers and review authors. Redefinitions of managerial ideals in a more 'pro-female' direction may improve the self-confidence of the female managers. Writers on the topic of women and management may also feel that the case is no longer one of 'proving that women are people too' (Calás and Smirich, 1996), but that there is space for women's voices on the topic. This may mean that what was earlier seen as 'no differences or relatively minor differences' supporting the similarity idea today tends to be expressed as 'some differences' supporting the idea that women manage in a different way. To determine 'objectively' when 'no', 'insignificant', 'minor' or 'some' is the best word to describe a relationship is hardly possible. When the research area is summarized, it is not easy to sort out new results, new analysis, new emphasis in conclusions from the changed use of words.

Of course, ideas and cultural norms do not exist on their own, but also affect the feelings, thoughts and actions of people in organizations – ideas on female leadership and the practices of women managers may therefore interact. If we learn from popular books and lectures that women lead in a particular way, female managers may adapt to that norm and subordinates may read the behaviour of the female manager accordingly, including devaluing behaviour perceived to break with the norm. In this way 'knowledge' of female managers creates its own 'truth effects' – it does not so much mirror as produce socially constructed 'reality'.[4] The general reservation we expressed in Chapters 1 and 2 about research mirroring objective reality and arriving at robust truths are valid here too.

There are also some more specific problems in sorting out how male and female managers may be compared. Managerial jobs differ tremendously. A complication is that many female 'managers' have positions of limited authority. The meaning of a 'manager' is often highly ambiguous and the title may tell us rather little – except about norms for classification. Sometimes the title just masks a position as 'glorified secretary' (Jacobs, 1992), although Jacobs himself found that this does not seem to be common or explain the rapid increase of women in managerial jobs. Survey studies may easily overlook the fact that classification hides diversity – what 'managers' really do and their 'real' social relationships to 'subordinates' may be very difficult to pinpoint – and such studies thus compare quite different phenomena. Another complication in drawing conclusions about sex and leadership is that the gender congeniality of leadership roles may be accompanied by different patterns. Eagly and Johnson (1990), for example, found that although male leaders were often more task oriented than females, the latter tended to be more so than males in a leadership role that was more congenial to women (e.g. head nurse). Establishing general, abstract correlations between sex and leadership may be a misleading or at least not very informative enterprise.

To summarize, the person wanting a clear and simple answer to the question of whether women manage in a different way to men is bound to be frustrated, not only by the research available, but also by the complexity of the issue. On the whole, male and female managers do not seem to differ very much in leadership behaviour, according to the heavily US-dominated research in the area, but also according to a few non-US studies. There may be some, but not significant, differences in terms of women being more personnel and democratically oriented. It is possible that many women are more inclined to adopt a democratic style than some men. How can we account for any possible tendency in this direction? It may be 'natural' for them, in the light of childhood experiences, female socialization or later experiences in family or at work. But it may also be an expression of their weaker authority, given the traditional image of leadership as a masculine activity. Or it may be a consequence of the stereotypical expectations of other people, assuming that female managers are more 'soft'. Given the unfruitfulness of keeping these aspects fully apart, one should not necessarily aspire to reach a final conclusion. If there are cultural stereotypes/ understandings about the way women 'are' in a particular sense, these may be self-fulfilling. The self is not developed in a social vacuum. We become men and women in the context of dominating masculinities and femininities and interactions partly guided by these cultural understandings.

One should also bear in mind that even if there should be some minor or moderate differences between the way in which male and female managers behave in a particular historical and cultural situation, this should not obscure the fact that there are wide variations within the two categories: some women managers may very well be seen as autocratic and there are male managers that can be described as democratic (cf. the Bayes study, referred to above). This may be obvious, but is ignored by a lot of writings on the subject trying to compare 'men' and 'women' in order to establish whether or not the groups differ.

Difficulties of women managers

Do females in managerial jobs face strains other than those encountered by their male colleagues? This topic may be summarized under the somewhat universal and broad-brush concept of 'stress'. There is a vast amount of literature comparing the stress levels of male and female managers.

The general impression is that there are significant differences. A British questionnaire (Davidson and Cooper, 1984) indicated that female managers experienced higher pressure levels from what is referred to as stress factors both at work, at home and within the individual herself. They also experienced greater manifestations of stress than did male managers. Women in junior and middle management experienced the highest occupational stress levels. They lacked female role models, and felt exposed to sex role stereotyping. They felt pressure to achieve and felt their treatment was unfair compared to men when it came to prospects of promotion and career. They experienced discrimination and prejudice and felt that their job-related training was inadequate compared to that of colleagues of the opposite sex. Finally, they felt that male colleagues received more favourable treatment by the management. 'In sum, the higher pressures at work which female managers are being subjected to, tend to be stressors beyond their control, i.e. external discriminatory-based pressures' (p. 193).

In the home there were also a number of factors which gave rise to 'stress'. Earning more than the husband/partner, lacking support for domestic chores, experiencing conflicting feelings of responsibility in coping with both family and career all gave rise to stress for female managers with families. Single women managers faced higher pressures than male managers, 'in relation to feeling an "oddity", being excluded from social/business events and career conflict over whether to marry/live with someone' (p. 193).[5]

As for the male managers, they experienced the greatest amount of stress arising from their authority/leadership role as well as from the (unsatisfactory) magnitude of their salaries. (Given that they presumably were much better paid than the average employee the lower than desired level of wage may be seen as a source of frustration rather than as 'stress'.) The female and male managers who were most exposed to stress showed symptoms like ill health, they smoked too much, consumed too much alcohol, were dissatisfied with their jobs and performed poorly at work. It is of course difficult to say what is the cause and what is the effect or to point at underlying significant factors.

According to Davidson and Cooper's study, the stress symptoms of the female managers were most often psychosomatic and found expression in inferior results in work performance. They lacked enough self-confidence to voice their opinions, according to the questionnaire responses. They reacted emotionally to problems at work and lacked self-confidence in the performance of their job. Headaches, migraine, irritability and anxiety were reported more frequently by women than by men. On the other hand the greatest stress symptoms of the male managers showed themselves as a nervous stomach and a larger consumption of alcohol. In only one area did they score higher than the female managers, namely in stress resulting from their inability to produce work at a satisfactory rate.

A study of middle managers at Volvo, the Swedish motor manufacturers, also showed that women suffered higher stress levels than men, they also complained more than men, especially about communication problems on the job and about lack of support from superiors. In addition one third of the women said that they had to perform better than the men in order to be evaluated as equally good (Frankenhaeuser, 1993). Women were seen as adopting the 'stress profile' of men, meaning that they tended to react in a similar way to men in relation to demands and challenges, and that they exposed the so-called A-type behaviour: competitive orientation, agressiveness, distrust and suspicion towards people around them. And they were even more competitive than their male colleagues. Frankenhaeuser suggests that this is due to their over-adaptation to the male values at the managerial level.

It appears that female managers also show more stress symptoms related to family/domestic issues than males. This tendency is presumably also valid for other groups of female employees, such as professionals (Etzion, 1987), especially if they have small children (Jick and Mitz, 1985).

The available research on male and female managers regarding stress appears to be consistent and indicates a higher level among the latter category. As with all empirical results, they are not as unproblematic as they appear to be. According to many students of female psychology, women are socialized into acknowledging vulnerability to a much greater extent than men (Fletcher, 1994). They consult physicians and psychotherapists more often. This could mean that they simply tend to respond to questionnaires in a way which emphasizes problems and suffering. The responses to questions, however, may not necessarily be seen as a mirror of the 'objective' level of stress or even genuine 'subjective' experiences about it. The responses may be an expression of the greater inclination of women to acknowledge or espouse problems than that of men, who may have adopted the norm that one does not acknowledge weaknesses or raise problems in ambiguous cases. Women may show better judgement and acknowledgement of problems than men in this respect. Frankenhaeuser (1993) refers to studies showing that women's own health reports are more congruent with medical diagnosis than men's are. Males may more often deny vulnerabilities. Still, it is possible that different responses to questions of health by men and women reflect different styles regarding denying/acknowledging and underreporting/overreporting problems as much as 'real' differences in 'objective' problems. But it is also likely that women experience more stress around work, in particular if they have children. Frankenhaeuser's (1993) study showed that women's level of stress – measured though biological indications (blood pressure, etc.) – remained high when they had come home from work, while men's fell significantly. For some women the level of stress even increased after the end of the working day, as a result of women's greater responsibility for most tasks in the home, including caring for children.

We do not want to discredit the reported results or seriously dispute that many women may well face strains in jobs calling for the exercise of authority and a high degree of engagement, especially in the context of deep cultural ideas giving women the principal responsibility for home, family and children. In addition, it seems reasonable to assume that cultural traditions may mean that women occupying positions of authority face more difficulties than their male colleagues. However, we must be receptive to the various ways in which seemingly robust and consistent empirical material may be interpreted, and realize that questionnaire responses seldom simply mirror 'objective reality' in a straightforward and simple way.

Subordinates, superiors and colleagues may evaluate female managers against the background of the traditional understanding that authority is a masculine position. Eagly et al. did a meta-analysis of available experimental studies: studies in which 'everything' is supposedly under control and where the only thing that differs is the sex of the leader. They concluded that these studies showed 'a small overall tendency for subjects to evaluate female leaders less favourably than male leaders' (1992: 1). But this tendency varied with different kinds of areas and leadership behaviour. In male-dominated areas, such as business and manufacturing, the tendency was more pronounced than in less masculine fields and organizations. When leadership or management was carried out in an autocratic way, that is, a way that is stereotypically masculine, females were evaluated less highly. When leadership was exercised in a gender-congruent way, females received a positive evaluation. But males did not receive a poor evaluation when engaging in 'non-masculine' leadership behaviour. In terms of difficulties for female managers, there seems to be a more restricted set of options that are fully acceptable for female than for male managers. As Eagly et al. (1992: 18) express it, 'they "pay a price" in terms of relative negative evaluation if they intrude on traditionally male domains by adopting male-stereotypic leadership styles or occupying male-dominated leadership positions'. It should perhaps be added that almost all the research is of US origin and one cannot generalize cross-culturally from this – which, of course, does not prevent Eagly et al., like other neo-positivists, from doing so.

Many female managers have traditionally been and are still supervising mostly women. Most people would predict that conventional ideas and expectations on the gendered nature of authority would sometimes make it a bit difficult for females to be managers of males, but the research on the topic does not seem to support this assumption (Eagly et al., 1992), at least not in terms of male subordinates being more inclined than females to give biased evaluations of a female manager. A non-female style, but not male subordinates, brings about a devaluing of a female leader, at least according to US studies on the matter. We should perhaps add that there are a variety of opinions on how this research should be summarized, from those believing that there are no negative evaluations of women managers to others concluding more far-reaching tendencies than what Eagly et al. think is the case. Many authors claim that female managers are caught between contradictory ideals of being feminine and being managerial, leading to great risks of negative evaluations for being either unfeminine or unmanagerial (Cockburn 1991; Stivers 1993; Wahl, 1996). The study by Eagly et al. indicates that this risk may be less significant than sometimes believed, if they adopt a non-autocratic style.

As always it is very difficult to estimate the relationship between experimental results and what takes place in 'real' organizational sites. The former may underestimate the degree of bias in judgements because in real settings people may feel less constrained by the degree of monitoring (by academics) in research experiments and thereby express their prejudices about sex more freely, although perhaps in a covert form. Or the experiments may exaggerate biases, because of the lack of broader information and a focus on sex in the research design, while in real settings the sex of a manager may be less central in evaluations, because other people have access to much richer and broader impressions of the person.

Summary

The research on women, managerial jobs and leadership is extensive, although – like leadership research in general – rather heavily dominated by North Americans. The great majority of the research consists of either positivistic or popularly oriented texts written for practitioners and mainly referring to anecdotal material. There is a shortage of careful qualitative studies in the field.

A review of the research indicates that the accumulation of studies has not so much meant convergence and agreement as increased variation and uncertainty. Until the late 1980s almost all research was interpreted as showing no or only insignificant sex differences in terms of leadership style. Recently, more indications of women adopting a somewhat different leadership style have been put forward (Eagly and Johnson, 1990; Lipman-Blumen, 1992). This may be seen as a response to a certain de-masculinization of traditional leadership ideals in ideology and perhaps also in corporate practice. However, most academic empirical research appears to support the no or only small difference view. While older studies of the 1970s pointed at evaluation bias against women, more recent work seems to indicate that such bias is more circumstantial than general. Only when engaging in leadership behaviour that was inconsistent with sex stereotypes were female leaders evaluated less favourably than males when acting in the same way (Eagly et al., 1992). Perhaps prejudices and biases against women in managerial positions have decreased over time. In terms of sex, stress and managerial jobs, the research findings are more consistent. Female managers show more stress symptoms than their male colleagues, which partly seems to be related to their taking more responsibility for children and home.

Children appear to have another meaning and other consequences for women than for men. As we will develop in subsequent chapters, many researchers believe that having children leads to experiences and orientations that make women in managerial jobs behave in a different way from men. A large number of female managers do not, however, have children. Many women with children seek balance in life between work and family, meaning that they may be less inclined to work more than 40 hours per week. Such an orientation or priority cannot, however, be seen as natural. It is not necessarily voluntary. It may well be because their husbands or partners do not seek such a balance, but are more willing to give priority to work and career. Senior managers and other people may also ascribe such a family orientation to women and act as if this were the case. This becomes self-fulfilling: if a person is denied promotion or challenging and meriting tasks because of anticipated motherhood and priority to children, that person will decrease work involvement and upgrade the family as a source of satisfaction.

Notes

1 The glass ceiling means that women may climb some way up the organizational ladder without too much problem, but that invisible barriers prevent them from reaching the top positions so that they reach a plateau at middle management level.

2 This label may appear pejorative, but we do not intend to give it a negative meaning. The label actually comes from Eagly and Johnson (1990), who found support for this view.

3 Respondents judged a leadership role as feminine if it was believed to require considerable interpersonal ability (for example cooperation), and masculinity if it required considerable task ability (directing and controlling people).

4 Of course, the truth effect of theories known to people also outside academia is often rather weak. It may affect beliefs and espoused theories rather than practices and theories-in-use. In particular, theories may affect how people account for their own or others' 'leadership' when interviewed – they provide scripts for talk – or offer guidelines for how to fill in questionnaires in, for example, scientific studies, but have less impact on everyday behaviour.

5 One may question the meaningfulness of the rather all-embracing use of the term 'stress' favoured in this study - it seems to be a synonym for frustration or dissatisfaction.

7

Women and Management II:
Four Positions

In this chapter we continue the review of women and management, but will change focus from an overview of empirical material to providing a review and discussion of ways of making sense of the area. As always, empirical results do not speak for themselves, but may be interpreted and evaluated in many different ways. The variation and inconsistencies in empirical findings – especially over time – in the studies of women and leadership (managerial jobs) also point to the need for considering various ways of making sense of the subject matter(s). In this chapter we identify and critically examine four fundamental stances on the subject of women managers that can be found primarily in the research community but also in the area of political and organizational policy-making as well as in other contexts when people think about women and management.

The four positions identified and discussed are associated with various arguments and rationales for the interest in increasing the opportunities for women to attain management jobs and exercise authority in organizations. These rationales correspond to different assumptions about gender and the nature of management/organizations. Rather than trying to find robust, definitive answers to questions about gender and management/leadership – as we doubt whether there are any, at least valid over a long time period – and irrespective of that, we think it is of greater interest to become more sensitive to different ways of looking at women and managerial jobs/leadership. Being open and reflective about various ways of interpreting and considering empirical results is more important than treating these as absolute truths or trying to determine such truths.

It should be emphasized that these positions, or perspectives, should not be seen as paradigms, but rather as lines of argumentation. Often they are motivated as much by tactical concerns – what appear to be important to emphasize – as by variation in world views, although the intellectual and political distance between some of the positions is considerable.

The equal opportunities position

The low proportion of women managers is seen by many as a reflection of fundamental inequalities and injustices in society and working life as a whole. In this perspective women are seen as being discriminated against, and denied the same opportunities as men both in a general career context and specifically with regard to the possibility of attaining managerial positions. Conservatism and prejudice prevent women from reaching the higher positions in organizations or in working life in general. Sometimes the interests of some men in keeping women out of the competition are referred to.

The advocates of the equal opportunity position to some extent consider 'legitimate' explanations for the smaller number of females in senior jobs, such as lower investment in a managerially relevant education and other priorities than a managerial career. However, these arguments explain only some of the underrepresentation of women in managerial jobs. Studies comparing men and women with the same background and qualifications, age, experience and time devoted to work suggest that women's success rates are lower than those of their male colleagues: 'It would seem that when women invest in the same education and skills as men, they earn equal access to "male" occupations, but not equal treatment in the internal corporate labour markets' (Devanna, 1987). The discrepancy between a clear increase of female managers at junior levels and very modest changes in the promotion gap at top levels also shows the problems of advancing above lower managerial levels for females.

The lack of equal treatment of men and women often leads researchers to focus on stereotyping and discrimination as explanatory factors. The emphasis typically is strongly on factors external to women, while all references to their background, socialization, motivations or particularity in relation to men are downplayed. There are no real or significant differences in psychology or work orientation that account for the promotion gap. Reskin and Padavic (1994: 42), for example, say that 'childhood gender-role socialization is actually not very important for explaining women's and men's concentration in different jobs and their different rates of promotion'. They refer to a recent US survey in which 78 per cent of the women and 74 per cent of the men agreed that they were willing to devote whatever time was necessary to advance in their career. As human subjects, the two sexes are seen as similar and promotion chances are attributed to workplace conditions, particularly to the arrangements and actions of employers and senior managers.

The finding of the majority of (positivistic) research on women, men and leadership that there are no significant differences also fits nicely with the equal opportunities perspective. When men and women manage in a similar way, there is no reason why they should not occupy managerial positions in large numbers, it is argued.

The reasons for taking an interest in the topic are typically moral ones, associated with fairness. Women should have the same opportunities as men to gain privileges. Reskin and Padavic (1994: 85) rhetorically ask if it matters that women are locked out of the higher-level jobs. They think it does, for three reasons. This practice is unfair, given the equal interest also of women to be promoted. Absence of women in senior posts depresses their wages. Having authority is a value in its own right, involving freedom, increasing work satisfaction and displaying talents (pp. 85, 95). Reskin and Padavic do not mention any consequences for others than the women concerned – such as other women or organizations as a whole. This is consistent with a downplaying of any kind of sex difference: female and male managers do not differ in leadership style.

A great many studies indicate the widespread existence of stereotyped thinking about women, and make a strong case for the assumption that sexual discrimination reduces women's opportunities for attaining management positions.

> Despite contradictory evidence, stereotypes concerning female inadequacy as managers persist and act to distort perceptions of male and female performance and potential. One obvious consequence of these ideas is that a man is more likely to be selected for a managerial position than is an equally qualified woman. (Dipboye, 1975: 7)

Stereotypes do not only influence recruitment and selection to a particular position; they also affect ongoing career development and performance evaluation. Several studies show that assessors who believed that a particular paper was written by a woman rather than a man judged it to be of a lower professional quality (Dipboye, 1975). Sex bias was also documented in science teachers' ratings of pupils' work (Spear, 1983), and in a number of other situations (Nieva and Gutek, 1980). As mentioned above, more autocratic forms of leadership behaviour are evaluated more negatively when expressed by women than men (Eagly et al., 1992). Most of these results have been obtained in laboratory studies. It is not impossible that in real life situations – where the evaluator has access to more information about the people concerned – such a sex bias may be harder to detect (Powell, 1988), although some research indicates that access to broader impressions do not change sex bias (Eagly et al., 1992). It is also possible that the effect of sex in evaluations over time is changing. In Denmark, for example, more girls than boys have gone to college in recent years, which contradicts the idea that the performances of girls should be undervalued, at least in an educational context. However, there is still likely to be a tendency towards biased evaluations of women in working life, especially perhaps in conservative and masculine areas and environments (Eagly et al., 1992).

These tendencies, which are typical of many if not all sectors of society, create barriers to women acquiring high positions in organizations. Even when women have attained management positions, discrimination still prevails. For example, a study of French and Canadian female managers showed that the women felt they were often placed in a role traditionally appropriate to their sex (e.g. secretary).

> A Canadian corporate president said she was called 'dearie' and a senior executive in France recalled being referred to as 'ma petite' ('my little one'). Other ways in which gender is made a salient characteristic of interaction include

comments on the woman's appearance, or questions concerning her marital status, dropped in the middle of what is supposedly a business conversation. (Symons 1986: 387)

Other barriers are of a structural type: the gender-related division of labour means that women are in a minority higher up in the hierarchy; this makes them highly visible as category members, with the risk of being treated as symbols rather than as themselves as individuals, as well as making it difficult for them to gain access to important informal settings because of their lack of network contacts (Kanter, 1977).

From an equal opportunities perspective, the fundamental problem is structural conditions, stereotypical cultural ideas and irrational social processes which lead to a bias in favour of male candidates for, and occupiers of, managerial positions. The lack of equal opportunities could of course be attributed to all social institutions – the family, primary and secondary education, the general labour market – but when it comes to managerial posts, organizational and managerial practices are of paramount importance. At least, equal opportunity advocates often concentrate on this.

The strongest argument in the equal opportunities approach is connected with the assumption – and at best also the evidence – that men and women, at least those with the educational and other qualifications as well as personal resources that make them candidates for managerial jobs, are either the same or at any rate very similar to one another. The less differences there are between men and women in terms of personality, work orientations or other personal characteristics of significance for carrying out the job, the more difficult it becomes to refute the equal opportunities argument.[1] Any promotion gap is attributed to discriminatory practices in organizations.

Within the equal opportunities camp it is sometimes assumed that a certain degree of misfit exists between most women and the current world of management. There may be communication problems and difficulties for females to decipher cultural norms. The domination of men in the latter is not sex-neutral and it creates difficulties which are hard for women to cope with. From the equal opportunities perspective these differences are perceived as limited and accessible to correction, for instance with the help of equal opportunities committees monitoring practices, campaigns affecting attitudes, mentor systems, support groups for women managers or other kinds of arrangements aimed at counteracting obstacles. In other words, this formulation of the equal opportunities stance states that 'real' equal opportunity calls for action to counteract the specific disadvantages caused by the historical absence of gender equity. Women need to be integrated into the historically seen male world of management (Marshall, 1984). Education of particular relevance for a managerial career, such as an MBA, may have to be changed in order not to be biased against women (Sinclair, 1995). Some authors argue for the use of legal procedures to force employers to take action to remove obstacles and increase the number of female managers (Reskin and Padavic, 1994).

Of course, the difference between the two versions is marginal and more a matter of emphasis. The first version also views the removal of biases against women as significant, but complements this with measures aiming to 'empower', train or support women, while the other exclusively emphasizes external constraints and goes beyond the level of the subject in accomplishing change.

The equal opportunities argument for paying attention to the problem of female leaders and their low numbers is basically of a political and moral nature. In modern society there is a strong conviction that everyone should have a fair chance, irrespective of gender, race and so on. It is considered unfair and immoral to prefer men for higher positions just because they are men, and the well-founded reasons for expecting that this is often the case provide a theoretical and – even more – a practical reason for examining the barriers to equal opportunities and leadership positions for women. This argument is perhaps most common in the USA where the interest in managers and upward mobility is pronounced (Adler, 1986/87).

The meritocratic position

While the equal opportunities argument looks at obstacles and possibilities from an ethical–political point of view, a meritocratic argument is interested in combating the irrational social forces which prevent the full utilization of the qualified human resources, thereby increasing effectivity. The fact that only a limited number of women have so far been recruited to management positions indicates that there is a large social group from which many more people could be drawn to occupy higher positions in business, government, politics and so on. The larger the reservoirs from which bright and highly motivated individuals can be recruited, the better these spheres of society can function. The meritocratic perspective consequently adopts a managerial rather than a moral approach to the subject matter.

In a meritocracy people move freely up and down the occupational hierarchy, according to personal merit and to the contributions they can make to the organization in which they work and to society as a whole. In a meritocratic society organizations will thus look for qualifications and will disregard gender, class, background, race, religion and other characteristics irrelevant to qualifications. Historically these characteristics have been the most significant factors in career building, but they are basically outdated in a modern, meritocratic society – at least according to the ideology of such a society. Recruiting women to management jobs can be seen as a natural result of the changing sexual divisions of labour in post-industrial societies (where women are 'moving', although slowly, from female to male work, for example).

Meritocratic societies will clearly recognize the drawbacks of under-utilizing resources, mainly on competitive grounds (for profit motives).

Another reason might be a male labour shortage which would cause companies to look in other untraditional directions for resources (among women). More generally, people taking this approach view the rational use of female labour in managerial ranks as a way of increasing management competence in organizations. Many authors relate this to international competition. P.Y. Martin (1993: 289) refers to competition with German and Japanese corporations; US corporations 'cannot afford to exclude from full participation the talented, intelligent women and minority men'. One could add that German and Japanese corporations seem to be doing well, despite a much lower number of female managers than in the USA. This does not, of course, contradict the idea that improved use of talents may strengthen business. Loden (1986) is worried about the crisis in US business and feels that feminine leadership could play an important role in revitalizing enterprises. Adler (1986/87) regards a greater number of women managers in US corporations as 'one of America's few remaining competitive advantages' at a time when the global environment has become exceedingly competitive.

> A top-quality human resource system provides strategic advantages, yet companies world-wide draw from a restricted pool of potential managers. Although they represent over fifty per cent of the world's population, in no country do women represent half, or even close to half, of the corporate managers. (Adler, 1986/87: 3)

Many authors argue that organizations are becoming increasingly aware of the talents of women.

> There is evidence that some organizations are already realizing that developing women managers can increase *both* their total pool of talent and *widen* the range of abilities and skills which their men as well as their women will then bring to the task of managing. (Hammond and Boydell, 1985: 77)

Such indications are also prevalent in Scandinavia. In an interview a Swedish bank manager declared that the bank quite simply needed the resources of women as well (*Veckans affärer*, 1986). We participated in a project involving a series of seminars for a subsequent book in which a group of Swedish executives from large organizations defined topics they felt were important in private as well as public management. One of these was the issue of female managers. The attendance rate of the executives at this particular seminar was high, indicating a serious interest in the topic.

Various opinions exist as regards both the nature of modern meritocratic societies in general and the virtues of the ideal of meritocracy. According to French, our society's claim to be a meritocracy is problematic because:

> The very word conceals layers of falsehood; it implies that all members of society have equal access to all doors of development and all avenues of practice; and that those who are most excellent rise to the top. It implies that the unskilled and unsuccessful deserve their fate, that they are less able *by nature*. In addition, our society praises those with power – as gifted when in fact no one develops and uses a talent without assistance from others at every step: from family, friends, and educators; from trainers and coaches; and from a larger community, which

accepts a person's exercise of an ability. An ability, like a person, requires nourishment and scope if it is to grow. It reflects not just individuality, independence, and a drive to excellence, but also dependency, interconnection, and the acceptance of society. (French, 1986: 550)

However, the meritocratic argument for taking up the problem of women managers and investigating the obstacles to a full realization of the human resource potential of the female population is not necessarily tied to an abstract individualistic view of social stratification and career patterns in society and working life. It could be argued, for example, that the effective use by society and its organizations of women's qualifications requires specific attention to be paid to circumstances which prevent women achieving optimal career patterns. Factors such as those indicated by the equal opportunities stance, such as discrimination, could be relevant here. Research on gender and mentorship could foster an interest in examining ways of counteracting this type of problem.

The interest of the meritocratically oriented writers in female managers and related processes both inside and outside organizations, and in the recruitment (and otherwise) of women to managerial positions, has much in common with the equal opportunities approach. Both perspectives are interested in what is preventing women's access to managerial jobs on equal terms with men. Both recognize the shortcomings in contemporary practices in equal opportunities and the realization of the meritocratic principle. The approaches differ radically, however, in terms of the underlying interest pursued. While the equal opportunities orientation stresses the interests of women and fairness primarily for women's sake or for reasons of democracy, meritocrats are concerned with the maximum efficiency of social institutions. The meritocratic approach is thus a stance more typical for business school academics and companies than for sociologists and politicians. Efficiency is something quite different from ethics. While meritocracy is not only a technocratic principle but can also be a component in an explicit political ideology, such concerns are not a key factor in the areas of business and organizations, and our argument here highlights the technocratic motive for fully utilizing the 'human resources' of organizations, irrespective of gender. This means that the whole issue is understood as a matter of 'inefficient human resources management', and not as 'discrimination' (nor, somewhat similarly, as 'immoral'). This can be illustrated by the following concluding comment in a study of myths about women managers:

> It is recommended, therefore, that organizations begin treating women as equals, not because of moral obligations or pressures from outside interest groups to improve female/male ratios, but because they would more effectively utilize valuable human resources. (Reif et al., 1975: 79)

The rationalization and improvement of recruitment, promotion and leadership in organizations, the counteracting of 'old-fashioned' and irrational cultural patterns, and the launching of progressive organizational socialization processes can all serve to promote a more efficient and sex-neutral utilization of management candidates as well as other significant employees.

In addition to these means for improving the supply of human resources, two practical implications of the meritocratic perspective can be emphasized, as compared with the equal opportunities approach. One of these concerns the actors involved in the correction of existing problems. According to the meritocratic approach, it is assumed that maximum (or at least a high level of) efficiency in the functioning of an organization is in the interest of top management, and that an enlightened top management is in the best position to handle the problem. Market competition and the struggle between companies to attract and utilize the best personnel will provide an incentive to counteract ineffective promotion practices and personnel policies. The equal opportunities position which is often very sceptical about the abilities and interests of top managers, particularly when it comes to pursuing a gender-neutral promotion policy, normally calls for broader societal involvement in the equality issue, including legislation and bringing cases to court. Some equal opportunities advocates even think that employers are willing to sacrifice efficiency gains in order to keep women out of top jobs (Cockburn, 1991).

The second practical difference between the equal opportunities and meritocratic approaches concerns the tolerance of deviations from the ideal of evaluation and promotion based purely on merit and qualifications. In an equal opportunities perspective even the slightest deviation to the disadvantage of women is intolerable. From a technocratic point of view a problem arises if a significantly less competent person is preferred to a more qualified candidate. In many cases two or more applicants for a certain job may be roughly equally competent, and it does not matter very much which of them gets the job. From a managerial point of view slight discriminatory practices which mean that males are preferred to equally qualified females are normally not a problem. Getting a sufficiently qualified and committed person is the priority, not perfect justice. If women are handicapped by having children and as a consequence may be at the employers' disposal for overtime or travelling to a reduced degree, a meritocracy position would see that mainly as a private concern – even though some companies may be prepared to assist in integrating private and working life for key employees – while equal opportunities advocates would not tolerate women falling behind due to a moderate disadvantage in terms of opportunities to prioritize work. Clear differences in terms of policy follow from the fact that the meritocracy advocates view more women managers as a *means* for organizational functioning, while equal opportunities proponents see this as the *goal* in itself. They will consider ambiguous cases in very different ways and have rather different levels of tolerance for a promotion gap between men and women. Meritocrats have less interest in aiming for a 50/50 sex ratio in promotions and also are less interested in taking actions for the long-term increase of promoted female employees.

The special contribution position

We have seen that the equal opportunities and meritocratic approaches emphasize the common traits of the two sexes; the problem as they see it is that men and women are not compared on fair and equal terms and thus do not have the same chances (they are not being evaluated and utilized strictly according to merit). The two approaches discussed in this and the following section, on the other hand, draw attention to the dissimilarities between the genders.

In the literature concerned with women's life situations and career patterns a shift has occurred during the last 20 to 25 years. During the 1970s the majority of writers on women attempted to minimize the differences between men and women in order to achieve equal opportunities. Androgyny was seen as a universally good category, both for men and women. During the last 10 years or so an increasing number of feminist writers have begun to emphasize the position that generally speaking 'the female experience' in childhood, family and community, etc. is different from 'the male experience' and that a female perspective may differ from the dominating, male one. 'This woman-centered perspective celebrates and exonerates female difference, instead of suggesting that women imitate male agenic features with an androgynous sprinkling of communal qualities' (Grant, 1988: 58).

The emphasis can be placed on women's differences in terms of experience, values, ways of behaving, feeling and thinking with varying force. A moderate position will first be discussed, while a stronger case for far-reaching differences will be examined later in the chapter. According to the approach discussed in the present section, it is suggested that due to moderate but significant differences compared with men, women possess complementary qualifications and, thus, the potential for making new and important contributions to the field of management. This can be referred to as the 'special contribution argument'. Some authors refer to it as 'female leadership' or as 'feminist management' (P.Y. Martin, 1993). Some even talk about the 'female advantage' (Helgesen, 1990). This approach may be seen as an applied but weak version of the feminist standpoint perspective covered in Chapter 2. It is adjusted to, and integrated with, the mainstream managerial preoccupations that most hardcore feminist standpoint advocates strongly dislike.

In general in contemporary society, there seems to be a fairly widespread belief (mainly among women) that women can contribute something essential to organizations. Women are believed to prefer a people-oriented and democratic leadership style, to make the social structure less hierarchical, and to change the workplace climate so that empathy and intuition become more significant. An investigation of female and male managers in the private and public sectors in Denmark found that 62 per cent of female managers and 33 per cent of male thought that as managers women could contribute something special, for instance using 'typical' female traits in cooperation and influencing the organizational climate (Carlsen and Toft, 1986). As we have seen from the review of the positivist research on the topic, there is some, but relatively weak, support for this view. The rather large body of studies concluding that there are no or only minor gender differences may be interpreted as an outcome of the relative lack of female managers (especially some time ago, when large parts of the research were carried out), selective recruitment and the pressure of female managers to adjust to dominating norms and expectations on leadership. With other options to express feminine forms of leadership and expansion of female managers, women may make a stronger difference in managerial practice.

The popularity of the special contribution perspective can be seen as a reflection of a broad societal trend. As mentioned above, changes in society and in organizations are broadly thought to require new styles of leadership which are seen as more congruent with women's orientations (Fondas, 1997). The organizations are changing, it is argued, for business reasons as well as in response to the demands of employees. Business reasons are related to a call for more flexibility and more rapid reactions, associated with new production and information technology and faster market changes. A possible consequence is that participatory styles of management are seen as increasingly significant. The old authoritarian style does not work, we are repeatedly told. All these changes are reflected in many new theories on leadership (for example, Kanter, 1983; Smircich and Morgan, 1982). Communication, teamwork, cooperation and the creation of meaning are issues that are regarded as important in leadership at the present time. The leadership ideas and styles popular during recent years are not necessarily explicitly pro-women, but they accord ill with traditional ideas of the masculine character of the good manager: technocratically rational, aggressive, competitive, firm and just. At a minimum a masculine bias is reduced. Some organizations indicate that they are actually looking for certain new values which are associated with women, such as flexibility, social skills, team orientation.

Of course, this kind of rhetoric does not stand in a one-to-one relationship to the complexities of organizational conditions and changes. Most likely it exaggerates and idealizes current trends. Of greater interest in the present context than to try to evaluate what is really going on out there – this lies anyway partly in the future – is to note the expressed interests in certain themes and assumptions of changes and the relevance for bringing forward ideas of a distinctive feminine leadership or a female advantage in organizations.

Grant (1988), among others, suggests that women managers may contribute in particular in the following important ways: communication and cooperation, affiliation and attachment, power, and intimacy and nurturance. She argues, for example, that because women have had a lot of practice from an early age in communicating and caring for others, they are often good at it. From this follows an ability to facilitate cooperative behaviour, which is of course important in terms of consultation, democratic decision making, work climate, and so on. According to Grant and many other female writers, women often have a different attitude to power compared with men. Unlike men, women tend to see power not so much as domination and an ability to control, but rather as a capacity, and particularly as a capacity stemming from and directed towards the entire community. Women's view of power is thus more relational and less purely individualistic. Some authors suggest that compared with men, women possess more flexibility, more intuition, and a greater ability to be empathetic and to create a more productive work climate (for example, Schmidt, 1987); they could exercise power in a more constructive way, mobilize human resources better, encourage creativity and change the hierarchical structures (Haslebo, 1987). A particular aspect here concerns recognition of vulnerability. Unlike men who are socialized to deny such feelings, women are more open to feelings such as self-doubt and inadequacy. This may reduce self-confidence, but also promote self-disclosure, addressing one's own and the work units' weaknesses, establishing contact, building networks, monitoring problems and thus learning and development (Fletcher, 1994). Lipman-Blumen (1992) talks of a 'connective leadership' in which networking and shared responsibilities are central, encouraging people to connect to others and others' goals.

Arguably, much of what is said is somewhat imprecise and refers to a rather idealized view of the positive contributions of women. In general, though, it makes sense to stress that women have often been socialized according to different values, norms, orientations and psychological characteristics, which could be seen either as complementary to existing values, or perhaps even as replacing some of them. Female characteristics, according to the authors referred to, indicate a certain discrepancy between what they believe are typical women's orientations and common organizational practices. The latter seldom promote empathy, attachment, nurturance, etc. It still remains to be seen what difference it would make if women were in senior managerial positions. There is little in the contributions mentioned to question seriously the commitment of the organizations (shareholders, top management) to profit, growth and other traditional goals. Capitalism and market economy, the complexity of large-scale organizations and other constraints may mean that any genuine female orientation – if one accepts this notion – may not come through very clearly in most managerial contexts, at least not as long as there are only relatively few female managers. Fierce competition between companies is not abolished by female forms of leadership. The specific qualities ascribed to women may have some importance, but in many corporate contexts it is an open issue whether there is space, within the capitalist economy, for these to become really significant. Thus women could very well come to provide the necessary oil to make the machinery work better; and/or their interpersonal and persuasive skills could be exploited as a potential tool for carrying out unpopular rationalizations more smoothly, with women acting as mediators between the top management and the workers (Calás and Smircich, 1993). Kolb (1992), for example, shows how women may be inclined to work with conflicts behind the scene, doing important work, but remaining invisible and also potentially preventing conflicts surfacing in cases where airing these may be positive. Such points of view are relatively seldom put by the writers arguing for the special contributions that women can make.

On the other hand, from a special contribution point of view it could be argued that the presumed different psychologies of men and women will mean different approaches to problems, whereby women coming from the outside will introduce a different set of beliefs; accepted norms may also be questioned, thus promoting a progressive development. The idea that 'the exaggerated male psychology of autonomy and separateness' leads to 'an overvaluing of rationality, objectivity and analysis, and again, to an undervaluing of nurturance, skill in interpersonal relations, and creativity' (Grant, 1988: 62) may represent a change, bringing complementarity and balance to bear on the managerial practices prevailing hitherto. But it could also be seen as conflicting sharply with these and with the dominating male organizational principles. Whether complementarity or conflict predominates will of course depend on how far the ideas associated with a special contribution are taken. Some degree of complementarity is facilitated by contemporary popular ideas on management, but a peaceful co-existence with concerns for productivity, growth, careers and profits, and reform based on special contributions would presumably call for a relatively careful, tactful and moderate introduction of these.

The special contribution position is not, of course, in total opposition to the two approaches discussed earlier in this paper – they all share the commitment to facilitate women's options in managerial positions – but the relationship between the equal opportunities and meritocracy perspectives on the one hand, and the special contribution argument on the other, is not without friction. The former emphasizes the similarity between the sexes and calls for 'gender-neutral' career patterns and managerial recruitment. The special contribution approach indicates certain aspects that call into question the possibility of 'gender neutrality'. The claimed significant differences between the sexes could make it difficult to evaluate 'typical' males and females according to a single scale. Rather, given their assumptions, it appears more reasonable to assume that many women and men have characteristics that make them suitable for different types of positions or jobs. The kind of 50/50 norm advocated by equal opportunities proponents is weakened by the special contribution argument. The emphasis on gender difference would mean that gender division of labour appears as to some extent natural. The special contribution stance does not of course suggest that the traditional male hegemony of leadership positions is reproduced; rather it promotes career patterns for women which helps them to achieve higher positions. (We are not concerned here with the possibility that the special contributions might be unacceptable to dominant groups of managers; if this is so, the contributions are probably best regarded as alternative, not special.) Of course, it may be likely that the special contribution idea would legitimate the fact that women are primarily represented in certain kinds of managerial jobs, in which people and human relations are central, while others, such as the more influential ones associated with production, finance and strategic management, are still seen as naturally male work. This kind of thinking would reproduce the current gender division of managerial labour. A positive difference would, however, be to anticipate a general, although unevenly distributed, increase of female managers. Even in the light of a continued absence in certain managerial jobs in which the female characteristics may be seen as less central, such a development would still be considered progressive.

The strategy that follows from the special contribution argument is not, as in the two earlier cases, that women should compete with men on 'equal' terms; instead it emphasises that women can contribute something different from what is assumed to be the typically dominating male characteristics and skills. A practical consequence of this approach appears to be that 'Recent developments in training for women aim to discover women's strengths, skills and management style, in order to change the male models of effective management. Clearly, women are no longer willing to let the organization mould them' (Clutterbuck and Devine, 1987: 6).

Rather than special arrangements for integrating women or the modification of human resource management to remove bias, the specific qualifications and orientations of the women should be built upon as the primary vehicles for their attainment of leadership positions. Rather than the same set of criteria, the use of dimensions for assessing women specifically considered for female psychological characteristics and work orientations would be developed.

The alternative values position

The point made here is that the two genders differ substantially. The key assumption is that in general women do not share the interests, priorities and basic attitudes to life that are common among men – or perhaps rather dominating groups of men. This approach has some similarities with the special contribution view discussed above, but the 'alternative values' position stresses the differences between typical 'male' and 'female' values more strongly, and also emphasizes conflicts between the two. This approach is a direct offspring from the feminist standpoint perspective and thus basically critical to male-dominated institutions.

According to this position, traditionally women have been socialized to live by the values of the private sphere, to be nurturing, to serve others, to be emotional, while men have been socialized to live by the values of the public sphere, to deny vulnerability, to compete, to take risks, to want to control nature. It could be claimed that the cultural norms and values characterizing the socialization of women and men belong to two different and more or less polarized worlds, one feminine and one masculine, one intuitive–communal and one logical–instrumental.

As briefly mentioned in Chapter 3, an important stream here is psycho-analytic feminism, which emphasizes early childhood and the different nature of mother–child interaction for girls and boys. Other authors ground a distinct feminine orientation less in early socialization and psychology than in shared female experiences associated with the historical position as subordinated or an orientation developed as a consequence of experiences of mothering (Cockburn, 1991). While special contribution authors typically view female early socialization as crucial for the gender difference, alternative values advocates more clearly invoke social con-ditions, including political positioning. It is the, in many respects, marginal position of women which brings about a specific set of orientations. One could also here imagine the significance of general cultural constructions of masculinities and their negations in terms of femininities. The variety of processes tying women to primarily embracing and defining themselves through what is seen as feminine are crucial for an alternative orientation to the one of dominating masculinities (Fletcher, 1994).

Irrespective of the specific background to gender differences, many writers see women as bearers of a rationality different from that of men. Some describe it as a rationality of responsibility (Sørensen, 1982) which is regarded as characterizing the female culture. This rationality is sometimes conceptualized as another morality (French, 1986) or as female forces of production (Prokop, 1981). It involves the capacity for taking care of other people's needs, a morality of responsibility and caring (Gilligan, 1982). That women develop a capacity for need-oriented communication is obviously most visible in the mother–child relationship. It is also possible to exploit this capacity, however, for example when a secretary is supposed to do 'mother work' for the boss, looking after his needs (Pringle, 1989; Sokoloff, 1981). Healy and Havens (1987) view the traditional female socialization as antithetical to leadership, at least in the way this is conventionally understood.

If we accept the idea of different rationalities, it may become easier to understand why women often choose to work in fields that deal with human beings, in the social and humanistic fields, and in the health and service sectors. From the stance discussed here, it could be argued that women work in these areas mainly because they provide a better fit with women's perceived needs and wants, and not so much because women are excluded from other areas or because they make choices regarding educa-tion and work based on traditions and internalized stereotypes.

The priorities of women mentioned above imply occupational choices (which are also largely a result of the socialization process) which lead to jobs oriented to human needs; such jobs seldom offer career opportunities on the same scale as the areas of engineering and business for example. Many women may not generally be attracted to managerial jobs in a com-pany, something which could be seen as a rather passive way of protesting against a managerial career, at least under contemporary conditions. They would be less willing either to make all the personal sacrifices demanded to achieve power, prestige and high wages, or to give priority to an instrumental orientation, central to the realization of productivity, growth and profit ends.

The notion of instrumentality marks a strong difference between the special contribution and the alternative values approaches. Fletcher (1994) criticizes the former, which she labels 'the female advantage', for pursuing a 'castrated' version of it. She argues that central in the mutual vulnerability, openness and mutual influence of the female orientation is reciprocity. This is 'antithetical to achieving pre-ordained instrumental goals. By its very nature, the outcomes of a mutual interaction are fluid, unknowable – the essence of creativity rather than management by objectives' (p. 79). Fletcher emphasizes the difference between using relational skills to achieve instrumental ends, as characterized by special contributions authors, and using relational skills to relate and then make instrumental decisions based on that interaction. Fletcher views the open, unpredictable nature of women's ways of being as central, and does not think that outcomes may be specified. Still, there is a clear radical element in a privileging of connection and openness. Minimizing status differences, a recognition of interdependence and an awareness of the costs of doing business for family, society and the natural environment are likely consequences, antithetical to the functioning of most organizations.

If these distinctions are taken seriously, it is obvious that men and women in general will come to the organizations with very different psychological and value orientations. Women will bring with them the view of the periphery, perhaps even threatening existing norms in many organizations. On the other hand, the act of entering a 'male world' such as the corporate world of management will probably be not so much a challenge as a repeated frustration to most women, as there will often be conflict between the female orientation and male-dominated organizational practices. As most business and public sector organizations have been designed by men as the bearers of technological rationality, and as most of them are dominated by males, it is obvious that they will suit many men better than most women – that is to the extent that women differ from men. They will fit masculine work orientations and male interests (cf. Jackall, 1988).[2] The antithetical position in relation to present institutions from a feminine point of view is also expressed by Ressner (1986), who talks of 'the institutionalisation of female interests and rationality' as an overall objective for most women. Such an objective may have great difficulty in co-existing with traditionally dominating male, technological and capitalist values and priorities. It may well be that fundamental changes in organizations are needed if more than a minority of women are to fit into higher organizational positions, if their different priorities and interests are taken seriously (Ferguson, 1984).

Similarly, a radical feminist position may see the issue of leadership not as a matter of promoting a female version of it as much as a questioning of the emphasis on leadership. As Stivers (1993: 132) says, (some) feminists raise the question of 'whether female leadership styles simply mask hierarchy more effectively; they would want to explore whether we need leaders at all – in the sense of someone who defines the meaning of situations, shows others the right way to approach problems, and makes them want what the leader wants (motivates them)'.

Ferguson (1984: 4) and other radical feminists reject the exclusive focus on integration in organizations because they regard 'the existing institutional arrangements as fundamentally flawed'. They believe that the price of success is to abandon any thought of changing the system. Therefore it is naive to hope that once women have made their way to the top, they will then change the rules. Ferguson asks, 'after internalizing and acting on the rules of bureaucratic discourse for most of their adult lives how many women (or men) will be able to change? After succeeding in the system by using these rules how many would be willing to change?' (p. 192). One could add that they have already changed through adapting to the rules.

The empirical results suggesting either that there are no, minor or moderate differences in the leadership style between men and women may seem to indicate similarity rather than radical difference but may also be interpreted as supporting the alternative values approach. Females have to adjust to organizational practices and make no real difference, if they get into positions of power. The results of stress research provides perhaps a more distinct support for the thesis that adjustment to organizations is accompanied by suffering for women to a higher degree than for men. Of course, as with all empirical results they may well be interpreted in accordance with all the approaches treated here.

Authors who lean towards this view suggest that women in organizations, and especially those entering the male-dominated management sphere, should act in accordance with their own needs and wishes without trying to adapt to the dominating values and standards, and that in this way they can try to achieve a radical change. P.Y. Martin (1993: 288), whose position lies somewhere between the special contribution and alternative values approaches, believes that this could bring about far-reaching improvements in almost all respects of corporate functioning, involving everything from democracy and worker safety to protection of the physical environment and preventing closing factories for tax reasons or moving them to the Third World, where cheap labour may be found. This probably appears as far too optimistic and naive for most people, including most alternative values proponents, who typically have few illusions about corporations or the leeway in a capitalist market economy. Even though she, referring to Jackall (1988), correctly points at weaknesses of male-normative management leading to ineffective forms of individualism, self-interest, covering up, suboptimization and short-sightedness it is also likely that feminist management, if put into action, has drawbacks in the context of corporate performance. And a wider set of organizational objectives may easily lead to conflicts between them. Conflict of (legitimate) interests cannot simply be defined away with idealistic definitions of management promising harmony and optimization on all accounts. Calás and Smircich (1993: 79) ironically notice the 'unique "all heart, all peace" managerial goodness assumed to come from women's qualities'. A more realistic evaluation of the options for alternative values to put an imprint on mainstream organizational culture is less optimistic.

> In this view, women who claim their individuality and difference, and so become more visible to each other and to men, are more likely to impact the deep structure of embedded values and so to contribute to creating organizations which are at least women-friendly. (Marshall, 1987: 30)

However, hopes in this regard are also typically modest. Most alternative values advocates would view painful personal transformation in a way that minimizes the distinctively female as a high price to pay for a 'successful' career or even adaptation in most organizations.

From the perspective on women in managerial jobs discussed here the barriers to women attaining higher positions are not only a matter of the lack of equal opportunities, of prejudice, of small numbers; they are also a result of many women's lack of real interest in adapting themselves to the demands made by corporations and management jobs. This emerges from insight and alternative commitment, and is thus not a weakness which can be repaired through more rational forms of social engineering, such as the use of mentors, training or less biased recruitment procedures.

Alternative values proponents take an anti-management stance and are more interested in developing alternative social institutions than integrating women in the existing ones. Ferguson (1984) argues for alternative organizations that are 'genuinely egalitarian'. Examples may be feminist organizations such as book stores and health clinics. They are decentralized, and 'they rely on personal, face-to-face relations rather than formal rules' and 'they see skills and information to be shared, not hoarded' (p. 190). There are two profound problems with this solution. The first is that such organizations are often emotionally demanding and frustrating to work in, contingent upon uncertainties, ineffective management, financial difficulties and a tendency to personalize most issues (Morgen, 1994). The second is that it means that women are concentrated in financially and technically weak and peripheral areas, while the large and powerful organizations are left in the hands of a group of men and a few like-minded women (Billing, 1994). A more moderate response to the alternative values critique in terms of women's career orientations would be to work in organizations that are more attuned to female orientations than most large-scale corporations. Some public sector, service companies and knowledge-intensive companies may be less alien to the alternative values, as portrayed by Ferguson and others (Billing and Alvesson, 1994: chapter 7; Blomqvist, 1994).

A dilemma for the alternative values approach is that it is of great political and social importance that women should attain decision-making positions to a much greater extent than they do at present. The obstacles and informed reluctance to do so lead to a paradoxical situation. The same factor that makes it especially important for women to be represented in decision-making groups, namely the assumed difference between female and male values and priorities, also makes it less likely that women will embrace or feel comfortable with careers leading to top jobs in business and government. Those who succeed are atypical in relation to broader groups of women, either from the start or as a result of organizational socialization and disciplining processes which means that they are not capable of speaking with a distinct female voice, at least not so that people in noisy organizational environments can hear it.

Comparing the approaches

Of course, far from all authors and texts can easily be plugged into any of the four alternative positions on the subject matter here discussed. Some texts represent a combination of arguments and views from these different perspectives. Martin (1993), for example, argues in between the special contribution and alternative values camps but also draws on meritocracy arguments pointing at the significance of using female talent in management. Occasionally writings appear as inconsistent or confused, for example if they strongly emphasize the existence of deeply rooted cultural beliefs negating women as managers, but still say that there are no sex differences in interest, ability or style (e.g. Reskin and Padavic, 1994). Given that cultural beliefs also affect the subjectivities of women, the consequences for women's self-confidence, career intentions and self-image – crucial pre-requisites for being a manager – may be considerable.

Related to problems in treating the leadership and gender topic coherently is the impossibility of stressing only similarity or only difference in all or even some profound respects. Some would argue against framing the issue in such a way that one has to emphasize either position (Scott, 1991). Most people would probably agree that men and women, of a particular age, ethnic group and class, during a particular historical time, tend to be similar in certain respects (situations) and different in others. This does not, of course, prevent us from recognizing the analytical value of identifying the four 'pure' forms. Although doing so inevitably involves the creation of order out of chaos, dominating lines of thinking and the majority of writings in the area lend themselves rather nicely to be mapped with the framework used here. Most authors emphasize either what they think tend to be similar or different, in terms of what is relevant for understanding the phenomenon treated. Equal opportunities authors also recognize that boys and girls experience different socialization, but they do not believe that this is very important for understanding gender and leadership.

The four perspectives are summarized in Figure 7.1 which combines the two central dimensions involved: emphasis on similarity/dissimilarity between the two sexes, and focus on ethical or efficiency concerns.

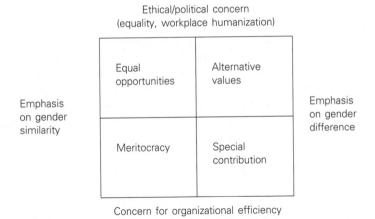

Figure 7.1   *Approaches to the understanding of women and leadership*

The two dimensions in the model must of course be seen as continua. The (dis)similarity between the sexes can be stressed more or less strongly. Alternative values advocates typically stress it more strongly than special contributions authors, but the specific qualities emphasized are more significant than quantities. Within all the boxes, there are a variety of opinions, although some aspects are of course not considered in the model. A mixture of efficiency and moral concern can probably be found in most authors, although some alternative values feminists do not express an interest in efficiency issues.

Various kinds of critique could be, and are to some extent, directed at the different approaches. Much of the critique of the variable and standpoint perspectives covered in Chapter 2 is highly valid here, but will not be repeated. Equal opportunity advocates would see the special contribution and alternative values approaches as reinforcing stereotypical views on women, which they would feel run against the struggle for gender equality. If female psychology and feminine values circling around connection, nurturance and vulnerability are seen as central, women may appear as more fitted as leaders of day care centres or personnel managers than as executives in industrial or financial corporations. The critique the other way around would say that similarity-focusing researchers do not take women's voices seriously and are caught in a defensive battle, trying to prove that 'women are people too' (Calás and Smircich, 1996). Marshall (1993: 125) writes that 'until recently, many researchers have emphasized women's similarities to win the former's acceptance'. Alternative values advocates would criticize special contributions authors for 'castrating the female advantage' (Fletcher, 1994) – selling out the distinctiveness of feminine orientations for the sake of integration and careers – while special contributions people may counter by arguing that alternative values thinkers locate themselves outside any form of realistic practical impact or, if successful, place women in the periphery of society – in marginal institutions – thereby reinforcing male domination in core sectors of society.

A big problem in discussing similarity/difference is that the male has typically been and still is the norm in organization and management, meaning that talk about difference often appears as negative and harmful for women; difference may be read as deviation (Cockburn, 1991; Scott, 1991). Precaution and tactic then appear as necessary. If one changed starting points and looked at what may be typical for men as the interesting issue, things might turn out quite differently. But the general interest in, and research literature on, 'men and management' – where gender is taken seriously – is still very meagre (for exceptions, see Collinson and Hearn, 1996).

A number of interesting research questions can be formulated, based on the relations and tensions between the four perspectives. The following are some examples.

One question starts from a comparison between the first two and the second two perspectives. Are women and men who represent potential candidates for middle and top leadership jobs on the whole basically similar or dissimilar? Few people claim any general difference in intellectual skills, for example, but as we have seen opinions vary about the socialization background and the psychological characteristics of men and women. This question is naturally a tremendously complex one. It is likely that research will produce a variety of answers depending on what empirical methods are used, what psychological and social dimensions are in focus, which groups are investigated and when, and so on. If we compare women and men in general, for example, we are likely to detect greater differences than if we look at the limited number of women who are managers today and compare them with their male colleagues (Eagly and Johnson, 1990). The picture could change when it becomes less unusual for women to reach higher positions as less 'atypical' women would make a larger part of the category. Research results on the subject will probably only provide temporary answers.

Another question that we feel is important concerns the significance of an increase in the number of women leaders for organizations and society as a whole; this could lead to a general increase in equality between the sexes in society, or the possibility that women's points of view would be better represented in decision-making circles or, if one accepts the special contribution position, that the subordinates will be more satisfied. But this is not necessarily so. It is only a small percentage of the population that attains higher management positions, and an equalization of the gender ratio here does not necessarily reflect or affect the situation as regards the majority of a population. It is also a disputed topic whether the sex of a manager has any consequences for subordinates. Some equal opportunities proponents, such as Reskin and Padavic (1994), view the closure of the promotion gap as beneficial for those specific women at present disfavoured (managerial candidates), but do not mention any consequences for other women (or subordinate men). Still, one could argue that an increase in the number of female managers may have a positive effect for other women, in that they will have more role models signalling that 'woman' does not only mean subordinate positioning, and that more female managers may also reduce sexual harassment. These are, however, minor advantages compared with the possibility that female managers would mean a specifically female form of managing corresponding to the wants of many female and some male employees. A trend towards more female top managers may be cut off from, or at least loosely related to, other gender issues in working life, if female managers do not differ from their male colleagues.

Even if one would assume that female and male managers differ in work orientations, it remains an open question whether this has any significant consequences. Certain factors and mechanisms could neutralize such different orientations and prevent women leaders from having a significant influence on organizations in a way that is representative of broad population groups. Some would argue that the scope for action for many managers is limited, and it does not then matter whether the top boss is a man or a woman. Profit-maximization and external resource dependencies may make the sex distribution in managerial jobs of limited significance. Some researchers downplay the role of managers (cf. Pfeffer, 1977; Pfeffer and Salancik, 1978). The general norms and practical constraints – heavy workload, deadlines, skills of personnel, amount of resources, bureaucratic regulations – on managerial behaviour may also sometimes prevent any possible effects of the sex of the manager.

Of course, it is not unlikely that there are great variations in this respect – as may be the case in all social issues. Sometimes in organizational contexts there are discretion and options for change that may provide fertile soil for a distinctive form of 'female leadership' or 'feminist management'.[3] There may be differences between different organizations or different situations. Some people – due to exceptional qualities and/or specific circumstances – may put specific 'gender imprints' on the work contexts in which they occupy a senior position, but the average manager presumably has a limited influence.

Another possibility is that the organizational socialization process associated with management positions, at least until now, has led to the mainstreaming of candidates, so that women-specific attributes, values and ambitions are lost and gender-neutral or masculine aspects are reinforced. Any sex difference emerging from upbringing or general cultural ideas may not be robust enough to withstand powerful corporate and occupational socialization and the rewards/punishments accompanying the road to as well as work in senior managerial positions. A related possibility is that mainly women managers are recruited in such a way that only women who do not deviate from traditionally dominating organization and leadership patterns ever attain – or aspire to – management positions. The many studies indicating that no significant differences exist in leadership style would be consistent with this opinion. But as we have said, it is an open question what would happen if women had better access to higher positions or if, as some people claim (e.g. Fondas, 1997; Gherardi, 1995), many organizations are going through transformations involving 'de-masculiniza- tion' (which does not necessarily directly involve changes in sex com- position – de-masculinization does not automatically mean an increase in the proportion of women, only that work principles are no longer constructed in distinctly masculine ways).

Regardless of whether or not women managers differ from their male colleagues – in their responses to questionnaires or in their everyday actions – either now or in the near future when a larger percentage of all managers probably will be women, it is important to consider the question of (an increasing number of) women managers in relation to the broader issue of the quality of working life (QWL) and workplace democracy. (Under this heading we address questions of need-orientation, cooperation, integration of the everyday life and the instrumental spheres, participation, etc.) This last can be assumed to be in the interests of most people and perhaps especially of women, since they are often over-represented at the lower levels of organizations (although this would change with the increase of the numbers of female managers). For most female employees the quality of working life is a much more urgent issue than the number of women in higher positions. The latter is of interest mainly insofar as it influences the former.

The four perspectives discussed in this paper represent very different attitudes to the question of QWL/democracy. The *meritocratic* approach, which is the social-selection aspect of the technocratic view of society and organizations that dominates present-day society (Habermas, 1971), considers QWL/democracy only as a potential means for achieving the smooth functioning of organizations and promoting efficiency. The question of leadership recruitment and gender has no direct bearing on this. The *equal opportunities* perspective tends to define its basic objective in terms of giving women a fair and just chance to climb the organizational hierarchy ladder. Here we can identify a remote connection with a broader humanistic concern, but the implications of this for the majority of women are rather weak. The *special contribution* perspective suggests that a strong link exists between female leadership and the concerns of most employees. Women's greater concern for need fulfilment, empathy, participation and commu- nication is of key importance here. The *alternative values* view differs quite radically from this third perspective by playing down the leadership issue and paying attention directly to improving the working conditions of the majority of the women in the workforce. In this perspective the humanistic and democratic questions are crucial and leadership as such is less important. A de-emphasis of the role of the individual leader – which may be seen as a male construct – may encourage maturity in, and initiative from, others. From this position, the well-being of employees is seen as a primary goal in itself, possibly at the expense of economic success and monetary rewards, although most feminists are pretty vague on how they see these issues.

Poststructuralist and critical–interpretive comments

All theoretical perspectives by definition privilege some aspects and obscure variety, not only in the sense that one may easily find empirical examples supporting each of the four approaches, but because a perspective easily obscures alternative ways of making sense of an empirical phenomenon. From a poststructural view, central concepts are often used in a totalizing manner, repressing alternative understandings and drawing attention away from the local context in which they may achieve a temporary, if fluid meaning. When Eagly and Johnson (1990: 249), for example, conclude that 'women's leadership styles were more democratic than men's' there is, from a poststructuralist standpoint, a rich variety of problems worth pointing at. The idea that words (signifiers) like 'women', 'leadership', 'style', 'more', 'democratic' and 'men' stand for some objective, universal, homogeneous, robust and easily comparable phenomena out there, mirrored in questionnaire responses or observation protocols, is not accepted. 'Leadership' and 'democracy', for example, may refer to language use, where unstable meanings cannot be lifted out of the specific context in which a speech act takes place and the words are used. One could also, again from a poststructuralist view, question the assumed coherence and static nature of 'leadership' and, even more so, of 'leadership style' – perhaps human actions are more processual, fragmented, varying, inconsistent and open to alternative interpretations than these concepts, and the statement quoted, suggest (cf. Alvesson, 1996b; Calás and Smircich, 1991; Chia, 1995). Talking about democratic leadership may be seen as confusing, as the idea of leadership tends to contradict democracy. One may argue that leadership marks an asymmetrical relation in which the impact of the leader is far-reaching while democracy stands for equality in terms of influence. The more of democratic 'leadership', the less of 'leadership'. The statement cited indicates a crude effort to universalize across history and culture, not to say local context. The law-like nature of the statement implies that there is a fixed causal relation between sex and a 'leadership style' called 'democratic'. That research according to Eagly and Johnson (1990) has shown a certain relationship between the variables involved is not a proof acceptable to the sceptical proponents of poststructuralism. In the first place, there are also different opinions among positivists; most refute the idea of a clear difference. In the second place, much of the proof is limited to the outcomes of questionnaire-filling responses. All empirical material – including laboratory studies – relies on ratings of individuals, that cannot totally avoid reflecting stereotypical cultural beliefs. Thirdly, the efforts to find regulatories mean that the opposite – variation and inconsistencies – receives little attention. (For a further critique of positivist leadership studies, see Alvesson, 1996b.)

Despite our sympathy with a lot of the poststructuralist critique, we feel that it perhaps pushes the case a bit too far. Modest generalization and local grounding are to be preferred. Rather than establishing a final truth, variation in the cultural constructions of what may be referred to as 'leadership' and how females and males act in, and give meaning to, asymmetrical work relations could be studied. Gender-stereotypic as well as counter-stereotypic actions and relations are both worth examining.

Poststructuralism as well as critical–interpretive thinking would question the attempts to fix and essentialize gender that is inherent in the two difference approaches, but to some extent also in the other two. Rather than saying something definite about the subject matter, it could be argued that gender – like leadership as well as all social phenomena – is discursively and culturally constituted and not given once and for all. Gender as well as leadership must be considered in terms of context. One could point at historical and societal–cultural variation, but also emphasize variety within a society or an organization at a particular time. Emphasizing variety may be more or less extremely local. One version is to point at variation between occupations, ages, classes and industries. Another is to see the individual subject as discursively constituted and also view the subject as inconsistent and varying according to the different discourses addressing her as woman, manager, engineer, middle-aged, mother or organizational employee. For example, sometimes a female manager may act in accordance with 'feminine' ideals, sometimes not contingent upon whether other people address her as a female or in other respects. A female manager is then a subject position, not a fixed essence. The latter, strong version of postmodernism goes beyond the four perspectives reviewed here – all would argue for a certain level of coherence and direction as characterizing subjects – but one may imagine a response to the critique of essentialism saying that the field of inquiry and validity of the perspective is constrained by the present societal context, that is, the latest decades and the nearest future. It would then not be the 'nature' of women *per se*, but the contemporary forms of socialization and value-orientations of women, that the various approaches address. An even less generalized approach could be imagined, in which the researcher studies local beliefs and arguments about gender and leadership, e.g. in an organization or a work group. Having said this, we must emphasize that this is a possible answer from authors adhering to a fixed position on the subject matter. Most do not treat it explicitly. Whether they would actually agree that research ideas and results are historically and culturally situated, or if they try to mirror universal or at least broad, long-term conditions, we cannot know.

Summary and final comment

The four positions presented here indicate the variety of ways in which the topic of women and leadership (management) may be considered. Equal opportunity expresses a variable view, while special contribution and alternative values are respectively weak and strong applications of the feminist standpoint perspective. Meritocrats may not be feminists at all; if they are, the variable perspective is closest. The questioning and playing out of all approaches without advocating any 'best one' would be in line with postmodernist thinking. From a critical–interpretive point of view one may also argue for a relaxation of the focus on men and women (as defined according to biological criteria). It would be a benefit to study how gender norms regulate managerial conduct and how different kinds of leadership actions contribute to the construction of masculinities and femininities in workplace cultures.

The four positions may be summarized through asking the Why, Where and How of female managers and forms of leadership.

The 'Why?' (more female managers) question is answered by equal opportunity as a matter of fairness, by meritocracy thinkers for the sake of efficient utilization of human resources, by special contribution for the promotion of new, progressive forms of leadership for the good of companies and all employees, but perhaps in particular women. The alternative values position does not argue for more female managers, but rather fewer managers and more female ways of managing or – and better – organizing, that are mainly in the interests of women.

On the 'Where?' (should female managers/feminine leadership be located) question, the two similarity-oriented approaches would answer 'Everywhere' – half of all managers should, in principle, be females. Even though special contribution advocates would hesitate to say so, their approach would imply that females should primarily be employed in people-oriented managerial jobs. (All managers deal with people, but in many jobs also technical expertise is an important ingredient in work.) Alternative values writers would either say that there should not be many female managers in dominating organizations – as managers are a part of a bureaucratic society based on hierarchy and careerism and particularly exposed to its negative features – or that there could be female 'leaders' in anti-bureaucratic, non-profit-oriented organizations.

'How?' (is it possible to increase the number of female managers or, in the alternative values case, promote more feminine ways of organizing). Most proponents of at least the three conventional approaches (alternative values is more radical) would presumably be open to a variety of different means. However, there is different emphasis. The equal opportunity approach would rely on feminist struggles within and outside organizations, legislation and, in the USA at least, bringing cases into court. Meritocrats would argue that effectiveness considerations and competition would provide sufficient incentives for changes. Improved human resource management would be the major vehicle. Special contribution advocates would also rely on competition-induced pressure for effectiveness as well as the demands of particular female (but also male) subordinates, some of them aspiring managers. Rather than gender-neutral HRM, analysis of the appropriateness of various styles of managing and an appreciation of the unique style of women would be seen as the way forward. For alternative values writers, the suggested route would be to develop alternative institutions, rather than try social engineering in the existing capitalist bureaucracies.

Finally, we would add a comment regarding the importance of promoting female managers to senior positions. As long as there are (or were)
relatively few women also in junior and middle-level managerial jobs, it
might be argued that obstacles for women comprise a substantial problem.
A relatively large number of women may then suffer deprivation in work
tasks and a general impression of the woman's natural place as subordinate
is re-created. Male domination is thus reproduced. If and when the
proportion of females occupying junior and middle-level managerial jobs
increase and the problem primarily concerns senior management positions,
the social significance of the issue becomes debatable. In the absence of
clearer indications that the ratio of female top managers makes a difference
for their subordinates, the relevance for the great majority of people is low.
In the USA over a couple of decades there has been a rapid increase of
women in low- and middle-level manager's jobs. The large body of texts on
women in management focusing on a glass ceiling preventing them
reaching the top, strikes us as somewhat narrowly focused, given the
limited and privileged group this concerns. Still, the symbolic significance
of the absence of women in the highest and most visible positions should
not be ignored (Ely, 1995).

Of course, we do not want to deny that the theme of gender and
leadership is of great interest. Of perhaps greatest interest is the critique of
dominating ideas on management and leadership (for example, Calás and
Smircich, 1993; Lipman-Blumen, 1992). It would be even more interesting,
however, if the field moved beyond measuring what is taken for granted as
distinct and robust 'styles' of men and women as well as producing positive,
often popular texts idealizing feminine leadership or feminist management.
Most work in the area falls into these two streams. What is needed and is
currently lacking are in-depth case studies of processes of organizing/
leadership in which gendered (masculine/feminine) meanings and their
consequences are identified and sensitively theorized. One could, for
example, study managers as 'active gendering agents' (P.Y. Martin, 1993:
281), i.e. investigate how these subjects contribute to creating or reproducing, or perhaps even disrupting and challenging gendered organizational
practices, meanings and subjectivities. Such studies, according to our view,
would call for an appreciation of the cultural context, of the workplace level
as well as the macro-level. Relatedly, a weaker interest in 'men' and
'women' as variables or carriers of distinct, homogeneous standpoints/voices
would be preferred. Also an open orientation regarding how to understand
'leadership' – including a reluctance to nail it and take its existence and
usefulness for granted – would do the field good (Alvesson, 1996b).

Notes

1 One option is to talk about comparable worth rather than equality in the sense of
similarity. An emphasis on the latter is seen by many as problematic, as it excludes
consideration of modest differences (e.g. Scott, 1991). A problem with the comparable worth

version of equality is that if gender difference is maintained, it becomes more difficult to make strict comparisons and argue for closing of the gender gaps in pay, promotion, etc. In addition, the notion of comparable worth is rather vague.

2 To talk about men's interests is of course a problem. They diverge as much as women's. A Swedish questionnaire (white-collar workers in an insurance company) showed that the number of married/cohabiting men who wanted increased responsibility (become managers) had decreased from 86 per cent in 1962 to 58 per cent in 1991. The decrease was not found for single men (Nilsson, 1992).

3 This is presumably often the case in typical female work organizations, such as kindergartens and social work, but occasionally organizations not dominated by women may also facilitate feminist management. According to some authors, contemporary, post-bureaucratic organizations actually do so (Fondas, 1997).

8

Broadening the Agenda: From Women to Gender Relations

In the two final chapters we will relate to the themes of gender sensitivity discussed in the introductory chapter and parts of the other chapters. We will *not* try to summarize the 'results' or even the major insights that the massive body of theoretical and empirical studies on gender and organization have produced to date. Instead, based on the reviews and critical comments in the earlier chapters, we will discuss how the field may be developed. We argue for an integration of gender and other organizational themes, in the light of the present division of labour within organization and social theory where gender is defined as a subspeciality regarded as marginal by most researchers and where the interplay between gender and other themes is on the whole rather poorly developed. We also discuss women's issues and interests and argue for paying more attention to men in gender studies. To understand women calls for understanding men and, in particular, gender relations. An interest in gender relations includes taking men more seriously, not just as beneficiaries of patriarchy, stereotypical carriers of masculinities or as people standing in a harmonious relationship with dominant working life conditions, but also as a broad and divergent category whose members also experience mixed feelings, thoughts and orientations, a variety of interests and preferences and who are sometimes constrained by current gender patterns. We will argue in this chapter for a more nuanced and sensitive approach to men – without in any way suggesting that gender studies should concentrate on this category.

We do also argue in a different direction – that categories like men and women should not be given too much attention. It easily leads to one-eyedness, a focus of attention on what is common for and specific to females and males and possibly an overemphasis on difference. A broader interest in the gendered nature of organizational life may lead to less emphasis on men and women *per se* in the interests of paying attention to gendered organizational processes, practices and values. Changing the emphasis from a focus on women to considering men also would be one move; being somewhat less concerned with people *per se* and directing attention to gender aspects of values, goals and interests would be another one. As will be argued here, we feel that both may increase the range and impact of gender studies.

On the problems of drawing firm conclusions

As we pointed out in the first two chapters, social science rarely produces conclusive results from empirical studies. Gender studies is no exception. There are some areas on which there is agreement about social reality at a descriptive level. It is thus fairly clear that women are worse off than men in terms of wages, that they are strongly under-represented in higher level jobs and thus access to formal power, that they hold more of the lower-level jobs, experience sexual harassment more frequently, take more responsibility for home and family and that, partly contingent upon the last issue, female managers seem to experience more stress than their male colleagues. The subordination of women and the devaluation of women's work are partly associated with these conditions. That gender is of central importance for social relations and interaction is also agreed upon in the majority of gender studies.

Apart from that there is not much agreement, either in terms of basic theoretical approaches or consistency of empirical findings. There is also much diversity in terms of attempted explanations; pay and promotion gaps may be seen as pure discrimination, as an expression of cultural inertia (affecting not only those in positions of formal power but women as well who sometimes behave in a gender-stereotypical way), or as women prioritizing other values than those of competition, productivity and a wish to become managers. In terms of theory many see the categories 'women' and 'men' as representing robust, objective reality, as starting points for empirical investigations beyond any need for consideration. Others, drawing upon recent, poststructuralist theorizing, view intellectual inquiry as flawed from the start if these categories are accepted as universal notions and uncritically applied. As Gergen writes, 'a once obdurate and unquestionable fact of biological life – that there are two sexes, male and female – now moves slowly toward mythology' (1991, cited in Gherardi, 1995: 108). We will return to this point, arguing that gender studies may progress through downplaying the interest in 'women' and 'men' (although we do not aim for consistency on this issue or propose that these categories should be totally abandoned).

In terms of less philosophical matters, what may misleadingly be seen as down-to-earth empirical studies – many of which function at the rather abstract and remote level of questionnaire-response counting – do not score much better in terms of unity and consistency. Take the area of women and leadership for example. As we have seen, a large body of literature suggests that women and men do 'lead' in basically similar ways. In the same area another somewhat smaller, but still substantial and increasing, stream argues that there certainly are differences and that women leaders are more network-oriented, skilled in dealing with relations, democratic and so on. Similar diversity is produced by the literature on the effects of changed sex composition on pay. While Pfeffer and Davis-Blake (1987) found that an increase in the number of women in the field of college administrators was followed by a decrease in wages, Jacobs (1992) and Wright and Jacobs (1995) found no such effect in managerial jobs, or in computer work. (All three studies are from the USA.)

This may be very frustrating for those who value agreement, straight accumulation of knowledge, order, predictability and 'truths'. For the believer in the opposite – the value of productive conflict, disruption of a common world view, the appreciation of ambiguity, variation and the evanescence and uncertainty even of well-argued or in other ways supported positions of validity claims – the state of the art is more positive. It is as one would expect. As we argued in Chapter 1, there are no reasons to expect strong consensus in this field – or in any other field in social studies, for that matter.

Rather than viewing the individual researcher – or (social) science as a whole – as an authority, offering theoretical and empirical knowledge to experts and lay-persons as guides to how to think and act, social science may be seen as offering a broad set of insights and impulses to aid reflective thinking. Reflective thinking is something quite different from adaptation to the truth claims of authorities. We see several advantages following from plurality in the development of knowledge. The major job of making sense of gender aspects in the specific organizational context must be carried out by the thinker/actor him- or herself. Variation in the input of viewpoints and empirical results offered may inspire creativity and critical reflection; it may also counteract people taking certain assumptions and frameworks for granted. Most importantly, while gender is socially constructed and varies not only over history and between macro social cultural configurations such as nation, class, age, ethnicity, sexual orientation, occupation and organization but also *within* these, any understanding of a specific empirical context must draw upon a body of vocabularies, ideas, theoretical explanations and relevant – parallel or contrasting – empirical illustrations in a context-sensitive way. Of course, delimitation and focus is necessary, but concentration should be balanced against careful consideration of alternative perspectives and interpretations and the problems of reductionism.

Rather than viewing theories as to be validated or falsified – as true or false – in an abstract or universal sense, it is better to see them as, in the best case, offering partially valid insights and explanations. Most theories are sometimes true and sometimes false or, better, sometimes a theory may offer an improved understanding of a particular situation, sometimes it does not work in this way. (Of course, what works and what does not is not only a matter of the compatibility between theory and empirical phenomenon – even though they cannot be fully separated, a particular theory may work badly with a certain empirical material – but is also an effect of the skills and creativity of the person who is to use the former to understand the latter and to persuade readers about what works.) Even the most committed adherent to patriarchy theory may have problems accounting for the rise and success of a small, but increasing, number of women in politics, public administration and, although to a lower degree, business, and very few psychoanalytic feminists would try to explain why female workers moved over to previously male-dominated jobs such as coal mining when the jobs became available in relatively large numbers, which happens at least once in a while (Reskin and Padavic, 1994). (The appeal of higher wages seems to offer a better explanation than the psychodynamics of early mother–child interaction.) In terms of leadership behaviour, it is rather obvious that irrespective of the degree of support for the hypothesis and theory of a specific female leadership style, there are females who act in autocratic and task-oriented ways and men who do the opposite. Of course, it is of interest to find out if there are tendencies to specific gender-leadership behaviour patterns – perhaps in a certain cultural and historical context rather than in terms of an eternal law – but the limits of such abstract variable correlations must be considered, otherwise they reinforce stereotypes and rigid expectations and may bring about category mistakes, such as the automatic association of a woman with a democratic leadership style. As mentioned in Chapter 6, according to Eagly et al. (1992) it is in particular when female managers deviate from a 'soft' style that they are evaluated in a biased way. A problem is that *if* the women-in-management literature suggests that women's leadership 'is' democratic and relational, this may be defined as 'natural' and 'normal' for women and may thus reinforce tendencies to evaluate women behaving in other ways more negatively and further constrain their opportunities to adapt to a range of leadership behaviours (which are viewed as acceptable for men).

There are several good reasons for adopting a 'non-fundamentalist' position on this subject of convergence of empirical studies and the establishing of 'truth'.[1] Besides the arguments for variation mentioned above connected to historical and social variation, the significance of paradigmatic assumptions for the results produced, and the fusion of social studies and what we are studying, all speak for non-fundamentalism. In particular the internal relationship between social science and gender phenomena shows the impossibility of establishing how 'it is' in any universal, ahistorical sense. The massive number of gender studies – distributed to the public through mass media and education – are an integral and productive part of the culture that constructs gender. All the writings and discussions about female managers, most of them promoting women in management, have consequences for the number of female managers – which is steadily increasing in most countries. The writings and talk also affect the self-understanding of female managers and the scripts they follow as well as the expectations and interpretations of people around them. A study done 25 years ago and a similar one produced today might give different results, if not for any other reason than because research subjects would talk about the subject matter in another way and would respond to similar wordings in questionnaires in a different way today than 25 years ago. But more profound changes are also likely to have happened. Female leadership is socially constructed in different ways over time, affecting not only talk and expectations but also cognitions, values and actions.

The historical nature of gender does not mean that everything changes rapidly – some things do, others change slowly, still others tend to be more persistent. An ahistorical approach is, however, totally misleading in the area of gender and organizations. We have mentioned this before, but the point is worth repeating. Even within a given historical period, it is important to be open to the possibility of variation. Why should one expect a uniform pattern regarding, for example, possible negative effects on pay of an increased representation of women in an occupation? Rather than any hard-and-fast rule, variation seems more likely.

It is important to emphasize that non-fundamentalism does not imply relativism in the sense that we cannot say anything valid about social reality or back up statements with empirical evidence. (For an overview of relativism, see Hollis and Lukes, 1982.) Whether there are any serious relativists in any strong sense of the term we do not know – the term is often used to accuse others of being extremists or, if one is in danger of being accused thereof, to assure the reader that one is *not* a relativist. Here we follow the latter, perhaps unfortunate, convention, and state that openness to diversity and incoherence in results produced, contingent upon variation in researchers' preferences and procedures as well as in the empirical objects studied, does not prevent the use of criteria for the evaluation of the results such as trustworthiness, theoretical novelty, added knowledge, useful addition to or contrast to other empirical studies (Alvesson and Sköldberg, forthcoming; Guba and Lincoln, 1994; Van Maanen, 1995). We also think that one should strive for high standards when judging studies and claims, critically addressing weak empirical material and biased interpretations and letting empirical studies kick back against ideas and theories when they run against empirical material. There is no opposition between advocating high standards and criteria for evaluating research and acknowledging the value of variation in viewpoints when studying a complex and multi-level area like gender.

There is a strong pressure in mainstream social science for emphasizing patterns, regularities and unity at the expense of fragmentation, variation and ambiguity. The latter qualities are to some extent also recognized by mainstream researchers, but mainly on the way to the discovery of patterns or mechanisms that explain surface level variation and inconsistencies. A valuable counterforce is poststructuralism, which stresses aspects such as multiplicity, pluralism, multiple voices, fragmentation (Calás and Smircich, 1987; Chia, 1995; Linstead, 1993; Rosenau, 1992). These qualities are, however, viewed as values and ends in themselves. Often this approach emphasizes language and texts as the focus of attention – it is the disclosure and differentiation of language (discourse) that is aspired to rather than the social reality 'beyond' language: feelings, actions, social practices. The approach taken in this book is only modestly inspired by poststructuralism/postmodernism. It is not so much a philosophical–linguistic position as an interpretive–empirical interest that lies behind taking variation seriously. Rather than one-sidedly pushing for multiplicity, we think that it is important to balance between the two extremes of seeking pattern–unity–result and celebrating diversity–fragmentation–pluralism. It is not necessary to choose between or privilege any of these 'ideals'. Interpretations in specific cases, as well as summaries of individual and aggregates of studies, should be conducted and based on considerations of a loose framework (interpretive inclinations) in which neither patterns nor diversities are privileged.

This view of the nature of knowledge – less of robust truth than a framework for reflection and interpretation – is of course close to the ideal of intellectually and practically conducting sensitive readings of gender in organizations and avoiding the pitfalls of one-eyedly reducing everything to gender or missing gender aspects.

Integrating gender and organization

The problem of isolation in gender studies

Despite its increasing significance in social science, education and to some extent politics during recent years, at least in some countries, feminism does not appear to be very popular among broader groups (Barnard, 1989). Cockburn (1991) and Stivers (1993) refer to a number of women in the organizations they studied or in other ways interacted with, almost all of whom distanced themselves from the label. We share the impression that feminism has an 'image problem'. Cockburn attributes this unfavourable evaluation to patriarchy. But it is also possible that the entire blame should not be ascribed to an abstract system that has managed to produce a negative image of its enemy. The women expressing a negative view on feminism in Cockburn's study still embraced many of the ideals of gender equality, suggesting that 'patriarchy' is not very successful in affecting the attitudes of these women. Therefore there may be drawbacks in the feminist projects, partly responsible for this 'image problem'.

From a more academic perspective, feminism appears rather isolated. Acker (1989: 65) thinks that 'feminist thought has been co-opted and ghettoized'.[2] To the extent that gender has had a broader appeal, it is as a variable rather than as a central theoretical concept. Acker feels that feminism has been partly successful in illuminating and theorizing about the situation of women, but that feminists have 'not, as yet, been able to suggest new ways of looking at things that are obviously better than the old ways for comprehending a whole range of problems', for example how gender is fundamentally involved in the way organizations function. She also thinks that feminists, with a few exceptions, have not developed many original contributions to methodology (pp. 72, 73). Acker believes that the reason for this unsatisfactory state of affairs is the difficulties in transcending the gender subtext of central theoretical categories and concerns.

To talk about gender, too often meaning women, is to take the theorizing from the general to the specific, and this appears to undermine the theorizing about the abstract and general. Consequently, talking about gender and women can be seen as trivializing serious theoretical questions, or it can be seen as beside the point. All of this rests upon obscuring of the gendered nature of fundamental concepts under the cloak of gender neutrality. (1989: 74)

This evaluation of the limited success of feminism, outside its core area, may not be shared by others. We also think that during recent years gender studies in organization theory have made progress and include more and more interesting contributions. McGrath et al. (1993) note that there is much overlap between the feminist and non-feminist critique of (positivist) methodology, but think that feminists have devoted more attention to developing alternatives. The novelty and success of this enterprise is, however, not easy to evaluate. Part of the problem is that feminist authors are often reluctant to take non-feminist work seriously, for example in methodology (and vice versa), at least in terms of acknowledgement, references and explicit dialogue. For example, in an article reviewing feminism and qualitative research (Olesen, 1994), about 200 works are referred to; of these less than 10 are non-feminist and nothing is said about the distinctiveness of feminist methodologies in comparison to other methodologies and their contributions to the development of method more generally. This is perhaps reasonable, but it makes it difficult to estimate the contributions of feminism to methodology.

Many other areas of feminism are also characterized by a somewhat one-sided interest in gender and feminist work. Other areas and theoretical orientations receive little attention – except as objects of critique. Ferguson's (1984) critique of bureaucracy, for example, takes only a moderate interest in the extensive existing bureaucracy critique, from radical Weberians, critical theorists and human relations people, arguing that her approach differs through using the experiences of women as the point of departure. Ramsey and Calvert (1994) offer a feminist critique of organizational humanism, in which the extensive earlier critical work which made the same or similar points is hardly mentioned and is not drawn upon (for example, Alvesson, 1987; Burrell and Morgan, 1979; Perrow, 1986).

It is certainly true that an increasing amount of feminist work is conscious of the problems of taking the white middle-class woman as a universal standard, and is also trying to address class and race, but typically as subvariables and variations of a gender focus. Gender is seen as the fundamental organizing principle; others – when not entirely neglected – are usually viewed as secondary.

The lack of interest in feminist or gender issues is obvious in most 'mainstream' research areas. We mentioned the general neglect of gender-in-organization studies in Chapter 1. For example, review articles of leadership intended to cover the most significant aspects of the field do not even mention gender or refer to the literature on women and leadership (Andriessen and Drenth, 1984; Bryman, 1996; Yukl, 1989). To the extent that authors outside the gender specialism take an interest in gender, it is only as a variable and not as a theoretical concept capable of illuminating any broader or deeper meaning of a phenomenon. The interplay between feminism (or gender studies, more broadly) and other academic streams consequently appears to be far from successful. A mutual disinterest characterizes many gender studies and other areas, especially in management studies.

There are thus reasons to agree with Acker (1989) when she describes feminism as ghettoized in certain respects. Gender is marginalized in, for example, organizational analysis (J. Martin, 1994), even though (other) critical organizational theorists have typically taken it into account, at least during recent years. Although ideas on equal opportunities are increasingly shared by large parts of the population and backed up by government policies in many countries (at least at a superficial level), this is associated with the variable view and does not mean that feminism as a theoretical project – going beyond body-counting – is very influential. Let us explore the ghetto metaphor a bit more systematically.

Counteracting ghettoization in gender studies

In the present context, a ghetto may be seen as an intellectual domain that is isolated, self-contained, holds a socially subordinate or low-status position, and is well demarcated. This characteristic appears to fit nicely with dominant views on feminist studies, both within and outside the domain.

There are advantages and disadvantages to such a position. The former include a relative safety, feelings of community and a clear identity. It is possible to develop one's own norms and values and identity diffusion is avoided. Some protection from the broader academic community may also be offered. Also the (self-)image of an outcast or victim may be positive in some ways, as it offers a kind of moral authority and indication of authenticity (cf. Elshtain, 1981). The problems include intellectual isolation, limited influence, power and prestige within the academic community. The lack of debate and mutual influence across gender studies and other areas may also lead to quality problems. (This is not typical only for feminism. Most areas are characterized by paradigm isolation and a lack of interest in different orientations.) Within gender studies there are constant discussions about whether the area should develop as a specific discipline, with its own departments and courses, or whether gender should be dispersed in traditional disciplines and integrated into research and education.

Labelling the current position a ghetto is, of course, to indicate that its position *vis-à-vis* other intellectual territories is unsatisfactory.[3] The limited impact of gender studies on most other areas in social science, including organization studies, calls for rethinking. This is to a high degree something for which the mainstream authors, unwilling or unable to take gender seriously, may be blamed. From the point of view of gender studies, critique of this neglect must be complemented with constructive proposals for how to bridge the gap between gender and conventional concerns.

One option here is to advocate that any book or curriculum includes a specific section on gender or women. But that would be to continue the ghettoization or at least compartmentalization of the topic. A more radical proposal would be to suggest that the artificial separation of gender issues from other issues should be dropped. Perhaps one should even entirely resist compartmentalization and stop writing books such as the one you hold in your hand. Instead of treating gender or women as a theme for specific courses, parts of courses or even parts of books or research projects, gender could be treated as an integrated part of the knowledge developed and taught. When treating management for example, one may discuss a variety of different aspects in terms of gendered meanings and not reduce these to the particular topic of women in management.

The research strategy of Calás and Smircich (1992a) of using 'gender' in order to rewrite 'organization' (mentioned in Chapter 2) may be called upon here. This strategy is interesting. It does not necessarily mean a total rewriting of any history of organization in terms of gender. Such an enterprise may lead to important aspects being lost. There are, as we mentioned in Chapter 4, considerable problems with an undiscriminating approach to gender concepts. Masculinities may easily be stretched or multiplied so that they cover everything and nothing. As with all meta-phors, there is the risk that they will command the world. Wherever the gender researcher directs attention, he or she sees masculinities and – although less frequently addressed – femininities appearing.[4] Alternatively a large number of significant aspects disappear because they are not easy to plug into a gender-theoretical interpretation. It is hardly possible, at least not given the knowledge so far produced, to imagine that management or organization studies or any of the subdisciplines could be clearly under-stood solely through gender concepts and ideas. That would mean a great risk of gender reductionism.

Combining gender and other perspectives

How can we avoid these problems of compartmentalization or one-sided gender focus? The problem may be formulated as a matter of trying to go beyond a rigid division between gender-blind and gender-one-eyed knowledge development and transmission. The ideal is to be able to see gender also where one does not expect it (avoiding blindness and devel-oping sensitivity), at the same time as one resists seeing it everywhere (avoiding one-eyedness and over-sensitivity). We think that a move in such a direction may be taken through the close cooperation of gender and other ways of interpreting phenomena. Through integrating – or perhaps rather paralleling – a gender perspective with some other perspective(s) or bodies of knowledge, themes may be treated where gender is sometimes central, sometimes less so. Through the development of a sufficiently broad interpretive repertoire – a set of theories, vocabularies and some meta-theoretical principles for regulating the diversities involved (Alvesson, 1996a; Alvesson and Sköldberg, forthcoming) – gender theory and other forms of understanding guide the approach.

This would mean that interpretations in gender terms – for example masculine cultural meanings, homosocial reproduction, sex boundary heightening, female ways of organizing – would move back and forth in terms of centrality and explicitness in research projects, in texts and in education (in for example research and teaching of organizational culture, strategic management, business ethics or whatever). Arguably, the study of organizational culture would be greatly improved through the application of a gender perspective, but there are certainly aspects of any organizational cultures that are lost or treated in a highly reductionistic way if gender is the only perspective used. It only marginally helps if class and race are added to gender. A well-functioning cooperation between gender and other perspectives may be hard to achieve, but if and when successful it may come to terms with the three crucial problems of gender/organization studies: the gender-blind mainstream, the tendencies to one-eyed gender reductionism in parts of feminist studies and, partly as a result of these two problems, the ghettoized nature of the latter. In terms of the problems we addressed in the introductory chapter of this book, we believe that the approach suggested here means increased possibilities in manoeuvring between gender under- and over-sensitivity, between denial and totalization in approaching issues of gender, between blindness and one-eyedness.

We will come back to how this may look. A possible effect – that some people may see as negative – of bringing gender issues out of their somewhat isolated existence in education and research would be to weaken the identity of gender studies (and gender scholars). Given the scepticism and sometimes hostility of a large number of academics (and non-academics also, for that matter) to gender studies this may be problematic for individual researchers and thereby weaken the presence and development of gender aspects. Another possibility is that if gender is an integrated part of research frameworks and parts of the results are gender-informed, this partiality of gender-imprinting in empirical projects and theoretical work may satisfy neither those interested in gender (they may feel that there is too little of it) nor those guided by conventional concerns ('Why is this funny stuff included here?'). A third drawback would be the high demands on the researcher; working with a broader frame of reference and moving beyond the reductionism, allowing one to neglect all but one set of aspects, is not easy.

The move suggested here would break with the commitments of many versions of feminism, oriented to developing knowledge by women about women for the sake of women.[5] This would call for a rather distinct, hardcore approach different from the integrative, boundary-crossing one suggested here. With the increased recognition of diversity and the negative image of feminism even among those supporting equal opportunity (reported above), the unitary and unique view of women and their interests has lost space. It is increasingly realized that gender cannot be seen isolated. It never appears in a pure form, except perhaps as an outcome of the manipulations of an experimental study. In the context of organizations not only class and ethnicity must be considered, but also issues such as economic context and competition, performances, technology, occupations, etc. The ideal is, of course, not that every study tries to address many aspects, but that the entire research field does and that the individual researcher is careful about what he or she chooses not to address. To reduce gender to only or mainly being about women is highly unsatis-factory, as Acker also notes in the citation above, but it is common. The large US Academy of Management, for example, has one division labelled 'women in management'. Similarly, the increasing interest in men and masculinities is a mixed blessing. It addresses a white spot on our knowl-edge map, but it is not possible to understand men without women, masculinities without femininities. The words gain their very meaning through their relationship to each other. Strictly speaking, one can really not say anything about women's (distinct) experiences without knowing something about men's (apart from a few sex-specific issues such as childbirth and some diseases) and the other way round. But this does not prevent researchers from sometimes doing so. Researchers interview a number of women and then claim gender-specific experiences without any real information about whether the experiences are very different from those of men. Sometimes it is, of course, possible to use judgements or background knowledge and argue for the gender-distinctiveness of certain demands, constraints and experiences. But there is too easily a tendency to fall back on taken-for-granted assumptions, for example, about women typically having a lot of domestic duties, and men being more or less totally unconstrained in devoting their energy to work. Thomas (1996: 153), for example, interviewed 19 female academics about appraisals and reached the conclusion that in a performance-oriented culture, 'those who thrive are childless, mobile and, or, male'. But in the absence of empirical material about the male academics' viewpoints, one cannot say much about how they feel about the situation involving 'highly intensified work rates'. According to our impressions, far from all male academics are comfortable with high demands on performances. (By definition, only a minority may perform well, if well is defined as above average.) To rely solely on some female respondents' perceptions of men and their assumptions on gender differences is, we think, unsatisfactory, but not uncommon.

Claims about the situation, experiences and preferences of women – treated as a specific group – call for careful comparisons, although we would suggest a greater interest in relations than comparisons. Rather than treating women as if they developed and lived in relative isolation from men, and vice versa, gender relations are crucial to investigate in order to understand the context and processes behind the presumably gender-specific. We therefore advocate gender relations rather than women or men

as the principal target of study, especially in the context
organization studies.

Two issues are crucial for the project of integrating gender i
knowledge area – in relation to other fields as well as in t
relations between men and women. The first concerns the view c
the fundamental organizing principle, claimed for example by a
patriarchy theory. The second concerns the issue of the interests or men and
women.

Gender as the fundamental organizing principle?

Most feminists claim that gender is the fundamental organizing principle,
either in the sense of a rigid distinction between men and women as social
categories and the privileging of the former, or the tendency to divide the
social world into masculine and feminine meanings and viewing the former
as superior. A more historical version of this would be that this has been
the case up to now and is likely to be at least in the near future. A less
universal approach would be to say that the centrality of gender is also a
matter of the particular domain addressed. Sometimes gender is absolutely
central, such as in sexuality, marriage, early childrearing, and, in many
countries, household work. One may also argue that a person's gender
is crucial for his or her identity, although a person's self-understanding
may be more or less consistent and stereotypical in terms of maleness/
femaleness. Gender is also, as we have seen in this book, highly significant
in very large parts of the labour market. The picture is often not that
simple, however. In Denmark, for example, even mothers with small
children work full-time, which probably means that gender as an
organizing principle for housework and paid labour may be of diminishing
importance, at least in some groups. We personally know several couples
who share housework and childcare equally.

In the world of organizations, it is easy to produce empirical evidence for
the view that gender is a central organizing principle, although one can
always dispute whether it is fundamental or not. Despite this, one must also
recognize the possibility that gender might not be very central in specific
sites. One option is to use the following two criteria for evaluating the
significance of gender as an organizing principle: sexual division of labour
and variety in the statements of experiences expressed by male and female
organizational members. If one uses these criteria it appears that sometimes
gender is a central organizing principle (most gender studies, for example,
Cockburn, 1991; Reskin and Padavic, 1994, and some of our own studies,
for example, Alvesson, 1997; Billing and Alvesson, 1994: chapter 9 point in
this direction), but sometimes it is not (Bergvall and Lundquist, 1995;
Billing and Alvesson, 1994: chapter 7; Blomqvist, 1994). In a questionnaire
study of Swedish female civil engineers and MBAs, Wahl (1992: 298) found
that only two per cent felt ('to a high degree') that they were in general

treated differently from their male colleagues, 33 per cent experienced that they were 'to a certain degree' while 64 per cent answered, 'No, not at all.' Despite this and similiar findings, Wahl also found indications of discrimination, giving the impression that the overall picture of the study is far from clear-cut. Often it is far from obvious how one should evaluate the significance of gender as an organizing principle at the level of workplaces (for example, Billing and Alvesson, 1994: chapter 8; Powell and Butterfield, 1994; Sundin, 1993).[6] Sometimes gender may be organized before the entry into the workplace, such as through gender-stereotypical educations, career choices and family relations. This would suggest that gender as an organizing principle is not seen as a paradigmatic point of departure, as something to be taken for granted, but as a theme for exploration. It is not a matter of testing whether gender is a central organizing principle or not – the significance of assumptions and theoretical commitments as well as the constructed nature of all empirical material prevent a separation of 'theory' and empirical material and thus testing in the strict sense of the word. But the ideal may be embraced of being as open and reflective as possible about the relative centrality of gender as an organizing principle in specific empirical sites as well as being prepared to acknowledge the centrality of other organizing principles (class, race, meritocracy, professionalization, education, etc.), which may be intertwined with, but cannot be reduced to, gender.

Such an openness calls for a particular gender theory not for making up the entire interpretive repertoire. An approach to social phenomena involving the sensitive readings of gender as well as non-gender aspects would mean a more nuanced view on the diversity and diverse intensiveness/salience of gendered meanings, as well as an appreciation of other kinds of aspects.

On interests

Related to the issue of the centrality of gender as an organizing principle and the associated segregation and subordination of women is the issue of women's interests. Although social science in general tends to be somewhat reluctant to talk too much about interests, seeing the issue as contradictory and complex, and refraining from authoritative statements about 'real interests', most feminists do not suffer from lack of conviction when addressing gender and interests. Even poststructuralists such as Weedon – generally sceptical about claims of 'truths' – appear to view the subordination of the interests of women to those of men as an unquestionable fact (1987: 2, 3, 12). Cockburn (1991: 220) evaluates contemporary society as rather one-sidedly benefiting men: 'Women do win some advantages from their position in patriarchy. For example, they are not called on to be prepared to kill other people to prove their femininity, as men are their masculinity. Men, however, gain hugely from patriarchy.'[7] Most students of gender also emphasize the strong interest of men in guarding their access to good jobs, promotions and high pay and their generally higher status (Chafetz, 1989; Reskin and Padavic, 1994; Stivers, 1993).

The issue of interest may, however, be questioned in several ways. Is interest the same as what is espoused or conscious or is it the 'real' interests, determined in an objective way by the elitist researcher?[8] Women's interests – as with all interest – may be an area of ambiguity, disagreement and dispute. Variation is often acknowledged, but those few women with successful careers, having a conservative lifestyle or benefiting from their looks and sexual appearence tend to be seen as exceptions and the idea of shared interest is thus saved. Different interests may converge not only between but also *within* a group or even a person. Most women presumably want minimization of harassment and maximization of pleasurable sexuality. (One may say that they want it by definition, as harassment by definition is undesirable and pleasure desirable.) Just focusing on the former will unavoidably have some negative effects on the latter, while a 'liberated' climate may increase the risk of sexual harassment at the workplace. There may also be variation in interest with regard to workload for managers. Women, and men also for that matter, may for example want higher pay and promotion but not want to work long hours or travel in the job very much. Some feminists argue that managerial jobs should be changed so that they should not be adapted to the norm of a person, normally a man, who can devote most of his time and energy to the job, and that such a change would be in the interest of women (such as Cockburn, 1991; Wahl, 1996). Of course, reducing the costs and retaining the benefits of work would be in anybody's individual interest, but if compensation, power and status fell with the reduction of working hours and sacrifices such as frequent travelling, there would be much disagreement regarding whether the change is in the interest of a majority of women, in the group of potential and actual managers as well as women in general.[9] In addition, women without young children and with jobs in which they are highly engaged may not want to restrict their working week.

Another issue concerns the assumption of a kind of collective interest shared by men. It is often assumed that men as a group guard their interests against women as a group. It could be argued that men normally are not organized in such a way, but compete with each other for positions and status. A group may of course close ranks and act against outsiders – such examples are not uncommon (Reskin and Padavic, 1994). For those men in a direct competitive situation with women, it is a benefit if the chances of the latter group – as with all competitors – are weakened. For most men, including top-level managers, there is nothing of direct interest at stake. Different generations and levels of managers do not compete with each other (Kvande and Rasmussen, 1994). Top-level managers have no self-evident interest in supporting junior male employees just because of their sex. More broadly, executives have little to gain from supporting the status quo in terms of gender division of labour – except from an interest in having female labour power with low expectations and being prepared to accept low-paid jobs. It is not uncommon that higher managers support improved promotion chances for women (Billing and Alvesson, 1994; Sundin, 1993). Arguably, they often have a clear interest in promoting women to senior positions in order to comply with current norms advocating meritocracy and equal opportunity, thereby attaining legitimacy – an important goal for contemporary organizations (Meyer and Rowan, 1977). Today, in the Western world, men do not want to be charged with discriminating against women and most men probably feel that they do not, and may be inclined to take certain actions to show others and themselves that they are pro-equality. In particular in public sector organizations there may be a strong political pressure to recruit and promote a number of females to managerial jobs.

But the issue of interest is complex. Senior managers may want to interact only with members of their own sex. They may support equality on a general level but, in specific cases involving them personally, favour a person of the same sex. Men may be perceived to be more reliable, predictable and free from loyalty conflicts between home and work (Kanter, 1977). Bonds between men may lead them to prefer each other. Roper (1996: 224), using the concept of homosocial desire, believes that 'intimacies between male managers are crucially important . . . because it is through them that "exclusionary circles" are formed and maintained'. But often preferences for sex-mixed groups are being espoused. Many people believe that they lead to a better atmosphere and more varied experiences and viewpoints. Of course, male managers – and female also, for that matter – may act on the basis of preferences, prejudices, a wish to minimize the uncertainty involved in interacting with people expected to be different, or on other non-rational grounds, but this is not the same as men's shared interests. It is certainly not so in the sense of guarding economic and status privileges. Nor does it make sense to talk about 'non-rational' interests associated with preferences and emotions being fulfilled through men supporting each other. Men may want to minimize uncertainty or enjoy the fruits of homosocial desire, but learning to interact with and enjoying the company of others than those similar to oneself may also be in one's 'interest'. Of course, we can only point here at aspects important to consider before freezing a standpoint on men's shared interests, and make no substantive statements. Such statements may only be made in relation to local, empirical settings and then in terms of perceived wants and preferences rather than 'objective' interests. There is no reason to expect uniformity in this regard (cf. Blomqvist, 1994). In particular younger people, accustomed to interacting cross-sexually throughout education, may for example not experience worry or uncertainty in interacting with people of the opposite sex. In terms of uncertainty and discomfort, differences in age, cultural and professional background may matter as much as gender, but in most cases it makes little sense to talk about shared interests based on age as an important explanation behind significant organizational phenomena.

A perhaps more profound issue concerns what men gain from gender arrangements in present society. That many more men than women benefit from higher pay and high-level positions is beyond doubt, but it is not the whole story. There are other values and criteria for a good life. As mentioned in Chapter 1, men score more badly than women on some crucial issues, for example life expectancy. In the Western countries women live about six to seven years longer than men. In Denmark the increase in life expectancy of women with higher education and professional jobs has actually dropped, coming closer to that of men in the same social category. A possible interpretation could be that these women experience not only the privileges but also some of the strains that men encounter in working life.[10] Contrary to what most students of gender emphasize, the prestigious jobs in which men greatly outnumber women are not only characterized by privileges but also by burdens such as long working hours, a lot of travelling and various forms of stress, including a great risk of being fired if results are bad, if one loses in corporate politics, or due to reorganizations. In a situation of strong competition for a higher position – where the supply is much stronger than the demand – it is not easily reconcilable with positive social relations, at least not within the corporate context. The sharp portrait of the work situations of managers in US companies by Jackall (1988) gives an excellent account of some of the negative aspects of positions of 'privilege' in a male-dominated culture. In addition, relation-ships with children may suffer. There may also be little time for leisure and to maintain friendship relations. A UK study of middle managers con-cluded that they 'are more careful, perhaps, than in the past about becoming completely "psychologically" immersed in their occupations and seek, instead, to obtain a balance between their work and private lives. They are reluctant to strive for career success if this can be gained only at the expense of personal and family relationships' (Scase and Goffe, cited in Watson, 1994: 63). On the other hand, most people would probably think that the advantages are stronger than the costs, at least for men and especially in senior positions. In a Swedish study of top managers the respondents indicated a high degree of job satisfaction and a relatively low degree of stress (Olsson and Törnqvist, 1995). The costs of managerial jobs seem to be higher for women, as we saw in the review of stress research in Chapter 6. But for many women too there is a strong attraction in career advancement, particularly if the conditions are less one-sidedly adapted to people with no or limited family obligations.

There are some indications that the values of money, a high-status job and formal power do not play such a determining role for life satisfaction for many people, at least not in parts of Europe, as the focus on these issues in most feminist studies on work and organization may indicate. In a Danish study more women than men thought of themselves as 'winners' rather than 'losers' (in the Danish newspaper *Politiken*, 8 and 9 June 1996). Family issues were broadly, i.e. also by men, seen as much more significant than money and power as sources of satisfaction in life. These results can hardly be accepted at face value. To the extent that they say something else besides how people put crosses in questionnaires, it may be about expectations. Given low expectations, it is difficult to see oneself as a loser. Still, the results question whether women really are so badly off in contemporary (Western) society as suggested by many feminists. The emphasis on family relationships rather than money and formal power also indicates that the criteria for what is important for the good life and what is in the interest of women and men should be given a broader consideration than is the case in many writings on gender, work and organization.

The appeal of money, status and formally based power is strong in our Western culture (and in many other societies also, for that matter), although in the USA people appear to be more materialistic than in parts of Europe. The career-oriented values around pay and promotion appear to be more pronounced in US than European texts on women at work and in management. That these values are broadly embraced should of course not discourage a sceptical view of the centrality of these values. Gender studies should not just promote the possibility of increased access of women to such cherished goods but also critically examine the social and cultural processes affecting the significance of these values. Gender bias is perhaps not restricted to equal access to these benefits, but is inherent in the cultural values attached to these. An important aspect of power is that it does not only or even mainly operate through preventing people from getting the good things in life, but through affecting what they perceive as good things and do want – their motives, intentions and goals. The entire capitalist economic system, based on drives such as competition and efforts to eliminate competitors, profit-seeking, expansion and circling around the prioritizing of the cold, objective, seemingly neutral medium of money for one regulation of social relations, may be seen in terms of masculine domination.[11] The capitalist economic system and the cultural values it produces and by which it is supported, bring about a strong orientation to maximum pay and managerial careers. The grip of this orientation may actually be reinforced if large groups of women are also encouraged to be heavily committed to these values. There are various opinions on how women relate to these values. For example, according to Reskin and Padavic (1994) there are no differences between men and women in terms of desire to have a career. Jacobs (1992) found no differences between US male and female managers in terms of ranking the most important things in work even though women rated meaningful work slightly higher and income slightly lower than men. Other authors say that there are differences between men and women. Often feminists emphasize that values such as good personal relationships for life-fulfilment, work done well for its own sake, helpfulness to others and the like are significant for women. Markus (1987), for example, found in a study of Hungarian women that the experiences of success for the large majority were connected to some form of concrete achievement rather than social recognition. Traditional 'external' success criteria of career achievement only surfaced among a few women in professional and managerial careers. Gender studies supporting an 'external success' orientation may actually reinforce masculine domination, even if the pay and promotion gaps between men and women could be reduced or even vanish. Gender equality and masculine domination – if equality is defined as how men and women score in quantitative respects and if masculine refers to social meanings and values and not to the positions of men – are thus not necessarily mutually exclusive phenomena. It is ironic that feminists in work and organization studies (as well as in other areas) often put forward values whose salience may be an effect of male domination as the ultimate yardstick of what is worth striving for.

Of course, this is not to say that women should be satisfied with work organizations and labour markets operating against them in terms of pay and promotion. The well-documented devaluation of women's work certainly runs against women's interests. There is every reason for women to demand the same wages as men for the same or similar work. A struggle for equality should, however, be conducted with a critical eye on the values involved. Changing organizations in a non-hierarchical direction and reduction of pay gaps in general could be objectives as important as increasing the percentage and number of female managers and reducing the pay gap only between people at a certain level, for example, between male and female executives, or between male and female unskilled blue-collar workers.[12] There is, however, no reason to assume fixed interests or goals associated with gender. What is important is to be open to historical and cultural variation of interests and values. Gender studies should neither take current values and priorities for granted nor impose a standard solution from above, but combine sensitive attention to the voices, experiences and espoused interests of people (men and women) being studied at the same time as the cultural meanings and mechanisms of power (for example capitalist institutions such as advertising) are critically evaluated.

As said in Chapters 1 and 2, an important contribution to gender studies could be to produce qualified input to critical reflection and debates about interests and values.

On alternative agendas

The issue of women's interests is of course closely related to what is on the agenda for feminist and gender studies.

Feminist demands on organizations and organizational changes may be described in terms of different agendas, for example a *short* and a *long* one (Cockburn, 1991). Liberal feminists, often heavily overlapping with the variable view, advocate the first one. Equal opportunity means that women should share the same privileges as men and be spared sex-specific sufferings. Equal pay, equal access to positions of formal power and liberation from sexual harassment and other kinds of degrading behaviour would then be the major demands. A longer agenda would call for changes so that women's self-confidence and positions are strengthened in many ways. Cockburn writes (1991: 159), for example, that women could express their specific circumstances in terms of bodily needs around pregnancy and menstruation, and be unconstrained by conventional norms dictating when a woman should express her femaleness and when to hide it. It would also address the sharing of home and family obligations and, more relevant in the organizational context, develop arrangements for facilitating the integration of work and family, such as day-care and parental leave possibilities, flexible work hours, working at home and so on.

While the short and the long agenda emerge from ideas about the specific interests of women, one may also talk about a *broad* agenda, linking a radical interpretation of women's interests with broader concerns. Such broader concerns may more or less clearly emphasize 'female values' or transcend the connection to women's distinct interests/voices/experiences/ perspectives and instead relate to more universal concerns. While acknowledging the diversity within the women's movement, Benhabib and Cornell (1987: 4) nevertheless claim that there is a 'minimal utopia of social life characterized by nurturant, caring, expressive and nonrepressive relations between self and others, self and nature'. Ferguson's critique of bureaucracy is women-focused in the sense that it claims to draw upon the experiences of women but it illuminates injuries also, although perhaps less pronounced, affecting men. Calás and Smircich (1993) criticize the current ideas about the feminine-in-management and argue for social considerations which are hardly exclusively beneficial for women, such as care for the third world and ecological consciousness, considerations that barely surface in the mainstream literature. This broad agenda is thus quite different from the focused one targeted primarily at pay and promotion equality and some other women's issues.

Broadening the agenda for gender studies of organizations may be seen as risking losing any foundation in broadly shared interests or experiences of women – although the idea of such a foundation is rather shaky. The position taken may be viewed as masquerading as feminist, but uncoupled from broadly agreed concerns and perhaps best labelled in other terms. On the other hand, it may also be argued that the purpose of feminism is to question dominating, masculinistic ideals, goals and ways of relating to the world, rather than to focus only on issues easily recognized as 'women's'. Rather than taking for granted the most apparent effects of centuries of male domination, institutionalized in social practices and goals, as liberal feminism and variable thinking tend to do, a broadened agenda would mean a less constrained scrutinizing of masculine domination. This would increase the risk of missing crucial but hidden forms of such domination. Here it makes sense to refer back to Acker (1989) who argues that a significant problem in feminism is the tendency to take for granted major theoretical concepts and the implicit ideas they carry and thus compartmentalize gender studies as a subfield addressing women-only concerns. Both the short and the long agenda contribute to such a marginalization.[13]

They focus on certain issues, but may suffer from and reproduce gender under-sensitivity on other issues. Their advantages are, of course, a clear identity and a focused policy. The broad agenda may easily be seen as too diffuse and over-ambitious, reducing the chances of doing something about what many people see as the core issues (pay, promotion, harassment) and increasing diversity of opinion and conflict in gender studies.

When considering the benefits of broadening the agenda the issue of interest in relation to men and women must be considered. Not only women-specific issues and experiences would be in focus, but social relations between men and women and the gendered nature of social institutions would be investigated. However, such a broadened view would call for a careful balance between sensitive readings of the gendered nature of all aspects of social reality and avoiding the trap of allowing the masculine domination metaphor to dictate our understanding of social reality, colouring everything in the field of gender studies.

To conclude, it seems problematic to assume that gender is a fundamental organizing principle as well as that there are broadly shared and distinct women's interests in a specific society. Openness about the significance of gender as an organizing principle and acknowledging the complex nature of interests, problems in substantiating a set of interests shared by all or most women and the reasons for addressing gender issues also from the viewpoint of men, throw doubt on the need for an exclusive, women-focused stream. The necessity of gender studies as a distinct field of inquiry isolated from other streams may thus be questioned. With the increasing awareness of diversity and conflict not only between groups of women, but also within feminism, the old ideal of a unitary and unique womanhood is discredited and an opening up of the intellectual agenda for interaction between different streams is encouraged. In addition, understanding the complexity of organizational life calls for an approach where gender thinking can enrich other streams and gender studies be enriched by these other orientations.

Some problems in 'anti-male' and 'anti-masculine' gender and organization studies

Some features in large sections of gender and organization studies run against integrating gender concerns with other aspects of management and organization. One is a bias for hypercritique, in which men are viewed as bad and women as good or innocent. This is often complemented by men being seen as active, doing things to/or against women, while the latter in most cases are passive – things are done to them. Here one significant effect is the potential alienation of a large audience. A second is an adaptation of the intellectual agenda and ways of doing research to political–tactical concerns associated with beliefs about what may serve women's interests.

Nasty men and innocent women

For many feminists – and some pro-feminist or 'anti-masculinist' men, such as Hearn (1993) – the identities of victim for women and oppressor for men seem to be the essential characters around which the story evolves. This fits also with the ghetto metaphor and legitimizes its existence. The vicious nature of men and innocence of women are moral themes in some writings. Of course, many gender texts are very careful and nuanced and critique of forms of domination often calls for unflattering accounts. But sometimes critique is taken a bit too far or is unsufficiently grounded. Rather extreme examples may be used and a 'negative' vocabulary favoured. The individual case receiving most attention by Collinson and Hearn (1996) concerns Howard Hughes, the American entrepreneur and tycoon. Hughes hated emotions and was apparently a very disturbed person. His detachment, isolation and obsession with control grew to the point where he could no longer interact with other people. Finally, he had his headquarters hermetically sealed and in his later years he lived totally alone in a room that was neither cleaned nor even saw the light of day. According to Collinson and Hearn, 'his life history illustrates the self-defeating consequences that can *ensue* from an obsession with personal control through autocratic management' (1996: 3). One may argue that Hughes is a very extreme example, telling us little about male managers in general, and that less atypical examples may be more informative to explore. Kerfoot and Knights (1996: 80) view the core of masculinity as 'a compulsive desire to be in control and thereby, to act instrumentally with respect to everything, including the self'. Masculinity is thus equated with a kind of compulsory neuroticism which is far less pathological than the one characterized by Hughes, but to indicate that people in management subordinate personal life, family, and even physical and mental health 'to the greater goal of control or mastery' (p. 80) may be somewhat harsh and lack nuances. Another type of 'anti-male' negativity can be found in the treatment of empirical material in some gender studies. It happens that highly pejorative statements about men are accepted as valid. Reskin and Padavic (1994: 138) for example refer to Segura, who cites a Hispanic women who, with irony, listed some stereotypes that disqualified her from promotion: 'That we like to be pregnant. We don't like to take birth control. We're "mañana" (tomorrow) oriented. We're easy. We're all overweight, and I guess we're hot (she laughed) and submissive.' Reskin and Padavic then comment that 'stereotypes like these seriously undermine women's authority on the job, as well as their chances for advancement'. That is, of course, true, but it is not easy to say how much the statement informs us about the stereotypes of other people at the workplace. It may be a bit stereotyped about stereotypes. In Reskin and Padavic's texts men come through with few exceptions as narrow-minded, prejudiced, anti-women and sometimes rather brutal creatures (1994: 72–4). Cockburn's text (1991) also portrays men in consistently unsympathetic ways. For example, she summarizes reactions to positive action for equal opportunity in UK organizations as follows: 'Many women may write this off as "mere" liberal feminism, women buying into the system. Men nonetheless often respond as though the end of the world were at hand' (Cockburn, 1991: 47).

> Men define 'women's difference' in terms that suit themselves. They play off one woman against another. Women are in a cleft stick. They do prefer what they call 'women's values' and share an idea of what they mean by that. 'I like to see a softer approach, less self-oriented', a women professional in the Service said. And in High Retail a woman distanced herself from men who treated their secretaries like dirt, 'It's just "Do" it!' Most women do not much like masculinity and do not want to emulate it. (1991: 70)[14]

The impression is that men are as unsympathetic as women are the opposite. When women appear authoritarian or in other ways masculine and negative, it is often seen as the effect of male structures and cultural norms:

> The environment they have joined, which is that of men of power, has threatened to repel them if they do not adapt to its culture. Life experiences makes us what we are and, one women said, 'Look what you have to do to get there'. Once such women have made a decision to compete with men there is a tendency for them gradually to take on masculine traits. (Cockburn, 1991: 69)

Stivers (1993: 22) says something similar when, referring to Kanter, she asserts that 'the bossiness of women supervisors about which both male and female employees complain is not a feminine trait but the behaviour of someone who has significant responsibility but little real power'. Alternatively, the perceptions are explained through references to prejudiced expectations of femaleness, making women in managerial positions appear as either too female, soft and insufficiently authoritative or as too unfeminine, bossy and too authoritative (Cockburn, 1991: 69).

In these cases pejorative statements about men are taken at face value while negative statements about women are seen as indicating the prejudices of the spokesperson and ascribed to male-dominated culture or social structure. The descriptions easily reinforce stereotypes. That some or many men are prejudiced and even nasty to women does not justify the fact that most times some research texts mention men it is done in a negative way, often in pejorative terms (for example, Cockburn, 1991; Hearn, 1993; Reskin and Padavic, 1994). The balance between fair and unfair critique is, of course, often difficult. Sometimes one gets the impression that negative stereotypical statements by women about men are accepted, while negative stereotypical statements by men about women are interpreted as proof of the prejudices of the former. Positive stereotypes of women are often accepted as 'true' (for instance, by most difference-oriented writers on women and leadership). Negative evaluations and critique should not be avoided, but a biased use of examples and an uncritical acceptance of unchecked statements of a pejorative nature do gender studies little good.

Of course, many texts in gender studies show little problem in this regard and it is very likely that this problem is diminishing as gender studies become less polemical and more reflective, but there are still some which are not far from the stereotypical image of feminism as anti-men and excessively negative which presumably has contributed to the way many women have distanced themselves from the label.

More generally, there is the problem with what may be called hyper-critique, that is, a one-sided and exaggerated focus on the negative features of a social order. (Here it is not human subjects but the 'system' that is in focus.) Many other critical theories, such as those that do not deal specifically with gender, suffer from this bias. In certain Marxist texts capitalism is viewed as nothing but the exploitation of workers. Critical theory sometimes views management as solely a matter of exercising domination and mind control, while radical feminism conceptualizes society as a patriarchy in which the suppression of women is the principal quality. In some gender studies, organizations seem to be understood solely as sites for the segregation, subordination and sexual harassment of women, not as institutions (also) producing goods and services. People do not seem to work or accomplish anything useful, but to be preoccupied by reproducing patriarchy. Masculinities are seldom considered as integral with or as crucial for technical, scientific or economic progress. Arguably, masculine orientations and ideals such as being impersonal, objective, explicit, outer-focused, action-oriented and analytic (Hines, 1992: 328) are necessary for carrying out many valuable, indeed indispensable tasks, from plumbing to housebuilding and surgery. In some gender studies it appears as if technical and scientific developments and productive work take place irrespective of, or even despite, masculine orientations being central in engineering, sciences and companies or that only harmful development and production may be ascribed to masculinity. When (male) managers and professionals work a lot, in gender studies this is typically not evaluated in terms of contribution to organizational performance, but as expressing and promoting a male norm preventing women from being promoted to, and functioning in, managerial and professionals jobs or as an effect of a neurotic obsession with control (Kerfoot and Knights, 1996; Thomas, 1996). (We suggest that both aspects are treated.) As we have said, one-sided attention to the negative is not confined to (sections of) gender studies. Despite our sympathy for critical theories, we feel that many theorists – and we are ourselves no exception – sometimes fall into the trap of excessive negativity and intolerance (see, for example, Alvesson and Willmott, 1996: chapter 7 for a discussion of critical theory-inspired management studies). This does not reduce the problem of over-criticism or hyper-negativity in parts of gender studies. As Elshtain (1981: 136) notes, over-inflated descriptions may backfire, and may lead to the reader being suspicious and the researcher losing credibility or, if the description is accepted, the female reader may define herself as 'victim' or 'the exploited', which means rather constrained and powerless identities.

Apart from the general problems of hypercritique, the emphasis on bad men and good and innocent women leads to the closure of the agenda in terms of women's issues. There appears to be little need to listen to the voices of those characters who are favoured over women and 'enjoy the benefits of being male without doing anything special to obtain these benefits' (Reskin and Padavic, 1994: 5). Why care about the opinions of men on positive action for equal opportunity if most of them are so crude and immature that they 'respond as though the end of the world were at hand' (Cockburn, 1991: 47)? The disadvantages of men in some crucial respects, such as less intense relationships with children, appear less relevant to consider if men are portrayed in negative terms. In addition to, and more significant than, this marginalization of men from gender issues, the brute–victim categorization draws attention away from highly significant areas of technological–capitalist society and its constraints for companies and pressure on working life. The sex of power holders is not the only important aspect; market logic, pressure for competition, profit, wage and consumption increases mean that many employees – male as well as female – enjoy little autonomy, status, and options for participation, creativity and job satisfaction in contemporary working life.

On the tactics of gender studies

A related problematic feature in gender studies concerns tactics. Many of the examples of bringing forward harsh critique, either of masculine domination as part of an abstract system (rather than related to men or women *per se*) or of specific men populating workplaces as employers, managers and workers, may emerge from tactical considerations regarding an effective critique. At least for those parts of feminism emphasizing political commitment and the contribution to social change it is important not only how informative a particular study or text is, but even more so how it can be used.

Within the literature on women and management the themes pursued may be understood in terms of promoting opportunities for women to be managers, the principal message being that women are as good or better managers than men. In the 1960s up to the 1980s researchers and other authors emphasized similarity, whereas it is now more common to indicate that women's style of leadership is superior – more democratic, flexible, etc. – to that of men. Both messages – at the time in which they were conveyed – may have contributed to the reduction of male domination in management and thereby have had constructive effects. It seems rather obvious that many of those pushing for a specifically female form of management and leadership (e.g. Helgesen, 1990) do so in an over-clear way in order to promote the cause. The message is simple and selling. It is difficult to evaluate whether those taking a hard-nosed similarity view (such as Reskin and Padavic, 1994, who view socialization as almost irrelevant for what takes place in working life and regard external constraints imposed, and biased treatment by employers and men, as the only significant obstacle for gender equality) 'really' believe in it or whether it has been adapted to tactical considerations for accomplishing change in an effective way. Mobilizing legislation and bringing cases to court may be an effective way of forcing employers to take measures, thus bypassing the conservative orientations of not only men but also many women in general.[15] Policies and changes from above are best initiated through powerful and clear-cut arguments emphasizing similarity (cf. Scott, 1991). Some commentators, like Marshall (1993: 125), think that 'many researchers have emphasized women's similarities to men to win the former's acceptance'.

This is not to say that the positions taken and theses argued are only efforts to make political points or that the proponents are deceitful. It is rather a matter of embracing a more straightforward, simplistic line of interpretation and argumentation than fully considering all complexities and uncertainties of the subject matter, of imposing order and downplaying ambiguity.

As with all positions taken, simplification and clarification may lead to unwanted side effects. A great problem for those studies arguing for specific female values or a specific version of the feminine-in-management is that they may express – or at least may be read as expressing – a conservative view on women and reinforcing stereotypes. The specific female qualities are defined through the experiences associated with the sphere of family and children and this may prevent the liberation of women from the household sphere. Household experiences and family obligations may be read as natural as well as good for women, a prerequisite for them developing genuine female work values and a female leadership style. However, the opposite view – emphasizing similarity – may also have unfortunate side effects. Marshall (1993: 125) believes that the 'rhetoric of equality for similarity has distorted many women's lives and left organizational cultures largely unchanged by their inclusion'.

Tactical considerations lead to a rather selective approach to the illumination of gender issues. Important aspects of gender relations remain obscured, for example conservative, anti-equality orientations of women. It could be argued that a history involving rigid gender divisions and the subordination of women has substantive effects on subjective orientations in terms of self-confidence, family orientation and ascribed significance of work and career to identity and life satisfaction. Such subjective orientations, contingent upon cultural traditions and not on any female essence, may sometimes be as important as employers' and men's discriminatory attitudes and actions for women's problems in working life. But such aspects are relatively seldom addressed in gender studies, perhaps less because they are not important or relevant than because they may be used against efforts to promote gender equality. Given the widely spread stereotypical ideas and arguments used against women in working life – for instance that they don't want a career, are more oriented to children and family, are too sensitive for managerial jobs – it is understandable that researchers carefully consider the risk of their results being misused (Scott, 1991). A problem, however, is the risk that we get an agenda and an intellectual style that are too strongly adapted to what is politically correct or informed by political–tactical concerns, while vital issues remain unexamined in research texts and are only aired in private conversations (Hirsch and Keller, 1991).

Especially if one views the change of gender relations as emerging from below, through development of new ideas and orientations among women as well as men, rather than as imposed from above through the effects of the pressures put on employers, legislators and policy makers (proposed by, for example, Reskin and Padavic, 1994: 177), investigations of forms of subjectivities that run against equality projects are important. Cultural norms preventing the progress of women do not just exist out there, among male bosses and workers, but are also internalized and expressed by women (Chafetz, 1989). Of course, such orientations and actions must be placed in a structural and cultural context and related to the dynamics of power – a multi-level, non-reductionistic understanding is called for. Gender studies facilitating the renegotiation and reduction of constraints on how we think, feel, value and act associated with gendered beliefs and norms call for attention to the complex interplay of structures, cultures and subjectivities. Here, we think, lies the potential for individual and collective learning and qualitative changes going beyond a redistribution of bodies in various work and activity fields. Policies focusing on body-counting may enforce the latter, but they leave most aspects of gendered organizational cultures intact and they may accomplish little of qualitative change.

Summary

A move from a focus on women to a broader consideration of gender relations seems indicated for gender studies to have a broader appeal and also to get better empirical information about the experiences, conditions and preferences of women, to the extent that these differ from men. The latter calls for some kind of comparison or listening to and incorporating a broader set of aspects than only those produced by one sex receiving all the attention. The claim that one is describing and drawing conclusions on women as women – and not as people – means that one claims that they clearly differ from non-women – men. This should not be assumed (apart from when biological difference is crucial, such as menstruation) but needs to be continuously rethought, empirically investigated or supported with convincing arguments. Despite the well-grounded argument that a lot of studies and theory are based on investigations of mainly members of the male sex – in conventional management and leadership studies – and that this raises important problems, one can hardly say for sure whether this means that the empirical basis leads to biased effects before one reaches the conclusion that the neglected sex is significantly different in this respect. If, for example, men and women behave pretty much the same in leadership situations then a one-sex only sample does not matter. If they differ, then generalization based on a males-only sample is deeply problematic.

It is also important to take an interest in men and masculinities; gender does not refer only or mainly to women. Also this subfield risks becoming a bit narrow by not taking gender relations and dynamics seriously enough. Masculinities only make sense in relation to femininities, men in relation to women. This suggestion for a change of emphasis does not of course mean that the interests and voices of the unprivileged group are taken less seriously – although one cannot always equate women and unprivileged or men and dominant group. A certain emphasis on women's issues may co-exist with a certain, albeit less salient, interest in the voices and experiences of men.

An important question is whether gender studies should cooperate closely with other streams and theories or maintain an independent status, claiming to be *the* framework for understanding social phenomena. This is contingent upon how fundamental gender is as an organizing principle: either in terms of a strong dualistic division between cultural masculine and feminine meanings or a strong segregation of men and women (and the subordination of the latter). In line with the more open-minded, reflective approach that we advocate here – and in social science in general, for that matter (Alvesson and Deetz, forthcoming; Alvesson and Sköldberg, forthcoming) – it is wise to be careful with very rigid or unchecked assumptions. Rather than assuming that gender is (always) a fundamental organizing principle in work organizations and then carrying out puzzle solving in which this is proved/illustrated or a specific version of it discovered, one may treat the possible fundamentality of this organizing principle as a theme for exploration, assessing it against other organizing principles (age, professionalization, organizational forms, class, ethnicity, meritocracy), of course bearing in mind that these other principles may be fused with, although not being reducible to, gender.

Having pointed at some problems with focusing on gender solely, raised questions about the uniformity and uniqueness of women's interests and experiences and argued for a kind of study where the assessment of the significance of gender as an organizing principle is partly an empirical question, calling for the consideration of other organizing principles as well, we think we have a case for integrating organization and gender studies, i.e. not treating gender and organization as a specific subfield, divorced from mainstream organizational concerns. This may reduce the risk for one-eyedness in gender studies and also encourage a broader sensitivity to gender aspects among those who are not specialists on gender. The next chapter will continue to explore this theme.

Notes

1 Fundamentalist here means that there is a firm basis in terms of valid core concepts, methodological procedures, unquestionable points of departure – such as men and women,

essentialist definitions of the masculine and the feminine or women's interests – and a common road towards accumulated knowledge and truth achieved through the assembling of a body of sound intellectual efforts and empirical studies. Non-fundamentalists doubt the robustness of these foundations.

2 Acker talks about sociology, but the situation is hardly better within other areas of social science such as management and organization studies (J. Martin, 1994).

3 That a ghetto may be viewed in different ways is excellently illustrated by a cartoon reprinted in Perrow (1978). A wealthy woman is looking at the horizon from her apartment and says: 'Oh, what a problem the ghetto is.' The husband, reading his newspaper, looks up and remarks: 'The ghetto is not the problem. It is the solution.' The ghettoization of feminism may be the solution for the enemies or those uninterested in gender equality but also for the feminists enjoying a stable identity and protection from the external academic world.

Of course, the joke may be interpreted in gender terms. The spontaneous, social responsibility of the female is challenged by the distanced, calculated voice of the male, who gets the last word. Whether such interpretations are best seen in terms of sex–role stereotypes or critical insights we leave to the reader to decide.

4 For example in a reader on men as managers, managers as men (Collinson and Hearn, 1996), masculinity is the key word, and not much else connecting men and management appears to be described or analyzed. One could argue that sometimes men do not manage or try to develop and sustain an identity in ways that are best described as masculine. Male managers may, for example, be relationship-oriented or adopt a 'soft', non-autocratic, relatedness-oriented style. According to our observations of Scandinavian managers, this is not uncommon.

5 Although this slogan is less often espoused today than in the 1970s and many feminists have broadened their perspectives, the formulation still captures the core of much feminist work, focusing the experiences of women and wanting to promote their interests.

6 Of course, empirical material should not be taken at face value in gender studies. (This is valid for all social research, but in particular for critical research.) If for example male and female managers appear to behave in a similar way, this of course does not necessarily indicate gender neutrality; instead a strong masculinist conception of management may also be imprinting itself on the female managers and the people in their environment, imposing a cultural standard for how to behave. The meaning of empirical material must almost always be treated as open. But just as unacceptable as treating empirical material as representing the truth is to be satisfied with a set of basic assumptions, embracing a closed theoretical system capable of ordering and domesticating all empirical material and avoiding using it as an input for rethinking.

7 There may be different opinions about whether the example shows an advantage or not. Reskin and Padavic (1994) view the fact that women in the US army do not have access to combat positions as discrimination and as a disadvantage as it means that they can't get experiences counting as a merit for promotion.

8 See for example Clegg (1989: chapter 5) for a critique of the notion of interests in critical research.

9 Among the group of women in general in a company, one could argue that most would have some interest – perhaps not fully recognized – in changes leading to 'women' not only symbolizing positions of service and subordination, but also being associated with prestige and power. (Whether they would manage in any specific 'women-friendly' way or not is uncertain, as we saw in Chapter 6.) On the other hand, it is possible that the company may perform better, that pay increases and safe employment for workers are more likely to be accomplished, if people in key jobs such as higher managers do work long hours and take on the travelling judged to be necessary for the business. At least in highly competitive and economically difficult sectors and periods, the interest in high performance would probably count more heavily for most people, while in other contexts, such as public sector organizations and companies in a secure position the evaluation of interests may look otherwise. Having said all this, it must be realized that a long working week does not stand in a one-to-one relationship to good performance. Long working weeks may symbolize commitment rather than represent

positive contributions (Jackall, 1988). It is also possible that utilizing more female talent, even if women work less than male colleagues during the time when they have children at home, may have qualitative advantages, e.g. better delegation, compensating for a shorter working week. Still, it is far from obvious that the majority of women in an organization have unequivocal interest in key people working no more than 40 hours per week.

10 Other interpretations are also possible, e.g. that women in male-dominated jobs suffer from being outsiders and face demands and constraints originating from male-dominated traditions.

11 Some of the warnings about overusing the masculinity concept that we discussed in Chapter 4 may be directed at our own argumentation here. Despite ambivalence, we still feel that the points we are making are valid and, above all, important to raise.

12 The gender and class interests may clash here. Even though women are, on average, paid less than men there are significant numbers of professional women earning more than the average man.

13 These agendas are reasonable and one may see feminist organization studies as addressing a limited set of women-specific concerns. As such this stream has its place in the academic division of labour. Our concern, and the reason for talking about 'marginalization', is the possibility of a broader impact.

14 A very small minority of the men interviewed in the study were evaluated more positively. In one of the organizations studied, Cockburn (1991: 66) 'met a few men – very few it has to be said – who were supportive not only of women's progress in the Service, but also of the aims of the equality policy and the women's movement, society-wide'.

15 Public institutions such as companies and other organizations are much more susceptible to government-induced change efforts than families. Employers may be obliged to demonstrate equality; husbands and families cannot be forced in the same way.

9

Reconstructing Gender and Organization Studies

In this chapter we develop some ideas for an integration of gender and other organizational themes, in the light of the present marginalization, even 'ghettoization' of gender theory (Acker, 1989). We link this to the problems of under- and over-sensitivity addressed in Chapter 1 as well as more or less explicitly in many of the other chapters. We also provide some suggestions for how a social constructivist understanding of gender can be developed through the avoidance of a focus on men and women defined through biological criteria. We thus suggest a move away from 'body counting' as a basis for gender studies. In order to develop gender studies, ways of de-familiarizing conventional assumptions, ideas and ways of making distinctions must be explored. Through this, we can sensitize gender thinking in new ways.

Let us briefly repeat that the purpose of this book is to advocate a critical, problematizing approach. That we direct critique at some salient ideas and lines of inquiry in gender studies should not of course be read as if we are saying that the area is particularly problematic compared to other fields. With political commitment perhaps a sense of moral superiority and some intellectual problems easily follow, such as unchecked assumptions, one-sidedness and premature conclusions. But basically all areas in social and behavioural science include much that deserve critical questioning and it is through ongoing questioning that progress is made (to the extent that we can talk about progress). A positive development is heavily dependent on raising critical questions and challenging established truths and points of departures. It is inherent in a more reflective approach to social science that one points to problems, blind spots, how certain lines of thinking and vocabularies draw attention to some aspects, but away from others. In this final chapter we continue this approach, but perhaps with an increasing emphasis on constructive proposals on how to illuminate organizational cultures and corporate practices in terms of gender.

Gendering organizational analysis and making gender studies sensitive for organizational issues

We suggest that researchers develop a sufficiently broad interpretive repertoire to make them capable of making interpretations in gender terms as well as in other terms. To be able to read gender aspects sensitively into phenomena when this is productive is balanced by the capacity to see other aspects. Gender-oriented interpretations are then produced while bearing in mind the possibility of making other interpretations.[1] From another angle, this would mean that other kinds of organization theory readings run less risk of being gender-blind. Gender theory may be mobilized to bring forward significant dimensions that remain hidden through other perspectives and to add to the understanding of phenomena partially highlighted in other ways. Hereby the dangers of under- as well as over-sensitivity of gender issues may be coped with.

Gender may thus be integrated with other ideas in studies of, for example, organizational culture and leadership. In Chapter 5 we showed how gender concepts may inform and enrich cultural analysis in the study of rituals, vocabularies, artefacts, etc. without necessarily focusing on men or women. Rather than what specifically concerns these two categories in terms of discrimination/bias, the entire cultural subtext of organizational life may be exposed in terms of how it creates certain meanings and orientation. Arguably, it is more often subtle, partly unconscious networks of meanings and symbols than crude 'I don't like women' or 'Women do not belong here' attitudes that are important themes to develop knowledge about. Learning how to read organizational cultures broadly rather than just around what are claimed to be women's unitary and unique experiences of biases against them is therefore important. Gender is all the time fused with age, occupation, level, class, department, task requirements, and one should also be very careful not to disregard other culturally meaningful distinctions besides gender, even if one wants to say something important about the latter. One can here add that women may also benefit from an understanding of cultural themes following other lines than gender. For example, studies of managerial cultures, uncovering implicit rules and symbolism (e.g. Jackall, 1988 and Watson, 1994), may be valuable for all groups that are underrepresented in, but aspire to, managerial positions (including women), even if they do not focus on gender. We thus recommend gender-sensitive but not gender-exclusive cultural studies.

A case study of an advertising agency by Alvesson and Köping (1993), introduced briefly in the final part of Chapter 5, illustrates this approach. The original intention was neither to study nor disregard gender. Gender was a part of the interpretative repertoire – together with cultural, linguistic and critical theories used by the senior author in earlier research projects. The approach was open: in an ethnography the key theme may emerge with increasing familarity with the case. The extremely gendered division of labour, the heavy sexualized nature of the workplace and the inconsistency between domination of men and the salience of what may be described as cultural feminine orientations led to an interest in gender issues. Gender is, however, only one of three key themes in the study. The other two are (occupational) identity and discourses (field-specific talk). The three themes interact and support each other in various ways. Different papers based on the project treat different themes (for example, Alvesson, 1994, 1997).

An interesting possibility of broadening the impact of gender reflection in the study of leadership would be to go beyond (or beside) the somewhat unproductive comparisons of male and female leadership and the slightly repetitive and stereotypical complaints about the man being the norm in management, and instead study specific examples of leadership processes.[2] Such processes could be investigated in terms of how gendered constructions are accomplished and expressed, rather than through a focus on the biologies of the people involved. The actions and interactions of manager X could then be read sensitively in terms of gendered subtexts, a variety of masculinities and femininities, which hopefully at the same time would add to knowledge about leadership (superior–subordinate interaction) and to gender processes in organizations.

We will use strategic management at some length as another example of how gender theory may be a resource for enriching 'conventional' subfields in organization theory. Mintzberg (1990), among others, has contributed to the critique of the design school, the dominant approach in strategic management. Its essence is 'the intellectual processes of ascertaining what a company might do in terms of environmental opportunity, of deciding what it can do in terms of ability and power, and of bringing these two considerations together in optimal equilibrium' (Andrews, cited in Mintzberg, 1990: 173). In the critique of the school, Mintzberg does not mention gender. As we see it, this is not an inherent weakness. We imagine, however, that exploring this theme could add important insights. Many of the premises of corporate strategies may be interpreted as expressing masculine meanings maintaining a firm hold over management thinking. Arguably, this is also the case with the premise that 'strategy formation should be a controlled, conscious process of thought', in the hands of the chief executive officer; 'that person is THE strategist' (Mintzberg, 1990: 176). Another example is the idea that full-blown and explicit strategies should first be thought out and formulated before they are implemented. Mintzberg criticizes this kind of approach for overemphasizing strategy, viewing it as something that can control organizational resources (rather than being affected by them in simultaneous interaction and mutual influence), promoting inflexibility and separating thinking from acting. He also suggests that people in a company differ in evaluations of strengths and weaknesses; such assessments may be bound up with feelings – aspirations, biases and hopes. Implicit is a critique of the notion of the lonely, strong corporate leader, in command of an organizational hierarchy which obeys. The ideal of proceeding through the sequence diagnosis, prescription, and then action is consistent with the classical notion of rationality, but stands in opposition to a more gradual and flexible approach, in which trial and error and learning are more significant than thinking out the major steps and routes in advance, assuming that the plan is correct and the world stands still for it to be implemented. This kind of highly rationalistic, detached, commander-oriented thinking fits military notions well and the masculine nature of it is worth expressing. Perhaps the school's assumptions, as well as its success, are rooted in the appeal of strong masculinity? Perhaps masculinistic orientations among the corporate actors responsible for what is called 'strategy' may encourage them to act in specific ways in terms of organizational development and change?

Mintzberg also discusses the effects of case study methods in business education (in which the design approach to strategic management is taught) and finds some disturbing features. The idea is that students, through reading short résumés of companies, may analyse their situation, assess strengths and weaknesses in relation to the environment and then formulate strategies. Here thinking and formulation are privileged while action, implementation and learning are not. An effect of this pedagogy, according to Mintzberg, is that people develop a belief that they can manage companies through using strategic management models with little and remote knowledge about the companies which are the objects of new plans, for example, involving mergers or aquisitions. The case study method in combination with the design model has promoted a mentality of, 'You give me a synopsis and I'll give you a strategy' (1990: 189). This mentality, encouraging managers to give priority to abstract thinking and analysis, and remain in their offices rather than getting into factories and talking to customers 'where the real information is to be dug out' (1990: 190), is seen by Mintzberg as a major cause of the problems of US contemporary organizations, which rely on short-term financial information at the expense of long-term development. The mentality expresses a model of the analytic, remote, socially isolated individual, imposing rationality, plans and order on the external world, denying feelings, intimacy, interaction and social responsibility. The strong masculine undertone may account for the appeal and spread of this model, despite, according to Mintzberg and many other commentators (Whittington, 1993), its profound weaknesses.

We thus feel that gender interpretations – here only briefly indicated – could enrich the critique and understanding of the design school and its impact. This does not mean that we would necessarily recommend a paper specifically on gender and strategic management, taking into account the ghetto problems mentioned earlier, and the indications that such a focus and labelling appeals to the 'right-minded' and scares all those uninterested in – and in need of – knowledge on gender away. In addition, gender concepts are only partially productive in interpreting the problems Mintzberg is addressing. (Some of these are not mentioned here.) It is better therefore to integrate the gender interpretations with other aspects (see for example Knights and Morgan, 1991).

Of course, the point made here is not only of relevance in an academic context. In organizational practice, actors may benefit from self-awareness, critical reflection and open discussions of how techniques and forms of knowledge may have a seductive appeal through a masculinity-reinforcing image at the expense of more thoughtful considerations and lines of action.

Insights on gender among managers and others may reduce a few of the sources of irrationality behind actions in organizations.

On the social construction and deconstruction of gender: beyond women and men

Perhaps the most crucial issue for gender studies is how to conceptualize women and men. Most authors in gender studies say that they reject a biology-based concept of sex, refuse to use the latter term and claim that they are interested in gender as a social construction. We think that in a basic respect most are *not* addressing gender in a social constructivist perspective, at least not in a consistent and elaborated way.[3] Biology (body characteristics) is central to most authors' ways of dealing with gender. Men and women are identified through bodily criteria, primarily sex organs and chromosomes. That variable research/number-counting studies do so is not surprising. All statistics on gender rely on the ability to identify subjects easily as men and women and here body and not social being is what counts. But even more sophisticated social constructionist gender studies appear to proceed from body criteria when talking about men and women, for example male and female waiters/waitresses (Hall, 1993). The social constructions of these males and females enter in the next phase, where the 'fact' that some are men and some are women leads to certain social processes in which these two sexes are turned into genders, for example friendly waitresses and less friendly waiters, according to the views of those involved. The problem is that body criteria are easily used in a self-evident way and imprint themselves too strongly on the way one interprets social constructions. Empirical material can easily be an outcome of the unreflective nature of the distinction between men and women shared by both the researcher and the 'natives', for example, the self-evident, body-based distinction between waitresses and waiters. That this distinction is also a social construction and that gender orientations may be uncoupled from bodies is normally not considered, although it is sometimes addressed in discussions of, for example, masculinity (for example, Connell, 1995).[4] It is, of course, possible that the subjects of Hall's study for example are very categorical in making distinctions between men and women (carriers of male and female bodies respectively), but we don't feel convinced that the research material could not be read as more ambiguous in terms of how the subjects construct their worlds. Perhaps some statements were less clear in the constructions of people as belonging primarily to the categories of 'men' and 'women' – rather than as experienced/unexperienced, outgoing/reserved, relaxed/energetic/lazy.

A problem with most of the gender research is that it has an inbuilt assumption as part of its design which privileges the men/women distinction and there is little chance of discovering if the people being studied divide up the social world in ways where the sex distinction is not particularly crucial.

There often appears to be little space in gender qualitative research for example for findings in which the distinction 'men' and 'women' is *not* crucial. In one Danish organization that we have studied, however, despite the interest of the researchers in addressing gender, the interviewees downplayed gender as significant and emphasized what was referred to as the A and B teams instead. The distinction was based on the common perception of whether people were suitable and had the potential for demanding tasks or not, and was, according to interviewees, unrelated to sex (Billing and Alvesson, 1994: Chapter 7). In another study, the management of some Swedish hospitals took the initiative of forming networks for female physicians. The initiative was met with mixed feelings among those concerned. Many of the women felt that it was not easy to define something specifically associated with being a female doctor. Some did not recognize themselves in the picture of women's difficulties that provided the rationale for the network: women as subordinated, as a unitary collective, as less individual, weaker and more burdened with difficulties than men. They were worried that the organized networks could reinforce stereo-typical ideas about women as a very specific group (Sahlin-Andersson, 1997). Others were more positive to networks, although informal rather than organized and public, and it is possible that some downplayed the specificity of being a female physician or head physician and denied the significance of gender (sex) as a defensive reaction against the risk of being linked to the low-status category of women in the eyes of others. Never-theless, this case also illustrates that the use of the distinction men/women as central in an organizational context may not reflect the understandings of those concerned and may have unfortunate effects. A considerable amount of openness about the meaning and significance of gender in a specific empirical context is therefore recommended – which of course does not preclude that the use of a distinction between men and women may well be worth examining in most organizational settings.

One possibility here is to try to take an open stance and investigate when social categorizations such as man, woman, masculine, feminine appear in the talk of those being studied – in everyday life and in research interviews. Here – as opposed to when the researcher makes subjects talk about gender – the focus should be on when and how the categorizations appear unobtrusively. This would allow a better empirical picture of the con-structions of gender in the setting being studied. A considerable problem is of course that gender constructions may not be made explicit in talk. Not all communication is verbal and explicit. Gendered meanings may also be hidden and hard to interpret. A related problem is that detecting social construction processes through the study of everyday life or listening to very open or only weakly directed interview accounts may be very uneconomical for the researcher. It may take a long time before interesting empirical material appears. This is, of course, of some interest in itself as it may indicate that gender construction processes are not very salient compared to other ways of constructing subjects, social relations and organizational practices. The frequency with which gender is mentioned in relation to other membership categorizations (age, profession and so on) may be studied. One option in interviews would be to start with relatively open questions which permit checking the frequency of gender categorizations and then, in the second half of an interview, more clearly address gender-relevant issues.[5]

Defamiliarization of 'men' and 'women'

Of course, few would argue against the view that men and women differ in terms of chromosomes, sex organs and a few other bodily respects. What is to be disputed is whether these differences are a particularly relevant starting point or focus for social analysis. The biology-based distinction may be more relevant for the gynaecologist than the student of gender. As Coser says:

> there is a tendency in feminist theorizing to extol one experience that women have in common: the experience of the female body and female sexuality. I believe that this is a variant of sociobiology, namely, the notion that women must be different because their body is different. Such an assumption, while being based on truth, is neither original nor helpful. (1989: 203)

It can, of course, be argued that the female biology is ascribed a particular set of psychological and social meanings, bringing about the social construction of women. Sex (biology) leads to gender (a specific social version of men and women). But the very idea of separating sex and gender is that there is a difference between what the words signify. Gender is not a distinct and uniform sex role imposed on the body through some form of standardized cultural mechanics. Nor is the distinction very meaningful if one assumes that there is a specific psychology being developed on the basis of biological sex differences, only marginally affected by cultural conditions. The social construction processes are complex, multifaceted, heterogeneous; they vary over time and with class, race, occupation, organization and age. The social construction of gender does not prevent some women from becoming tank commanders[6] and bank robbers, some men from becoming kindergarten teachers and strippers, and both male and female managers showing a spectrum of different kinds of leadership behaviour. (Perhaps female managers are, in their work contexts, at least sometimes constructed as managers rather than women.) There are good reasons for agreeing with poststructuralists when they point at the problems with the use of universal concepts of men and women (Fraser and Nicholson, 1988; Scott, 1991).

Almost every time signifiers as man and woman are used they impose a taken-for-granted unity. Normally it is assumed that identifying a subject in these terms is highly informative: 'Who has written this book? A man and a woman. Aha!' The assumption is shared by the public as well as most students of gender.

The fact that there are strong cultural beliefs that the man/woman signifiers are crucial for creating order and understanding among human subjects does not mean that gender studies should follow this, perhaps culturally prejudiced, assumption. Through doing so the researcher does not so much analyse cultural beliefs as reproduce them. A research focus on 'men' and 'women' may actually exaggerate or reinforce such beliefs through the tendency to assume and impose a fundamental division of human subjects into two sexes. When critically attacking the effects of the application of the distinction between men and women in social context, researchers sometimes reproduce or even reinforce the seemingly self-evident and inevitable nature of the distinction itself. One could, to continue the approach briefly sketched above, imagine gender studies in which any strong inclination to divide people into men and women is viewed as something worth systematically exploring. This is different from only looking at the (negative) effects of the distinction. When, how and why the natives refer, or do not refer, to 'men' and 'women' is then the object of study. The signifiers are the vocabulary of the natives, but not theoretical concepts used by the researcher in the efforts to accomplish an epistemological break and move beyond common sense knowledge.

The very idea of gender studies would be to contribute to reducing the significance, or even abolishing the identities, of man and woman, or as Deetz expresses it, to make the 'gender distinction irrelevant at the place of work so that the identity of people constituted as women, as well as pay and routine treatment practices, would be based on other dimensions of distinctions and other constituted identities' (1992b: 30). This would call for not using this kind of identification. Individuality would not be sacrificed to the definition of a person as a 'woman' – whether produced by others or by the person herself. On the other hand, the men–women distinction is an historical fact and effects such as sex segregation and pay discrimination have materialized in most organizations. In order to work against them, the woman identity is necessary for women to organize themselves and express their distinct group processes in a gendered society (p. 30). The 'woman' label contributes to socially separating women and men, marginalizing women's experiences and denying personal complexity but it also forms a basis for resistance and productive conflict, Deetz says. When feminists try to accomplish the latter, there are sometimes unintended effects in the direction of the former.

One possibility in gender studies would be to minimize the use of the labels 'man' and 'woman', except when used by the people being studied. This may be done through the concepts of masculinities and femininities, which may be employed without noticing the sex of the subjects involved. We have warned of the problems involved in the use of these notions: they may reflect one's own (group) idiosyncracies (what is masculine for one person or group may not be for another) and may easily be overused (almost everything in organizations may be seen as expressing masculine meanings). One may therefore also try other vocabularies for labelling what is conventionally, but unreflectively, ascribed to man and woman. If one is interested in identifying bodies through conventional criteria, one may talk about the bio-man and the bio-woman. One may also focus on the bodily differences which are perhaps most salient – different sex organs – thus referring to them as a P-person (biological male) and a V-person (biological female). P- and V-people figure in all gender statistics and in the majority of all gender research, taking some (biological) criteria as the crucial issue for addressing gender (or rather sex).

Many feminists have understood the specific female in terms of sets of 'motherly' experiences with children and nurturance bringing about a specific set of values or a leadership style; the interesting quality is the one of having been a primary caretaker (of infants/children) (Cockburn, 1991; Grant, 1988; Hartsock, 1987). Hartsock, for example, emphasizes the significance of a 'deep unity with another through the many-levelled and changing connections mothers experience with growing children' (1987: 167). This experience of reproduction is routinely equated with 'women', but our point here is that we in research work should be very careful about using this imprecise term, overburdened with unexplored meanings and ambiguously referring to biological and socio-cultural aspects at the same time. We should also hesitate to talk about 'mothers' for the same reason (Fraser and Nicholson, 1988). The primary caretaker may be a P-person (the P-parent rather than the V-parent). There may also be two, in such cases often perhaps one P- and one V-person or even two persons of the same biological sex (i.e. a homosexual couple). Any naturalization of it being a V-person should be avoided. That this has been the case historically and still is does not require that one reproduces it. The dominating vocabulary works in this way. (Sometimes psychoanalytic writers addressing the early mothering of the child realize that it may not necessarily be the biological mother and then use the mother label irrespective of the sex of the primary caretaker.) Childbirth is, of course, associated with V-people but what happens after this short period in terms of the division of labour between P- and V-people is not self-evident. One should also be careful about equating primary caretaking with V-people and seeing this as the source of women's (V-people's) specific orientations. Far from all V-people have had these experiences. Some V-people never have any children, many have not had any at a particular time (for instance, at the time when they are studied).[7] *If* these experiences were central for the formation of a woman's 'essence' (a set of qualities associated with being a woman), then perhaps 25 per cent of the V-population in a typical organization would *not* qualify for the label 'woman' (or, better, childbearer and primary caretaker), while a few men may do so.

There are, of course, other possible sources behind the construction of 'men' and 'women' (or how we label subjects) than those addressed here, for example, early psychosexual and object relations development, general socialization and/or role learning. It would take us too far to discuss all the versions of how the origins, development and 'content' of the possible men- and women-specific qualities may be understood. Irrespective of which version is preferred, there is not an automatic relationship between body, specific processes of social constructions and a set of characteristics/ orientations. And while internationalization, identification, learning, etc. do not stand in a one-to-one relationship to biology, emphasizing the latter criteria and defining people through their bodies is, at least occasionally, misleading. As cultural signifiers 'women' and 'men' are also often ambiguous and multifaceted: a 'woman' may mean highly different things in different contexts and for different groups (cf. woman as sex object and mother). For many feminists (Chodorow, Gilligan, Cockburn) 'woman' signifies something radically different from 'man' in terms of subjectivity and orientation; for others (Kanter, Reskin and Padavic) 'woman' is no different from 'man' apart from being unfavourably located in organizations and an object of discrimination. What 'woman' refers to, except a certain biological equipment, is thus notoriously ambiguous and, in social science, it often means a problematic tight linking of biological, psychological and social characteristics.

An interesting example may illustrate that social practice may carry more weight than body in how a subject is socially constructed. An American female director of a public relations organization, who was sent to Sudan, was invited for a meal at a businessman's home. He treated her as he would treat a man, 'brought her a cushion, served her food and washed her arms with rose water'. The female director asked him if this was not a violation of the cultural norms in Sudan. To this he replied, 'Oh, it's no problem, women do not do business, therefore, you are not a woman' (Solomon, cited by Fagenson and Jackson, 1993: 311). Here we see an example of the Western social construction of the subject as a female manager – here the female/she categorization is salient – while the Sudanese constructs the subject as a 'non-female' manager. Of course, within Western society too there are variations in terms of when and how the subject is constructed as a female manager. (The case also illustrates other aspects, for example, that being a business person and a foreigner may wipe out signs of femininity/womanhood and neutralize gender.)

Let us continue our exploration of how one may address gender without privileging biology as the *ultimate* characteristic or essence – viewing the body as the focal point of uniform social constructions – from which social analysis proceeds. We will then move over to qualities associated with P- and V-people of greater relevance in organizations. In Chapter 4 we addressed masculine/male and feminine/female values and cited, among others, Marshall (1993). She describes the relationship between these and the two sexes as follows:

> I see male and female values as qualities to which both sexes have access, rather than the exclusive properties of men and women, respectively. I believe that through biological and physical makeup, socialization, and social role, contemporary women are more often grounded in the female pole and men in the male pole. This patterning may well be contradicted or unclear for women with a strong patriarchal education. (1993: 125)

Although we would have perhaps expressed ourselves a bit differently, we accept this account. If we continue to refrain from using the conventional men and women labels, we could investigate the grounding of subjects in terms of male- and female-poling. It is possible, for example, to divide the human population into five categories: strong male-polers, weak male-polers, mixed (or neutral), weak female-polers and strong female-polers.[8] One could assume that men/P-people typically belong to the first two categories and women/V-people to the last two. Women with a strong patriarchal upbringing may be placed in the middle. One could, however, imagine the possibility, at present or in the near future, that P- and V-people would not be very clearly clustered around the first and the second pole, respectively. Sex may say little about a person's orientations. The trend seems to be that it tells us less and less. The divisional manager Gustaf and the advertising P-people mentioned in Chapter 5, for example, appeared to express female rather than male pole-orientations, at least in terms of certain work values and social relations. The 'bossy' female (V-person) managers, even though according to commentators cited in Chapter 8 they are not 'really' authoritarian but forced to behave in that way by male norms or structural problems, may have ended up at the male pole. It is an open question how much the P/V distinction says about male/female poling. In a work and organization context – for example in relation to leadership – how people are poled may be of more interest than their P- or V-identities, at least in some situations, but this may vary. Different distinctions may matter in different situations. V-people may be a relevant category for under-standing those exposed to sexual harassment. But perhaps male-poled V-people are less exposed? (Presumably the risk of being sexually harrassed is related to looks and appearance. V-people perceived as masculine may be less at risk? They may, of course, receive sanctions for not 'doing gender' according to norms, but perhaps in other forms than sexual harassment.)

If the reader thinks that all this sounds strange and unfamiliar it does not mean that we as authors have failed. Defamiliarization is an important part of critical research (Alvesson and Deetz, forthcoming; Marcus and Fischer, 1986). Rather than adopting and confirming established ideas and beliefs, these are disrupted. Taken-for-granted, commonsensical ideas are chal-lenged. The well-known, natural and self-evident should be approached in a manner making it appear strange, arbitrary and unfamiliar. There are, as Deetz (1992b) points out, some reasons for sticking to the established category of woman, but it is equally if not more important to disrupt ongoing discourses fixing human identities and social relations in 'men' and 'women', thereby weakening the impact of this organizing principle. This would mean a reduction of the polarization of differences, 'supporting instead a notion that gender categories are fluid and include behaviours, values, and attitudes from which men and women are equally free to draw' (Ely, 1995: 593). Access to an alternative vocabulary, such as the one suggested here, may be a way forward. One may argue that it is not vocabulary that matters as much as the reasoning and understanding of the words used. That is true, but what is important here is the discourse – the combination of the vocabulary and line of thinking. Words like 'woman' and 'man' hold a strong grip over thinking and that contributes easily to conservativism and muddled thinking, including the strong tendency to privilege biology even if one is interested in social construction. Experimenting with words, including using a defamiliarizing vocabulary, facilitates questioning established frameworks and is a part of the development of new discourses.

Our purpose is not, however, to claim that the vocabulary suggested here is necessarily the best or that 'conservative' signifiers such as 'man and 'woman' should be skipped altogether.[9] We are more interested in challenging some established ideas, suggesting rethinking and illustrating how this can be done. We realize that talk about 'man' and 'woman' also has some virtues, as Deetz (cited above) mentions. We can hardly completely avoid using them. One possibility is the use of alternative and varied vocabularies. One could imagine texts alternating between the familiar and the defamiliarizing vocabularies, between (cautiously) using the word 'women' to encourage women-oriented demands and to illuminate critically devaluations clearly directed against a category of people identified as 'women' by the devaluators and to use other vocabularies (bio-women, V-people) to encourage liberation from conventional wisdom and the conserving and stereotyping tendencies of privileging biology and the identities so forcefully imposed by it.

Defamiliarization may, of course, be accomplished in other ways. The use of cross-cultural examples is one possibility, underutilized in this book. The case with the American business woman in Sudan is, for example, instructive. Placing men and women in the 'wrong' settings may also be useful. Studies of men in 'women's occupations' and vice versa have gone some way along the road, but they do not always accomplish the effect of defamiliarizing the reader. The story sometimes appears as predictable, based on ingredients such as scepticism, resistance and problems facing the person crossing gender lines. Through paying attention to detail in ethnographic studies of specific processes – rather than summarizing interview responses – a better effect may be accomplished. A good example of this is Finder (1987, cited in Mumby, 1988), a man who worked as a secretary for a time. His fellow workers were unable to accept that he 'was just a secretary'. His accounts of their reactions are revealing. Another example is provided by Pringle, who reports from the setting of a university committee:

> At each meeting Pat, the secretary, not only took minutes but frequently left the room to make telephone calls and send faxes. Pat's role was clearly to do the bidding of the chair. Pat did all this cheerfully and was warmly thanked by members of the committee at the end for taking care of them. The work was secretarial in the broadest sense, including organizing lunches and daily travel arrangements, and helping to clear the cups away after morning tea. But Pat was a man. And nobody thought it at all odd that he should be doing this work. It was, after all, a high-level, confidential committee chaired by the Vice-Chancellor. Pat was a besuited, slightly swarthy man in his late forties, not in any

way effeminate. He was doing work that was clearly defined as appropriate to a man, and he was formally classified, not as a secretary but as an administrative officer. (1993: 128)

Another possibility would be to write studies in such a way so that the sexual physical characteristics of the subjects involved are not focused. Signifiers such as he, she, man and woman, P-person and V-person may just be left out. Gendered meanings and experiences may be addressed in other ways, for example, through describing and interpreting masculine and feminine meanings in talk, action and practices.

To round off, we make two overall suggestions in this section: avoid privileging the body as the ultimate criterion for making distinctions between subjects and aim for the defamiliarization of established lines of thinking. The first point may facilitate the latter, but there are, as briefly indicated above, other ways of accomplishing defamiliarization.

The social deconstruction of gender

If our interest goes beyond focusing on body differences and the accompanying law-like significance of the men–women distinction, it is important to ask where does gender – a set of regulatory ideas dividing up the social world in men and women, the masculine and the feminine and thus constructing human subjects and social relations – come from? Why is it so important? What are the effects? These are questions sometimes addressed by students of gender, although many look only at the effects. How may gender disappear? is less clearly addressed or analysed. As a social phenomenon gender does not just exist, but is created. According to most students of gender, the creations are grounded in two types of division of labour, in the household, including primary caretaking, and in the labour market.[10] Crucial for the former is that household work has traditionally been seen as primarily women's responsibility while labour markets are characterized by the segregation and subordination of women. Gender is then created through women/V-people being constructed as mothers and family-oriented, being located in 'female' jobs, in particular service jobs (including paid caretakers of children, the old and the sick) and in subordinated positions. In other words, the more V-people there are as primary (and secondary) caretakers (unpaid), household workers, in female jobs and in positions of relative subordination, the more gender – as a distinct, socially significant category. The less of these divisions there are between V- and P-people and other kinds of sex-specific positionings, the less gender. Gender may even vanish – as an issue of social interest – with social changes that cause a radical upheaval of divisions of household and labour markets. This would mean that, at least in these contexts, 'the code of sexual marks would no longer be discriminating' (Derrida and MacDonald, cited by Cornell and Thurschwell, 1987). It loses social significance. We are certainly far from that, and some would argue that biological or biology-based psychological differences will always create some consequences upholding the significance of gender (sex), but there may still be radical changes on the way. This is what equality policies try to accomplish, although often in a rather contradictory manner.

In Sweden, the policy of equality has two elements, one quantitative and one qualitative. The first says that there should be an equal distribution of men and women across all sectors of society, including education and occupations. This means around 50/50 (no less than 40 per cent of the underrepresented sex). The second element means that both women's and men's knowledge, experience and values are to be used and have an equal impact within all areas of society. The problem is that the first element contradicts the latter, if (which is normally the case) the qualitative element is taken to mean that men and women have different kinds of knowledge, experience, etc. (If they don't, there is little point in raising the issue.) Different types of knowledge, experience and so on are outcomes of participation in various areas in a society and if a 50/50 distribution were accomplished, knowledge and experience would not be gender specific.[11] Gender as an organizing principle would actually be gone (in the areas referred to), and there would be little point in studying gender. Sex would be relevant in the contexts of sexuality, childbirth and a few sex-specific diseases. The idea of addressing a feminine style of leadership or women's values in work would make little sense, except in the discipline of history.[12]

All this may sound to some people like a Utopian dream, to others a nightmare, and will be pretty confusing to most. Nevertheless, the relationship between the degree of segregation and the construction of gender may be of interest in a much more immediate context, for example to understand women and leadership. As we have said, a lot of talk about V-people having certain values and orientations in work is based on the idea that these are rooted in experiences from the family sphere, in particular with children, and from secondary socialization. Writers on women and leadership say that skills developed in the private sphere are not only transferable, but also an advantage in managing organizations. Bringing up children and managing home and family develops the ability to cope with stress and to manage diverse tasks, as well as intuition, problem-solving and skills in communication and coping with relationships (Helgesen, 1990; Sharma, 1990, cited in Townley, 1994). Leaving aside the issue of whether all or even most people are affected very positively by home and family life in terms of development of qualities – family life appears as rather neurotic sometimes – the idea of a connection between these experiences and a particular set of work orientations is interesting. Let us explore this line of reasoning in terms of tendencies to shake up gender and, relatedly, how meaningful it is to identify people as 'men' and 'women'.

Rather than assuming that there exists some democratic leadership gene in the biological make-up of women, the *specific experiences* associated with the location of V-people in the gender division of labour, in particular in the household/labour market divide, may account for the tendency for there to be a distinct female orientation, for instance in leadership.[13] These experiences should not, however, be equated with women (V-people) as a group. The qualities mentioned, or other family-based values or skills, may be viewed as outcomes of the depth and intensity of experiences of 'family work', including childrearing and household work. A career woman, with no or one child, having hired labour to assist with childcare and household work, and sharing the responsibility with her husband, hardly develops any substantial skills such as those mentioned above, at least not in the same way that a woman does who has several children, spends a lot of time with them and manages the entire household with little or no help. In this last case specific female experiences are profound and the chance of developing skills contingent upon them is high. Of course, general socialization effects may also matter for the development of female skills, but if not material-ized in gender-specific behaviour in relation to family work the effect may be weak, especially in terms of learning skills. As argued by Markus (1987: 96) it is 'real life-activities through which the typical and determinant experiences of different groups are being formed'. Given the far from perfect correlation between family work experiences and biological sex, emphasis on the former, for example for leadership style, would indicate that the focus is not on women (V-people) but on the intensiveness of the family work. Perhaps a better label than 'women' or V-people would be family work- or possibly childcare-experienced subjects. (Such work experi-ences may have been gained in family work or as paid labour, for example, through employment in a day-care centre.) According to the argument, it is really this quality rather than anything inherently female (connected to the female body) that accounts for a particular leadership style. It is possible that the insignificant or weak sex differences in leadership reported by the academic research, treating bio-women and bio-men en bloc, to some extent may be explained by the fact that a rather large group of female managers does not have children and therefore may not have developed the orientation and skills seen as so central for 'women' by authors on female leadership. It is possible that a comparison between 'family work-experienced' (most of these V-people) and 'non-family-experienced' (some of these V-people) would show clearer differences in leadership than a body-based comparison of V- and P-people.

Claims are made by advocates of female leadership that 'the full potential of feminine leadership will only be realized when a large number of women managers begin to assert their true identity and use their special talents' (Sharma, 1990, cited by Townley, 1994: 151). We doubt that it would work in this way, because the full utilization of any women-specific orientations in managerial labour would undermine the basis for developing these orientations. If women moved into managerial jobs in great numbers they would have limited opportunities to sustain or reproduce these special skills and talents. Their 'true identities' would change or be diffused – made 'untrue'. Extensive family work and managerial work are hard to combine, not only at the same time, but also in terms of transformations over time. In principle, one may imagine a woman (V-person) being strongly immersed in family work for a significant time period and then embarking on a managerial career. Such a development is presumably rare, even if authors celebrating the value of female skills for managerial work were successful in their rhetoric. The problem is that the female-specific orientations and skills are contingent upon sex-based household/employment division of labour.[14] If an increasing number of women occupied senior positions in organizations, it is likely that fewer younger women – at least among those who may be judged to have managerial talents – would be prepared to take primary responsibility for home and family to the extent needed in order to develop substantial female skills and orientations.[15] The very inclination of women to do major parts of the family work is based on a general division of labour in which women's 'natural' place is primarily to be responsible for the family and children and, contingent upon that, in relatively subordinated positions in organizations.

To summarize, gender-specific orientations are contingent upon the division of labour, meaning that the primary base for women's and men's different experiences and different orientations is the fact that men and women do radically different things within the family and in the labour market. If the division of labour – and thereby sex segregation and the subordination of women – were to be weakened, for example through more women occupying senior managerial jobs (and not only in 'soft' areas such as personnel or information), it would mean that the material basis for the development of gender-specific orientations would vanish. There may be a basis for 'female leadership', a distinct 'style' of female managers as long as women's (V-people's) more significant experiences follow from their *not* being or becoming managers (in great numbers or at a senior level, at least). To the extent that V-people were promoted to senior jobs, it would presuppose as well as lead to V-people being less engaged in family work – which would become less sex-specific and gendered – leading to a reduction of gender-specific experiences, orientations and skills.[16] The social importance of gender would then be weakened, as an organizing principle and a source of different orientations. Even though we are very far from it, gender – in the sense of a socially significant category accounting for division of labour and variation in values and styles in organizational and other social contexts – may even fade away over time. In a few organizations the significance of gender is not very great and one could say that gender here, compared to most other contexts, is deconstructed (or never constructed) rather than constructed (cf. Billing and Alvesson, 1994: chapter 7; Blomqvist, 1994). To support the opportunities of human beings to decide how they want to live their lives – without norms about sex and cultural definitions of what is 'masculine' and 'feminine' directing them – makes it important not to naturalize and eternalize gender, and privilege the biology-based distinction between men and women, but maintain an open perspective on the processes constructing as well as deconstructing it. A possible outcome would be to make the distinction not only less rigidly but also less frequently used.

Final words

In this and the previous chapter we have argued for trying to avoid gender and organization being reduced to a sub-speciality for the truly committed. Instead we have advocated the close interaction between gender and other perspectives. It is claimed that most areas of organization, management and working life studies may be enriched through considering gender aspects – remembering at the same time that focusing only on gender, or exclusively using a gender vocabulary may lead one to lose sight of important aspects. Not only class and race, often mentioned in gender research, but also organizational performance and survival need to be considered – of course without being privileged. This is seldom the case – apart from those texts arguing for the increased use of female managers and feminine leadership for improved performances. Also when researchers try to avoid 'gender reductionism' and stress a variety of considerations, issues of effectiveness and production are neglected. Collinson and Hearn (1996: 18) for example, in an introduction to a reader on men, masculinities and management, stress that the chapters 'do not suggest that management or indeed organizations are the product simply of gender relations – hence the interrelated focus on other questions such as class, culture, hierarchy and sexuality'. Apparently, management and organization are not seen as products of the tasks they are supposed to carry out or competition and other economic constraints and pressures. In particular, those more radical versions of gender and organization studies that challenge current forms of masculine domination and offer an important counterpicture to prevalent norms would benefit from more seriously considering organizational accomplishments not only in terms of oppression of low-level employees, the turning of citizens into consumers and exploitation of nature, but also as contributions to a high material standard of living. Materialist and consumerist values, orientation and the contemporary belief that a capitalist market economy is best capable of achieving them, may well be the major constraints to radical transformations of gender relations. Competition between companies means strong incentives for employers and managers to prefer employees that can give priority to work performance (although, of course, less rational considerations also affect recruitment and promotion choices). A person who has responsibility for small children will be at a disadvantage compared with somebody who does not have this constraint. This is not a matter of prejudice or bad will from an employer – although prejudices and other forms of biases may exaggerate the significance of this disadvantage – but is inherent in a market economy. The sex of the employer may be of little significance here.

Such issues need to be critically examined in gender studies, which at present pursue too narrow and selective a view on organizational matters. Only the negative side of dominant forms of management and organizational practices associated with inequality and subordination of women is highlighted. Transformations going beyond the more effective use of females in organizations governed by the same goals and technologies under the performance pressures of the market economy may well call for a radical change in which qualitative values such as balance between family and work life and ecological sustainable development are upgraded at the expense of affluent consumption. This seems to be implied in the ideas of the more progressive feminists, for example, alternative values, but the costs and conflicts associated with such a development are seldom sufficiently addressed. Ramsey and Calvert (1994) for example argue for nonhierarchical organizational structures, a new balance of organizational–individual relationships so that the needs of individuals are better served and so on, but there is no awareness or discussion of the fact that the realization of these principles may lead to some problems or call for a lower priority for other values, for example, organizational competitiveness and performance and thus secured employment and wages for employees. Some of the other critical organization theory, drawing on the Frankfurt tradition (for example, Habermas, 1971, 1984; Horkheimer and Adorno, 1979; Marcuse, 1964) is more explicit on this account (for example, Alvesson, 1987; Alvesson and Willmott, 1996; Deetz, 1992a), but this literature is seldom utilized by feminists not inclined to draw upon non-feminist literature, despite its apparent relevance.[17] If one comes from the critical theory tradition, some of the more radical feminist ideas feel similar, but less novel than they appear.

A development towards integrating gender ideas with other critical strands as well as more conventional approaches to organizational culture, leadership, strategic management and service management, may weaken the project of improving the conditions of women in core respects such as closing the gender gap in pay and promotion and counteracting sexual harassment and devaluation of women. This is a significant risk that needs to be taken seriously. But a heavy emphasis on these qualities may run against a broader consideration of forms of masculine domination that actually may have led to the strong significance of values such as pay and promotion. A strong pro-women orientation and an emphasis on V-people's issues and interests may also – apart from neglecting the enormous diversity among women and the complexity and inconsistency of interests – one-sidedly reinforce the image of V-people as powerless victims and men as, if not oppressors, then at least benefiting from and reproducing structures of oppression and inequality. Arguably, even though many men's better access to positions of privilege is beyond doubt and is a powerful source of gender conservatism, P-people's interests in reproducing the gender regimes which currently dominate are far from clear-cut. Strains leading to shorter lives and less fulfilling contact with children are substantive losses. Many gender studies come close to being blind and deaf when it comes to these issues as mainstream social science is to the subordination of women in a variety of social contexts. Rules for living gendered lives also constrain many men. To the extent that dominating masculinities play a role in developing money and consumption-oriented social institutions with severe effects on the environment and also on social relations, it is an open question whether most men (P-people) will necessarily want to reproduce them without any form of hesitation or ambivalence. It would be a bad mistake to write all or most men off as immune to critical reflection on gender issues – whether it is the thinner agenda of equal opportunity/changed sex distribution or the broader agenda addressing wider political issues, including less apparent forms of masculine domination – and only likely to be influenced through legislation or other means of compulsion. Perhaps very few people nowadays would claim such an immunity, but sometimes one encounters texts expressing such an orientation. In any case there is not much work that is sensitive to men (P-people) in organization studies, with the exception of some studies on blue-collar workers (for example, Collinson, 1988).

Gender organization theory should therefore be careful about expressing anti-male orientations that may well be one-sided and unfair and alienate men. This does not mean, of course, that we do want to discourage critical studies of men, masculinities and oppression. On the contrary, this is a crucial task for gender studies. But there are also other tasks and aspects to consider. As we have said, gender too often means women. Both sexes need to be invoked in developing capacities to reflect critically about the gendered nature of society – and how dominant forms of masculinities and femininities constrain our identities and pre-structure our orientations behind our backs.

Notes

1 A prerequisite here is, of course, that the empirical material is not too strongly structured. See Note 5 below.

2 Openness if and when 'leadership' is the best interpretation for what goes on is to be recommended here (Alvesson, 1996b). It is actually rather few actions or interactions that are self-evidently best understood as 'leadership'. As mentioned in Chapter 7, the inclination to focus on leadership may be an expression of dominant masculine ideas.

3 Inconsistencies are, of course, hard to avoid. Too much rigour may lead to narrow-mindedness and reductionism. We don't claim to have avoided inconsistencies either. Sometimes they are, however, important to address critically.

4 To repeat, that there are biological differences between 'men' and 'women' is beyond dispute, even though most of the criteria used are less robust than they appear (Kaplan and Rogers, 1990; Lorber, 1993). What is of interest in a social context is the meaning and consequence of certain differences. Constructions are partly a matter of picking out and privileging a particular distinction. The fact that the distinction between being physically strong or weak, or being large or small in terms of body size, is a less salient theme in social construction processes than the penis/vagina related distinction – at least in most contemporary work/organization contexts – tells us that 'objective', natural distinctions are in themselves of little significance.

5 One may for example start by asking, 'How do you experience your workplace?' (interactions with others, ideal job . . .) and, 'How do you think people feel about working in this organization?' Later more specific questions could be asked, e.g., 'How do you as a woman/man experience . . .?' One could then see if and when gender – in terms of statements about men and women or male and female values, orientations, etc. – emerges and then evaluate its significance. The latter, more directive question may be used in the final part of an

228 Understanding gender and organizations

interview in order to compare answers or get additional aspects. Of course, asking relatively open questions does not mean the absence of the pre-structuring of responses. A feminist researcher will by her (or his) very presence probably trigger partly different responses than a non-feminist even if the same questions are asked.

6 According to a newspaper interview, a Swedish 25-year-old woman sergeant and tank commander did not experience any significant gender-related problems with the male soldiers, although she thought that it was an advantage that her boyfriend was also in the army, as a man in a non-masculine occupation may feel his masculinity threatened by her job (in the Swedish newspaper *Kristianstadsbladet*, 16 May 1994).

7 In addition, it is possible that the experience of bearing and rearing children may differ considerably between people.

8 We use this example, and to some extent the entire section, for pedagogical purposes rather than as a definite suggestion for developments in the field. We have little sympathy for one-dimensional masculinity/femininity scales. Masculinities/femininities (male/female values) are perhaps better seen as dynamic, interactive orientations, invoked by social processes, rather than fixed attitudes or traits. In addition, the assumption that there is one male pole and one female pole is problematic. A person may be described as male-poled in some respects (orientations or actions), female-poled in others and hard to tell on others (most?).

9 To repeat, there is no automatic relationship between a certain biological (sex) equipment and the social construction of it. It becomes evident that this is not the case if we consider cultural, class, racial, etc. variation but also in a specific social group a particular body is not an object of standardized social construction processes. Not all carriers of female bodies become secretaries, nurses or kindergarten teachers, become subordinated to men or are understood by others and/or see themselves as oriented towards relatedness, empathy and nurturance. There may be tendencies for the cultural meanings ascribed to a carrier of a female body to trigger processes of this nature, but a specific person, having a female body, may well depart strongly from this path.

10 Psychoanalytic feminisms would see gender division of labour as only of indirect significance. They, as discussed earlier, emphasize early childhood–parent (mother) interaction. Changes in division of labour would slowly affect and change early development. Our discussion here is more sociological and social psychological than psychoanalytic and we discuss the standpoint taken by the majority of students of gender.

11 Of course, some body-related differences remain and affect some experiences, e.g. around childbirth and menstruation. Sex differences in these respects would probably lead to rather insignificant effects on knowledge, experiences and values in most respects, compared to the sex-similar experiences in education, work and other social areas.

12 In a developmental perspective, i.e. before the 50/50 representation of the two sexes is achieved (if ever), there would still be sex-different experiences and varieties of knowledge (if we accept that there are such), meaning that the second, qualitative part of the two goals of the gender quality policy would be relevant. In a development perspective, the qualitative differences may be crucial to incorporate on an equal basis for a period, although they would play a diminishing importance to the extent that the quantitative goal comes closer to realization. The problem is that the more that diverging experiences and knowledge are seen as characterizing men and women, the stronger the reason for considering these in various areas of everyday life and politics, but there is then less likelihood that equal representation in quantitative terms appears, as diverging experiences are an outcome of, at the same time as determinant of, gender division.

13 We are not stating that such an orientation does exist although women may sometimes exhibit a slightly more democratic and relationship-oriented style. Of course, there are many ways of accounting for a specific female orientation or psychology. Here we are discussing the linkages which might exist between a possible female leadership style and a set of experiences through which it may be developed.

14 As Calás and Smircich (1993) note, the idea of introducing the feminine-in-management is grounded in the feminine defined by patriarchy.

15 The assumption here is that such development takes considerable time. One could

perhaps imagine a quickie version, where a few months at home with the baby, supervising a maid or spending some hours per week doing housework would do, but the skills mentioned by Helgesen and other special contribution advocates call for considerable experience and also challenges in family work. Many modern men presumably have some experiences of the quickie version of childcare and household work experiences.

Of course, an appreciation of any women-specific skills contingent upon child-rearing and family work may to some extent compensate for a lower degree of involvement in the labour market for some years. But it is likely that having been at home with children, full- or part-time, for several years will harm career prospects. From the other angle, women with good career prospects are inclined to share child-rearing and family work with the husband, thus there will be less sex-specific development of skills and orientations. Realizing that there are exceptions, a strong connection of V-people with children/family work will be the factor behind, as well as an outcome of, their moving ahead and attaining managerial positions to a significantly lower degree than men.

16 To repeat, we are focusing here on what most students of gender see as the most significant aspect of gender relations, i.e. the relationship between the division of labour in the household and in paid labour (Chafetz, 1989; Coser, 1989, etc.). Other phenomena, such as early child–primary caretaker interaction, general sex stereotypes, are not directly considered here. Arguably, many of these other phenomena are contingent upon – as well as influence – gender division of labour in paid work and at home. Also feminist psychoanalysts agree that changes in child-rearing affect the psychosexual development (Chodorow, 1978). An upheaval of gender division of labour in organizations and home would also affect early parent–child interaction (the P-parent would be more central) and neutralize general gender stereotypes and sex–role-oriented socialization.

17 Some feminists outside organization studies draw upon critical theory, sometimes partly critical (e.g. Fraser, 1987; Meisenhelder, 1989) sometimes more positive (Benhabib, 1987; Elshtain, 1981). As we have said before, the disinterest in non-gender literature by many feminists is accompanied by a similar, if not even more profound, lack of interest in gender aspects by mainstream authors. Our purpose here, however, is not to discuss the latter, but reflect upon how gender studies may be developed.

References

Aaltio-Marjasola, I. (1994) 'Gender stereotypes as cultural products of the organization', *Scandinavian Journal of Management*, 10(2): 147–62.

Acker, J. (1989) 'Making gender visible', in R.A. Wallace (ed.), *Feminism and Sociological Theory*. Newbury Park, CA: Sage.

Acker, J. (1992) 'Gendering organizational theory', in A. Mills and P. Tancred (eds), *Gendering Organizational Analysis*. London: Sage.

Acker, J. (1994) 'The gender regime of Swedish banks', *Scandinavian Journal of Management*, 10(2): 117–30.

Acker, J., Barry, K. and Esseveld, J. (1991) 'Objectivity and truth: problems in doing feminist research', in M. Fonow and J. Cook (eds), *Beyond Methodology: Feminist Scholarship as Lived Research*. Bloomington: Indiana University Press.

Acker, J. and Van Houten, D.R. (1974) 'Differential recruitment and control: the sex structuring of organizations', *Administrative Science Quarterly*, 19: 152–63.

Adkins, L. (1992) 'Sexual work and the employment of women in the service industries', in M. Savage and A. Witz (eds), *Gender and Bureaucracy*. Oxford: Blackwell.

Adler, N. (1986/87) 'Women in management worldwide', *International Studies of Management and Organization*, 16(3–4): 3–32.

Allan, J. (1993) 'Male elementary teachers: experiences and perspectives', in C. Williams (ed.), *Doing 'Women's Work': Men in Nontraditional Occupations*. Newbury Park, CA: Sage.

Alpern, S. (1993) 'In the beginning: a history of women in management', in E.A. Fagenson (ed.), *Women in Management: Trends, Issues, and Challenges in Managerial Diversity*. Thousand Oaks, CA: Sage.

Alvesson, M. (1987) *Organization Theory and Technocratic Consciousness: Rationality, Ideology and Quality of Work*. Berlin/New York: de Gruyter.

Alvesson, M. (1993) *Cultural Perspectives on Organizations*. Cambridge: Cambridge University Press.

Alvesson, M. (1994) 'Talking in organizations: managing identity and impressions in an advertising agency', *Organization Studies*, 15(4): 535–63.

Alvesson, M. (1995a) *Management of Knowledge-intensive Companies*. Berlin/New York: de Gruyter.

Alvesson, M. (1995b) 'The meaning and meaninglessness of postmodernism: some ironic remarks', *Organization Studies*, 15(6): 1047–75.

Alvesson, M. (1996a) *Communication, Power and Organization*. Berlin/New York: de Gruyter.

Alvesson, M. (1996b) 'Leadership studies: from procedure and abstraction to reflexivity and situation', *Leadership Quarterly*, 7(4): 455–85.

Alvesson, M. (1997) 'Gender relations, masculinities and identity at work: a case study of an advertising agency'. Working Paper, Department of Business Administration, University of Lund, Sweden.

Alvesson, M. and Berg, P.O. (1992) *Corporate Culture and Organizational Symbolism*. Berlin/New York: de Gruyter.

Alvesson, M. and Björkman, I. (1992) *Organisationsidentitet och organisationsbyggande: en studie av ett industriföretag*. Lund, Sweden: Studentlitteratur.

Alvesson, M. and Deetz, S. (forthcoming) *Doing Critical Management Research*. London: Sage.

Alvesson, M. and Köping, A.-S. (1993) *Med känslan som ledstjärna: en studie av reklamarbetare och reklambyråer*. Lund, Sweden: Studentlitteratur.

Alvesson, M. and Sköldberg, K. (forthcoming) *Towards a Reflexive Methodology*. London: Sage.

Alvesson, M. and Willmott, H. (1996) *Making Sense of Management: A Critical Introduction*. London: Sage.

Andriessen, E. and Drenth, P. (1984) 'Leadership: theories and models', in P. Drenth, H. Thierry, P.J. Willems and C.J. de Wolff (eds), *Handbook of Work and Organizational Psychology* (vol. 1). Chichester: Wiley.

Aron, C.S. (1987) *Ladies and Gentlemen of the Civil Service: Middle Class Workers in Victorian America*. New York: Oxford University Press.

Barley, S. and Kunda, G. (1992) 'Design and devotion: surges of rational and normative ideologies of control in managerial discourse', *Administrative Science Quarterly*, 37: 363–99.

Barnard, J. (1989) 'The dissemination of feminist thought: 1960 to 1988', in R.A. Wallace (ed.), *Feminism and Sociological Theory*. Newbury Park, CA: Sage.

Barrett, F. (1996) 'The organizational construction of hegemonic masculinity: the case of the US navy', *Gender, Work and Organization*, 3(3): 129–42.

Bartol, K. (1978) 'The sex structuring of organizations: a search for possible causes', *Academy of Management Review*, (October) 3(2).

Baude, A. (1992) *Kvinnans plats på jobbet*. Stockholm: SNS Förlag.

Bayes, J. (1987) 'Do female managers in public bureaucracies manage with a different voice?' Paper presented at the Third International Interdisciplinary Congress on Women, Dublin, 6–10 July.

Benhabib, S. (1987) 'The generalized and concrete other: the Kohlberg–Gilligan controversy and feminist theory', in S. Benhabib and D. Cornell (eds), *Feminism as Critique*. Cambridge: Polity Press.

Benhabib, S. and Cornell, D. (1987) 'Introduction', in S. Benhabib and D. Cornell (eds), *Feminism as Critique*. Cambridge: Polity Press.

Bergvall, Y. and Lundquist, S. (1995) 'Jämställdhet på högskolan.' Unpublished masters thesis, Department of Business Administration, Stockholm University.

Billing, Y.D. (1991) *Køn, karriere, familie*. Copenhagen: Jurist- og Økonomforbundets Forlag.

Billing, Y.D. (1994) 'Gender and bureaucracies', *Gender, Work and Organization*, 1: 179–93.

Billing, Y.D. (1995) 'A nice union.' Working paper. Copenhagen: Pædagogisk Medhjælperforbund.

Billing, Y.D. and Alvesson, M. (1994) *Gender, Managers and Organizations*. Berlin/New York: de Gruyter.

Blomqvist, M. (1994) *Könshierarkier i gungning: kvinnor i kunskapsföretag*. Uppsala: Acta Universitatis Upsaliensis. Studia Sociologica Upsaliensia 39.

Borchorst, A. (1993) 'Arbejdsliv og familieliv i Europa', in S. Carlsen and J.E. Larsen (eds), *Den Suäre Balance*. Copenhagen: Ligestillingsrådet.

Bordo, S. (1990) 'Feminism, postmodernism, and gender-scepticism', in L. Nicholson (ed.), *Feminism/Postmodernism*. New York: Routledge.

Bourdieu, P. (1979) *Outline of a Theory of Practice*. Cambridge: Cambridge University Press.

Bradley, H. (1989) *Men's Work, Women's Work: A Sociological History of the Sexual Division of Labour in Employment*. Oxford: Polity Press.

Bradley, H. (1993) 'Across the great divide: the entry of men into "women's jobs"', in C. Williams (ed.), *Doing 'Women's Work': Men in Nontraditional Occupations*. Newbury Park, CA: Sage.

Bradley, H. (1994) 'Gendered jobs and social inequality', in *The Polity Reader in Gender Studies*. Cambridge: Polity Press.

Brewis, J. and Grey, C. (1994) 'Re-eroticizing the organization: an exegesis and critique', *Gender, Work and Organization*, 1(2): 67–82.

Brittan, A. (1989) *Masculinity and Power*. Oxford: Basil Blackwell.

Brown, H. (1992) *Women Organizing*. London: Routledge.

Bryman, A. (1993) 'Charismatic leadership in business organizations: some neglected issues', *Leadership Quarterly*, 4: 289–304.

Bryman, A. (1996) 'Leadership in organizations', in S. Clegg, C. Hardy and W. Nord (eds), *Handbook of Organization Studies*. London: Sage.

Burrell, G. (1984) 'Sex and organizational analysis', *Organization Studies*, 5: 97–118.

Burrell, G. (1992) 'The organization of pleasure', in M. Alvesson and H. Willmott (eds), *Critical Management Studies*. London: Sage.

Burrell, G. and Morgan, G. (1979) *Sociological Paradigms and Organizational Analysis*. Aldershot: Gower.

Burris, B. (1996) 'Technocracy, patriarchy and management', in D. Collinson and J. Hearn (eds), *Men as Managers, Managers as Men*. London: Sage.

Butler, J. (1990) 'Gender trouble, feminist theory, and psychoanalytic discourse', in L. Nicholson (ed.), *Feminism/Postmodernism*. New York: Routledge.

Butterfield, D.A. and Powell, G.N. (1981) 'Effect of group performance, leader sex, and rater sex on ratings of leader behaviour', *Organizational Behaviour and Human Performances*, 28: 129–41.

Calás, M. and Smircich, L. (1987) 'Post-culture: is the organizational culture literature dominant but dead?' Paper presented at SCOS Conference, Milan, June.

Calás, M. and Smircich, L. (1991) 'Voicing seduction to silence leadership', *Organization Studies*, 12(4): 567–601.

Calás, M. and Smircich, L. (1992a) 'Re-writing gender into organizational theorizing: directions from feminist perspectives', in M. Reed and M. Hughes (eds), *Re-thinking Organization: New Directions in Organizational Theory and Analysis*. London: Sage.

Calás, M. and Smircich, L. (1992b) 'Feminist theories and the social consequences of organizational research', in A. Mills and P. Tancred (eds), *Gendering Organizational Analysis*. London: Sage.

Calás, M. and Smircich, L. (1993) 'Dangerous liaisons: the "feminine-in-management" meets "globalization"', *Business Horizons*, (March–April): 73–83.

Calás, M. and Smircich, L. (1996) 'From the "woman's" point of view: feminist approaches to organization studies', in S. Clegg, C. Hardy and W. Nord (eds), *Handbook of Organization Studies*. London: Sage.

Calhoun, C. (1992) 'Culture, history, and the problem of specificity in social theory', in S. Seidman and D. Wagner (eds), *Postmodernism and Social Theory*. Cambridge/Oxford: Blackwell.

Campbell, D. (1984) *Women at War with America*. Cambridge, MA: Harvard University Press.

Carlsen, A.M.S. and Toft, L. (1986) *Køn og ledelse*. Copenhagen: Forlaget Politiske Studíer.

Carlsson, C. (1987) 'Kön och klass ur ett historiskt perspektiv', in H. Ganetz et al. (eds), *Feminism och marxism: en förälskelse med förhinder*. Stockholm: Arbetarkultur.

Chafetz, J.S. (1988) *Feminist Sociology: An Overview of Contemporary Theories*. Ithaca, IL: F.E. Peacock.

Chafetz, J.S. (1989) 'Gender equality: toward a theory of change', in R. Wallace (ed.), *Feminism and Sociological Theory*. Newbury Park, CA: Sage.

Chia, R. (1995) 'From modern to postmodern organizational analysis', *Organization Studies*, 16(4): 579–604.

Chodorow, N. (1978) *The Reproduction of Mothering: Psychoanalysis and the Sociology of Gender*. Berkeley, CA: University of California Press.

Clegg, S.R. (1989) *Frameworks of Power*. London: Sage.

Clutterbuck, D. and Devine, M. (eds) (1987) *Businesswoman: Present and Future*. London: Macmillan.

Cockburn, C. (1991) *In the Way of Women*. London: Macmillan.

Collinson, D. (1988) 'Engineering humour: masculinity, joking and conflict in shop-floor relations', *Organization Studies*, 9(2): 181–99.

Collinson, D. (1994) 'Strategies of resistance: power, knowledge and subjectivity in the workplace', in T. Termier, D. Knights and W. Nord (eds), *Resistance and Power in Organizations*. London: Routledge.

Collinson, D. and Hearn, J. (1994) 'Naming men as men: implications for work, organization and management', *Gender, Work and Organization*, 1(1): 2–22.

Collinson, D. and Hearn, J. (1996) 'Breaking the silence: on men, masculinities and managements', in D. Collinson and J. Hearn (eds), *Men as Managers, Managers as Men*. London: Sage.

Connell, R. (1987) *Gender & Power*. Cambridge: Polity Press.

Connell, R. (1995) *Masculinities*. Cambridge: Polity Press.

Cooper, C.L. and Davidson, M.J. (1982) *High Pressure: The Working Lives of Women Managers*. London: Fontana.

Cornell, D. and Thurschwell, A. (1987) 'Feminism, negativity, intersubjectivity', in S. Benhabib and D. Cornell (eds), *Feminism as Critique*. Cambridge: Polity Press.

Coser, R.L. (1989) 'Reflections on feminist theory', in R.A. Wallace (ed.), *Feminism and Sociological Theory*. Newbury Park, CA: Sage.

Crompton, R. and Mann, M. (1986) *Gender and Stratification*. Cambridge: Polity Press.

Cronberg, T. (1986) *Teorier om teknologi og hverdagsliv*. Copenhagen: Nyt Fra Samfundsvidenskaberne.

Cullen, D. (1994) 'Feminism, management and self-actualization', *Gender, Work and Organization*, 1(3): 127–37.

Czarniawska-Joerges, B. (1991) 'Culture is the medium of life', in P. Frost et al. (eds), *Reframing Organizational Culture*. Newbury Park, CA: Sage.

Dachler, D.H. and Hosking, D.M. (1991) 'Organizational cultures as relational processes: masculine and feminine perspectives and practices.' Paper presented at the 10th EGOS Colloquium, Vienna, 15–17 July.

Dahlerup, D. (1988) 'From a small to a large minority: women in Scandinavian politics', *Scandinavian Political Studies*, 11: 275–98.

Daly, M. (1978) *Gynecology: The Metaethics of Radical Feminism*. Boston: Beacon Press.

Davidoff, L. (1986) 'The role of gender in the "first industrial nation": agriculture and England 1780–1850', in R. Crompton and M. Mann (eds), *Gender and Stratification*. Cambridge: Polity Press.

Davidson, M.J. and Cooper, C. (1984) 'Occupational stress in female managers: a comparative study', *Journal of Management Studies*, 21(2): 185–205.

Davies, K. and Esseveld, J. (1989) *Kvalitativ kvinnoforskning*. Stockholm: Arbetslivscentrum.

Deetz, S. (1992a) *Democracy in an Age of Corporate Colonization: Developments in Communication and the Politics of Everyday Life*. Albany, NY: State University of New York Press.

Deetz, S. (1992b) 'Disciplinary power in the modern corporation', in M. Alvesson and H. Willmott (eds), *Critical Management Studies*. London: Sage.

Deetz, S. (1996) 'Describing differences in approaches to organization science: rethinking Burrell and Morgan and their legacy', *Organization Science*, 7: 190–207.

Deetz, S. and Kersten, S. (1983) 'Critical models of interpretive research', in L. Putnam and M. Pacanowsky (eds), *Communication and Organizations*. Beverly Hills, CA: Sage.

Denzin, N. (1994) 'The art and politics of interpretation', in N. Denzin and Y. Lincoln (eds), *Handbook of Qualitative Research*. Thousand Oaks, CA: Sage.

Denzin, N. and Lincoln, Y. (eds) (1994) *Handbook of Qualitative Research*. Thousand Oaks, CA: Sage.

Dews, P. (1986) *Logics of Disintegration*. London: New Left Review.

Devanna, M.A. (1987) 'Women in management: progress and promise', *Human Resources Management*, 26(4).

Dipboye, R. (1975) 'Women as managers – stereotypes and realities', *Survey of Business*, (May–June): 22–6.

Di Stefano, C. (1990) 'Dilemmas of difference: feminism, modernity, and postmodernism', in L. Nicholson (ed.), *Feminism/Postmodernism*. New York: Routledge.

Dobbins, G. and Platz, J. (1986) 'Sex differences in leadership: how real are they?' *Academy of Management Review*, 11: 118–27.

Doucet, A. (1995) 'Gender equality and gender differences in household work and parenting', *Women's Studies International Forum*, 18(3): 271–84.

Drenth, P. et al. (eds) (1984) *Handbook of Work and Organizational Psychology* (vols 1 and 2). Chichester: Wiley.

Eagly, A. and Johnson, B. (1990) 'Gender and leadership style: a meta-analysis', *Psychological Bulletin*, 108(2): 233–56.

Eagly, A., Makhijani, M. and Klonsky, B. (1992) 'Gender and the evaluation of leaders: a meta-analysis', *Psychological Bulletin*, 111(1): 3–22.

Eagly, A., Karau, S. and Makhijani, M. (1995) 'Gender and the effectiveness of leaders: a meta-analysis', *Psychological Bulletin*, 117(1): 125–45.

Ehn, B. and Löfgren, O. (1982) *Kulturanalys*. Lund, Sweden: Liber.

Eisenstein, Z. (1981) *The Radical Future of Liberal Feminism*. New York: Longman.

Elshtain, J.B. (1981) 'Feminist discourse and its discontent: language, power and meaning', in *Feminist Theory: A Critique of Ideology*. Chicago: University of Chicago Press.

Ely, R. (1995) 'The power in demography: women's social constructions of gender identity at work', *Academy of Management Journal*, 38(3): 589–634.

Engels, F. (1972) *The Origins of the Family, Private Property and the State*. London: Laurence and Wishart.

Eriksson, U. (1997) PhD project, Department of Business Administration, Gothenburg University.

Etzion, D. (1987) 'Career success, life patterns and burn-out in male and female engineers: a matched pairs comparison.' Paper presented at the Third International Interdisciplinary Congress on Women, Dublin, 6–10 July.

European Network of Experts (1996) *Women in the Decision-making Process*. Brussels: European Union.

Fagenson, E.A. (ed.) (1993) *Women in Management: Trends, Issues, and Challenges in Managerial Diversity*. Thousand Oaks, CA: Sage.

Fagenson, E.A. and Jackson, J.J. (1993) 'Final commentary', in E.A. Fagenson (ed.), *Women in Management: Trends, Issues and Challenges in Managerial Diversity*. Thousand Oaks, CA: Sage.

Fakta Europa (1993) *Kvinna i Europa: om EG och jämställdheten*. Stockholm: Norstedts.

Ferguson, K. (1984) *The Feminist Case against Bureaucracy*. Philadelphia: Temple University Press.

Ferguson, K. (1994) 'On bringing more theory, more voices and more politics to the study of organization', *Organization*, 1: 81–99.

Finch, J. (1984) '"It is great to have someone to talk to": ethics and politics of interviewing women', in C. Bell and H. Roberts (eds), *Social Researching: Politics, Problems and Practice*. London: Routledge.

Fine, B. (1992) *Women's Employment and the Capitalist Family*. London: Routledge.

Firestone, S. (1971) *The Dialectic of Sex*. London: Paladin.

Flax, J. (1987) 'Postmodernism and gender relations in feminist theory', *Signs*, 12: 621–43.

Fletcher, J. (1994) 'Castrating the female advantage: feminist standpoint research and management science', *Journal of Management Inquiry*, 3: 74–82.

Fondas, N. (1997) 'Feminization unveiled: management qualities in contemporary writings', *Academcy of Management Review*, 22(1): 257–82.

Forisha, B.L. (1981) 'The inside and the outsider: women in organizations', in B.L. Forisha and S. Goldman (eds), *Outsiders on the Inside*. Englewood Cliffs: Prentice Hall.

Forsberg, G. (1992) 'Kvinnor och män i arbetslivet', in J. Acker et al. (eds), *Kvinnors och mäns liv och arbete*. Stockholm: SNS.

Foucault, M. (1976) *The History of Sexuality, Vol. 1*. New York: Pantheon.

Foucault, M. (1980) *Power/Knowledge*. New York: Pantheon.

Foucault, M. (1982) 'The subject and power', *Critical Inquiry*, 8: 777–95.

Frankenhaeuser, M, (1993) *Kvinnligt, manligt, stressigt*. Höganäs: Bra Böcker/Nike.

Fraser, N. (1987) 'What's critical about critical theory? The case of Habermas and gender', in S. Benhabib and D. Cornell (eds), *Feminism as Critique*. Cambridge: Polity Press.

Fraser, N. and Nicholson, L. (1988) 'Social criticism without philosophy: an encounter between feminism and postmodernism', *Theory, Culture & Society*, 5(2–3): 373–94.

French, M. (1986) *Beyond Power: On Women, Men and Morals*. London: Abacus.

Frost, P. (1987) 'Power, politics, and influence', in F. Jablin et al. (eds), *Handbook of Organizational Communication*. Newbury Park, CA: Sage.

Frost, P. et al. (eds) (1985) *Organizational Culture*. Beverly Hills, CA: Sage.

Frost, P. et al. (eds) (1991) *Reframing Organizational Culture*. Newbury Park, CA: Sage.

Gagliardi, P. (ed.) (1990) *Symbols and Artifacts: Views of the Corporate Landscape*. Berlin/New York: de Gruyter.

Geertz, C. (1973) *The Interpretation of Cultures*. New York: Basic Books.

Gergen, K. (1994) 'The limits of pure critique', in H. Simons and M. Billig (eds), *After Postmodernism: Reconstructing Ideology Critique*. London: Sage.

Gherardi, S. (1995) *Gender, Symbolism and Organizational Cultures*. London: Sage.

Giddens, A. (1989) *Sociology*. Cambridge: Polity Press.

Giddens, A. (1991) *Modernity and Self-Identity*. Cambridge: Polity Press.

Gilligan, C. (1982) *In a Different Voice*. Cambridge, MA: Harvard University Press.

Gonäs, L. (1992) 'Kvinnors arbetsmarknad i det framtida Europa', in J. Acker et al. (eds), *Kvinnors och mäns liv och arbete*. Stockholm: SNS Förlag.

Gordon, F. and Strober, M.H. (eds) (1975) *Bringing Women into Management*. New York: McGraw-Hill.

Göransson, A. (1978) 'Den könsliga arbetsdelningen och dess strategiska konsekvenser', *Sociologisk forskning*, 15(3): 51–81.

Göransson, A. (1996) 'Kön som analyskategori i den ekonomiska historien', in E. Borgström and A. Nordenstam (eds), *Kvinnovetenskapens vadan och varthän*. Gothenburg: Länsarkivet.

Grant, J. (1988) 'Women as managers: what they can offer to organizations', *Organizational Dynamics*, 16(1): 56–63.

Guba, E. and Lincoln, Y. (1994) 'Competing paradigms in qualitative research', in N. Denzin and Y. Lincoln (eds), *Handbook of Qualitative Research*. Thousand Oaks, CA: Sage.

Gutek, S.A. and Cohen, A.G. (1992) 'Sex ratios, sex role spillover, and sex at work: a comparison of men's and women's experiences', in A.J. Mills and P. Tancred (eds), *Gendering Organizational Analysis*. London: Sage.

Habermas, J. (1971) *Toward a Rational Society*. London: Heinemann.

Habermas, J. (1984) *The Theory of Communicative Action, Vol. 1*. Boston: Beacon Press.

Hall, E. (1993) 'Smiling, deferring, and flirting: doing gender by giving "good service"', *Work and Occupations*, 20(4): 452–71.

Hallberg, M. (1992) *Kunskap och kön: en studie av feministisk vetenskapsteori*. Göteborg: Daidalos.

Hammersley, M. (1992) 'On feminist methodology', *Sociology*, 26(2): 187–206.

Hammond, L. and Boydell, T. (1985) 'Men and women in organizations: the issues', *Management Education and Development*, 2: 77–8.

Harding, S. (1987) 'Introduction: is there a feminist method?', In S. Harding (ed.), *Feminism & Methodology*. Milton Keynes: Open University Press.

Harley, S. (1990) 'For the good of family and race: gender, work and domestic roles in the black community, 1880–1930', in M.R. Malson et al. (eds), *Black Women in America: Social Science Perspectives*. Chicago: University of Chicago Press.

Hartmann, H. (1979) 'The unhappy marriage of Marxism and feminism: towards a more progressive union', *Capital and Class*, 8 (Summer): 1–22.

Hartsock, N. (1987) 'The feminist standpoint: developing the ground for a specifically feminist historical materialism', in S. Harding (ed.), *Feminism & Methodology*. Milton Keynes: Open University Press.

Hartsock, N. (1990) 'Foucault on power: a theory for women?', in L. Nicholson (ed.), *Feminism/Postmodernism*. New York: Routledge.

Haslebo, G. (1987) 'Kvinders magt og indflydelse', in G. Haslebo et al. (eds), *Magt og indflydelse: kvinder i job*. Copenhagen: Teknisk Forlag.

Healy, L.M. and Havens, C.M. (1987) 'Feminist leadership styles as a force for humanizing the workplace.' Paper presented at the Third International Interdisciplinary Congress on Women, Dublin, 6–10 July.

Hearn, J. (1993) 'Emotive subjects: organizational men, organizational masculinities and the (de)construction of "emotions"', in S. Fineman (ed.), *Emotions in Organizations*. London: Sage.

Hearn, J. and Parkin, W. (1983) 'Gender and organizations: a selective review and a critique of a neglected area', *Organization Studies*, 4: 219–42.

Hearn, J. and Parkin, W. (1986/87) 'Women, men and leadership: a critical review of assumptions, practices and change in the industrialized nations', *International Studies of Management and Organization*, 16: 3–4.

Hearn, J. and Parkin, W. (1987) *'Sex' at 'Work': The Power and Paradox of Organisation Sexuality*. Brighton: Wheatsheaf Books.

Hearn, J. et al. (eds) (1989) *The Sexuality of Organization*. London: Sage.

Helgesen, S. (1990) *The Female Advantage*. New York: Doubleday.

Hennig, M. and Jardim, A. (1977) *The Managerial Woman*. New York: Anchor Press.

Hines, R. (1992) 'Accounting: filling the negative space', *Accounting, Organization and Society*, 17(3–4): 314–41.

Hirdmann, Y. (1988) 'Genussystemet: teoretiska reflexioner kring kvinnors sociala under-ordning', *Kvinnovetenskaplig tidskrift*, 9(3): 49–63.

Hirsch, M. and Keller, E.F. (1991) 'Practicing conflict in feminist theory', in M. Hirsch and E.F. Keller (eds), *Conflicts in Feminism*. New York: Routledge.

Hochschild, A. (1983) *The Managed Heart*. Berkeley: University of California Press.

Hollis, M. and Lukes, S. (eds) (1982) *Rationality and Relativism*. Oxford: Blackwell.

Hollway, W. (1984) 'Gender difference and the production of subjectivity', in J. Henriques et al. (eds), *Changing the Subject*. London: Methuen.

Hollway, W. (1989) *Subjectivity and Method in Psychology*. London: Sage.

Hollway, W. (1996) 'Masters and men in the transition from factory hands to sentimental workers', in D. Collinson and J. Hearn (eds), *Men as Managers, Managers as Men*. London: Sage.

hooks, b. (1984) *Feminist Theory: From Margin to Center*. Boston: South End Press.

Horkheimer, M. and Adorno, T. (1979) *The Dialectics of Enlightenment*. London: Verso. (First published 1947.)

Hosking, D.M. and Morley, I. (1991) *A Social Psychology of Organizing*. London: Harvester Wheatsheaf.

Illich, I. (1982) *Gender*. New York: Pantheon Books.

Itzin, C. (1995) 'The gender culture in organizations', in C. Itzin and J. Newman (eds), *Gender, Culture and Organizational Change*. London: Routledge.

Jackall, R. (1988) *Moral Mazes: The World of Corporate Managers*. New York: Oxford University Press.

Jacobs, J. (1992) 'Women's entry into management: trends in earnings, authority, and values among salaried managers', *Administrative Science Quarterly*, 37(2): 282–301.

Jacobs, J. and Lim, S.T. (1992) 'Trends in occupational and industrial sex segregation in 56 countries, 1960–1980', *Work and Occupations*, 19(4): 450–86.

Jaggar, A.M. (1989) 'Love and knowledge: emotion in feminist epistemology', *Inquiry*, 32: 51–176.

Jick, T. and Mitz, L. (1985) 'Sex differences in work stress', *Academy of Management Review*, 10: 408–20.

Johns, G. (1983) *Organizational Behaviour*. Glenview, IL: Scott, Foresman.

Jonasdottir, A. (1991) *Love, Power and Political Interests. Towards a Theory of Patriarchy in Contemporary Western Societies*, Örebro Studies 7. Örebro: University of Örebro.

Joseph, G. (1983) *Women and Work*. Oxford: Philip Allan.

Kanter, R.M. (1977) *Men and Women of the Corporation*. New York: Basic Books.

Kanter, R.M. (1983) *The Change Masters: Innovations for Productivity in the American Corporation.* New York: Simon and Schuster.

Kaplan, G. and Rogers, L. (1990) 'The definition of male and female: biological reductionism and the sanctions of normality', in S. Gunew (ed.), *Feminist Knowledge: Critique and Construct.* London: Routledge.

Kauppinen-Toropainen, K. and Lammi, J. (1993) 'Men in female-dominated occupations: a cross-cultural comparison', in C. Williams (ed.), *Doing 'Women's Work': Men in Nontraditional Occupations.* Newbury Park, CA: Sage.

Keller, E.F. (1974) 'Women in science: a social analysis', *Harvard Magazine,* October: 14–19.

Kerfoot, D. and Knights, D. (1996) '"The best is yet to come?": the quest for embodiment in managerial work', in D. Collinson and J. Hearn (eds), *Men as Managers, Managers as Men.* London: Sage.

Kessler-Harris, A. (1995) 'The paradox of motherhood: night work restrictions in the United States', in U. Wikander et al. (eds), *Protecting Women: Labor Legislation in Europe, the United States, and Australia, 1880–1920.* Chicago: University of Illinois Press.

Kessler-Harris, A., Lewis, J. and Wikander, U. (1995) 'Introduction', in U. Wikander et al. (eds), *Protecting Women: Labor Legislation in Europe, the United States, and Australia, 1880–1920.* Chicago: University of Chicago Press.

Kirkham, L. and Loft, A. (1993) 'Gender and the construction of the professional accountant', *Accounting, Organizations and Society,* 18(6): 507–58.

Kimmel, M. (1994) 'Masculinity as homophobia: fear, shame, and silence in the construction of gender identity', in H. Brod and M. Kaufman (eds), *Theorizing Masculinities.* Thousand Oaks, CA: Sage.

Knights, D. and Morgan, G. (1991) 'Corporate strategy, organizations, and subjectivity: a critique', *Organization Studies,* 12: 251–73.

Knights, D. and Willmott, H. (1985) 'Power and identity in theory and practice', *The Sociological Review,* 33(1): 22–46.

Knights, D. and Willmott, H. (1989) 'Power and subjectivity at work', *Sociology,* 23(4): 535–58.

Kolb, D. (1992) 'Women's work: peacemaking in organizations', in D. Kolb and J. Bartunek (eds), *Hidden Conflict in Organizations.* Newbury Park, CA: Sage.

Kovalainen, A. (1990) 'How do male and female managers in banking view their work roles and their subordinates?' *Scandinavian Journal of Management,* 6: 143–59.

Kvande, E. and Rasmussen, B. (1994) 'Men in male-dominated organizations and their encounter with women intruders', *Scandinavian Journal of Management,* 10: 163–73.

Lakoff, G. and Johnson, M. (1980) *Metaphors We Live By.* Chicago: University of Chicago Press.

Laurent, A. (1978) 'Managerial subordinancy: a neglected aspect of organizational hierarchies', *Academy of Management Review,* 3: 220–30.

Lefkowitz, J. (1994) 'Sex-related differences in job attitudes and dispositional variables: now you see them', *Academy of Management Journal,* 37(2): 323–50.

Legge, K. (1987) 'Women in personnel management: uphill climb or downhill slide?', in A. Spencer and D. Podmore (eds), *In a Man's World.* London: Tavistock.

Legge, K. (1995) *Human Resource Management: Rhetorics and Realities.* London: Macmillan.

Leidner, R. (1991) 'Serving hamburgers and selling insurance: gender, work, and identity in interactive service jobs', *Gender & Society,* 5(2): 154–77.

Lerner, G. (1986) *The Creation of Patriarchy.* Oxford: Oxford University Press.

Lewis, J. and Rose, S.A. (1995) 'Let England blush: protective labor legislation', in U. Wikander et al. (eds), *Protecting Women: Labor Legislation in Europe, the United States, and Australia, 1880–1920.* Chicago: University of Illinois Press.

Lindgren, G. (1992) *Doktorer, systrar och flickor.* Stockholm: Carlssons.

Lindgren, G. (1996) 'Broderskapets logik', *Kvinnovetenskaplig tidskrift,* 17(1): 4–14.

Lindvert, J. (1997) 'Förändrad skolorganisation – makt och möjligheter', in E. Sundin (ed.), *Om makt och kön – i spåren av offentliga organisationers omvandling,* SOU. Stockholm: Fritzes.

Linstead, S. (1993) 'From postmodern anthropology to deconstructive ethnography', *Human Relations*, 46(1): 97–120.

Lipman-Blumen, J. (1992) 'Connective leadership: female leadership styles in the 21st-century workplace', *Sociological Perspectives*, 35(1): 183–203.

Loden, M. (1986) *Feminine Leadership, or How to Succeed in Business without Being One of the Boys*. New York: Time Books.

Löfgren, O. (1977) 'Arbetsfördelning och könsroller i bondesamhället', *Kvinnovetenskaplig tidskrift*, 3.

Lorber, J. (1993) 'Believing is seeing: biology as ideology', *Gender & Society*, 7: 568–81.

Loring, R. and Wells, T. (1972) *Breakthrough: Women into Management*. New York: Van Nostrand-Reinhold.

Maccoby, E.E. and Jacklin, C.N. (1975) *The Psychology of Sex Difference*. Stanford, CA: Stanford University Press.

McGrath, J., Kelly, J. and Rhodes, J. (1993) 'A feminist perspective on research methodology: some metatheoretical issues, contrasts and choices', in S. Oskamp and M. Costanzo (eds), *Gender Issues in Contemporary Society*. Newbury Park, CA: Sage.

Marcus, G. and Fischer, M. (1986) *Anthropology as Cultural Critique*. Chicago: University of Chicago Press.

Marcuse, H. (1964) *One-dimensional Man*. Boston: Beacon Press.

Markus, M. (1987) 'Women, success and civil society: submission to, or subversion of, the achievement principle', in S. Benhabib and D. Cornell (eds), *Feminism as Critique* Cambridge: Polity Press.

Marshall, J. (1984) *Women Managers: Travellers in a Male World*. Chichester: Wiley.

Marshall, J. (1987) 'Issues of identity for women managers', in D. Clutterbuck and M. Devine (eds), *Businesswoman: Present and Future*. London: Macmillan.

Marshall, J. (1993) 'Organizational communication from a feminist perspective', in S. Deetz (ed.), *Communication Yearbook, Vol. 16*. Newbury Park, CA: Sage.

Martin, J. (1990) 'Deconstructing organizational taboos: the suppression of gender conflicts in organizations', *Organization Science*, 1: 339–59.

Martin, J. (1992) *The Culture of Organizations: Three Perspectives*. New York: Oxford University Press.

Martin, J. (1994) 'The organization of exclusion: institutionalization of sex inequality, gendered faculty jobs, and gendered knowledge in organizational theory and research', *Organization*, 1: 401–31.

Martin, J.R. (1994) 'Methodological essentialism, false difference, and other dangerous traps', *Signs*, 19: 630–57.

Martin, P.Y. (1985) 'Group sex composition in work organizations: a structural–normative model', *Research in the Sociology of Organizations*, 4: 311–49.

Martin, P.Y. (1993) 'Feminist practice in organizations: implications for management', in E.A. Fagenson (ed.), *Women in Management: Trends, Issues, and Challenges in Managerial Diversity*. Thousand Oaks, CA: Sage.

Meisenhelder, T. (1989) 'Habermas and feminism: the future of critical theory', in R.A. Wallace (ed.), *Feminism and Sociological Theory*. Newbury Park, CA: Sage.

Meuser, M. (1996) 'Kønsforhold og maskuliniteter: et videnssociologisk perspektiv', *Dansk Sociologi*, 7(3): 7–30.

Meyer, J. and Rowan, B. (1977) 'Institutionalized organizations: formal structure as myth and ceremony', *American Journal of Sociology*, 83(2): 340–63.

Mills, A. (1988) 'Organization, gender and culture', *Organization Studies*, 9(3): 351–70.

Mintzberg, H. (1990) 'The design school: reconsidering the basic premises of strategic management', *Strategic Management Journal*, 11: 171–95.

Mohanty, C.T. (1991) 'Under western eyes: feminist scholarship and colonial discourses', in C.T. Mohanty, A. Rosso and L. Torres (eds), *Third World Women and the Politics of Feminism*. Indianapolis: Indiana University Press.

Morgan, D. (1992) *Discovering Men*. London: Routledge.

Morgan, G. (1980) 'Paradigms, metaphors and puzzle solving in organization theory', *Administrative Science Quarterly*, 25: 605–22.

Morgan, G. (1986) *Images of Organization*. London: Sage.

Morgen, S. (1994) 'Personalizing personnel decisions in feminist organizational theory and practice', *Human Relations*, 47(6): 665–84.

Morrison, A. and Von Glinow, M.A. (1990) 'Women and minorities in management', *American Psychologist*, 45(2): 200–8.

Morrow, R. (1994) *Critical Theory and Methodology*. Thousand Oaks, CA: Sage.

Mumby, D. (1988) *Communication and Power in Organizations: Discourse, Ideology and Domination*. Norwood, NJ: Ablex.

Mumby, D. and Putnam, L. (1992) 'The politics of emotion: a feminist reading of bounded rationality', *Academy of Management Review*, 17(3): 465–86.

Nicholson, L. (ed.) (1990) *Feminism/Postmodernism*. New York: Routledge.

Nicholson, N. and West, M.A. (1988) *Managerial Job Change: Men and Women in Transition*. Cambridge: Cambridge University Press.

Nieva, V. and Gutek, B. (1980) 'Sex effects on evaluations', *Academy of Management Review*, 5: 267–76.

Nilsson, A. (1992) 'Den nye mannen – finns han redan?', in J. Acker et al. (eds), *Kvinnors och mäns liv och arbete*. Stockholm: SNS Förlag.

Normann, R. (1983) *Service Management*. Chichester: Wiley.

Northcraft, G.B. and Gutek, B.A. (1993) 'Point–counterpoint: discrimination against women in management – going, going, gone – going but never gone?', in E.A. Fagenson (ed.), *Women in Management*. Thousand Oaks, CA: Sage.

Novarra, V. (1980) *Women's Work, Men's Work: The Ambivalence of Equality*. London: Marion Boyars.

Olesen, V. (1994) 'Feminisms and models of qualitative research', in N. Denzin and Y. Lincoln (eds), *Handbook of Qualitative Research*. Thousand Oaks, CA: Sage.

Olsson, E. and Törnqvist, U. (1995) 'Hur mår Sveriges toppchefer?' Unpublished masters thesis, School of Economics, Stockholm.

Ortner, S. (1984) 'Theory in anthropology since the sixties', *Comparative Studies in Society and History*, 26: 126–66.

Ott, E.M. (1987) 'Effects of the male–female ratio at work: policewomen and male nurses.' Paper presented at the Third International Interdisciplinary Congress on Women, Dublin, 6–10 July.

Perrow, C. (1978) 'Demystifying organizations', in R. Sarri and Y. Heskenfeld (eds), *The Management of Human Services*. New York: Columbia University Press.

Perrow, C. (1986) *Complex Organizations: A Critical Essay*. New York: Random House.

Pfeffer, J. (1977) 'The ambiguity of leadership', *Academy of Management Review*, 2: 104–12.

Pfeffer, J. (1981) *Power in Organizations*. Boston: Pitman.

Pfeffer, J. and Davis-Blake, A. (1987) 'The effects of the proportion of women on salaries: the case of college administrators', *Administrative Science Quarterly*, 32: 1–24.

Pfeffer, J. and Salancik, G.R. (1978) *The External Control of Organizations: A Resource Dependence Perspective*. New York: Harper and Row.

Pleck, J., Sonenstein, F.K. and Ku, L. (1993) 'Masculinity and its correlates', in S. Oskamp and M. Costanzo (eds), *Gender Issues in Contemporary Society*. Newbury Park, CA: Sage.

Pondy, L., Frost, P., Morgan, G. and Dandridge, T. (eds) (1983) *Organizational Symbolism*. Greenwich, CT: JAI Press.

Poster, M. (1989) *Critical Theory and Poststructuralism*. Ithaca, NY: Cornell University Press.

Potter, J. and Wetherell, M. (1987) *Discourse and Social Psychology: Beyond Attitudes and Behaviour*. London: Sage.

Powell, G.N. (1988) *Women and Men in Management*. Beverly Hills, CA: Sage.

Powell, G. and Butterfield, A. (1994) 'Investigating the "glass ceiling" phenomenon: an empirical study of actual promotions to top management', *Academy of Management Journal*, 37(1): 68–86.

Pringle, R. (1989) 'Bureaucracy, rationality and sexuality: the case of secretaries', in J. Hearn et al. (eds), *The Sexuality of Organization*. London: Sage.

Pringle, R. (1993) 'Male secretaries', in C. Williams (ed.) *Doing 'Women's Work': Men in Nontraditional Occupations*. Newbury Park, CA: Sage.

Prokop, U. (1981) *Kvinnors livssammanhang*. Stockholm: Tema Nova.

Ramsey, J. and Calvert, L.M. (1994) 'A feminist critique of organizational humanism', *Journal of Applied Behavioral Science*, 30(1): 83–97.

Rapoport, R. and Rapoport, R. (1976) *Dual-Career Families Re-examined*. London: M. Robertson.

Reed, M. (1996) 'Organizational theorizing: a historically contested terrain', in S. Clegg, C. Hardy and W. Nord (eds), *Handbook of Organization Studies*. London: Sage.

Rees, T. (1992) *Women and the Labour Market*. London: Routledge.

Reif, W., Newstrom, J. and Monczka, R. (1975) 'Exploring some myths about women managers', *California Management Review*, 17(4): 72–9.

Reskin, B. (1984) *Sex Segregation in the Workplace: Trends, Explanations, Remedies*. Washington DC: National Academy Press.

Reskin, B. and Padavic, I. (1994) *Women and Men at Work*. Thousand Oaks, CA: Pine Forge Press.

Reskin, B. and Roos, P. (1990) *Job Queues, Gender Queues: Explaining Women's Inroads into Male Occupations*. Philadelphia: Temple University Press.

Reskin, B. and Ross, C. (1992) 'Jobs, authority, and earnings among managers: the continuing significance of sex', *Work and Occupations*, 19: 342–65.

Ressner, U. (1986) 'Women and group organised work in the public sector', in J. Fry (ed.), *Towards a democratic rationality*. Aldershot: Gower.

Riley, P. (1983) 'A structurationist account of political cultures', *Administrative Science Quarterly*, 28: 414–37.

Rix, S.E. and Stone, A.J. (1984) 'Work', in S.M. Pritchard (ed.), *The Women's Annual*. Boston: G.K. Hall.

Roper, M. (1996) '"Seduction and succession": circuits of homosocial desire in management', in D. Collinson and J. Hearn (eds), *Men as Managers, Managers as Men*. London: Sage.

Rorty, R. (1989) *Contingency, Irony and Solidarity*. Cambridge: Cambridge University Press.

Rosen, M. (1988) 'You asked for it: Christmas at the bosses' expense', *Journal of Management Studies*, 25: 463–80.

Rosenau, P.M. (1992) *Post-Modernism and the Social Sciences: Insights, Inroads, and Intrusions*. Princeton: Princeton University Press.

Sahlin-Andersson, K. (1994) 'Group identities as the building blocks of organizations: a story about nurses' daily work', *Scandinavian Journal of Management*, 10: 131–45.

Sahlin-Andersson, K. (1997) 'Kvinnoyrken i omvandling: om förändrade gränser och relationer i sjukvården', in E. Sundin (ed.), *Om makt och kön – i spåren av offentliga organisationers omvandling*, SOU. Stockholm: Fritzes.

Sangren, S. (1992) 'Rhetoric and the authority of ethnography', *Current Anthropology*, 33 (Supplement): 277–96.

Sarup, M. (1988) *An Introductory Guide to Post-Structuralism and Post-Modernism*. Hemel Hempstead: Harvester Wheatsheaf.

Savage, M. and Witz, A. (eds) (1992) *Gender and Bureaucracy*. Oxford: Blackwell.

SCB (1995, 1996) *Statistics Sweden: Women and Men in Sweden – Facts and Figures*. Stockholm: SCB.

Schein, V.E. (1973) 'The relationship between sex role stereotypes and requisite management characteristics', *Journal of Applied Psychology*, 57: 95–100.

Schein, V.E. (1975) 'Relationships between sex role stereotypes and requisite management characteristics among female managers', *Journal of Applied Psychology*, 60(3): 340–4.

Schmidt, E. (1987) 'På vej til lederjob', in G. Haslebo et al. (eds), *Magt og indflydelse: kvinder i job*. Copenhagen: Teknisk Forlag.

Schmitt, S. (1995) 'All these forms of women's work which endanger public health and public welfare: protective labor legislation for women in Germany, 1878–1914', in U. Wikander et al. (eds), *Protecting Women: Labor Legislation in Europe, the United States, and Australia, 1880–1920*. Chicago: University of Illinois Press.

Schunter-Kleemann, S. (1995) 'Welfare states and family policies in the EU countries', *NORA*, 2: 74–86.

Schwartz, F.N. (1989) 'Management women and the new facts of life', *Harvard Business Review* (January–February): 65–76.

Schwartzman, H. (1987) 'The significance of meetings in an American mental health center'. *American Ethnologist*, 14: 271–94.

Scott, A.M. (1986) 'Industrialization, gender segregation and stratification theory', in R. Crompton and M. Mann (eds), *Gender and Stratification*. London: Polity Press.

Scott, J. (1991) 'Deconstructing equality-versus-difference: or, the uses of poststructuralist theory for feminism', in M. Hirsch and E.F. Keller (eds), *Conflicts in Feminism*. New York: Routledge.

Sculley, J. (1987) *Odyssey: Pepsi to Apple*. New York: Harper and Row.

Sheppard, D. (1992) 'Women managers' perceptions of gender and organizational life', in A.J. Mills and P. Tancred (eds), *Gendering Organizational Analysis*. London: Sage.

Shorter, E. (1975) *The Making of the Modern Family*. New York: Basic Books.

Shotter, J. and Gergen, K. (eds) (1989) *Texts of Identity*. London: Sage.

Shotter, J. and Gergen, K. (1994) 'Social construction: knowledge, self, others, and continuing the conversation', in S. Deetz (ed.), *Communication Yearbook, Vol. 17*. Newbury Park, CA: Sage.

Silverman, D. (1985) *Qualitative Methodology and Sociology*. Aldershot: Gower.

Silverman, D. (1993) *Interpreting Qualitative Data*. London: Sage.

Simpson, R. (1996) 'Does an MBA help women? Career benefits of the MBA', *Gender, Work and Organization*, 3(2): 115–21.

Sinclair, A. (1995) 'Sex and the MBA', *Organization*, 2(2): 295–317.

Smircich, L. (1983) 'Concepts of culture and organizational analysis', *Administrative Science Quarterly*, 28: 339–58.

Smircich, L. (1985) 'Is organizational culture a paradigm for understanding organizations and ourselves?', in P.J. Frost et al. (eds), *Organizational Culture*. Beverly Hills, CA: Sage.

Smircich, L. and Morgan, G. (1982) 'Leadership: the management of meaning', *The Journal of Applied Behavioural Science*, 18(3): 257–73.

Smith, D. (1989) 'Sociological theory: methods of writing patriarchy', in R. Wallace (ed.), *Feminism and Sociological Theory*. Newbury Park, CA: Sage.

Sokoloff, N. (1981) *Between Money and Love*. New York: Praeger.

Sommestad, L. (1992) *Från mejerska till mejerist: en studie av mejeriyrkets maskuliniseringsprocess*. Lund, Sweden: Arkiv.

Sørensen, B.Å. (1982) 'Ansvarsrasjonalitet: om mål-middeltenkning blant kvinner', in H. Holter (ed.), *Kvinnner i felleskab*. Oslo: Universitetsforlaget.

SOU (1993) 7. Stockholm: Fritzes.

Spear, M.G. (1983) 'The biasing influence of pupil sex in a science marking exercise', in Girls and Science and Technology: Contributions to the III Girls and Science Technology Conference. London.

Spender, D. (1981) 'Education: the patriarchal paradigm and the response to feminism', in D. Spender (ed.), *Men's Studies Modified: The Impact of Feminism on the Academic Disciplines*. Exeter: Pergamon Press.

Steier, F. (1991) *Research and Reflexivity*. London: Sage.

Stenvig, B., Andersen, J. and Laursen, L. (1991) 'Statistics for work and the family in Denmark and the EC', in J. Larsen and S. Carlsen (eds), *The Equality Dilemma*. Copenhagen: Equal Opportunity Council.

Stivers, C. (1993) *Gender Images in Public Administration*. Newbury Park, CA: Sage.

Sundin, E. (1993) *Ny teknik i gamla strukturer*. Stockholm: Nerenius and Santérus.

Sundin, E. (1997) 'Den offentliga sektorns omvandling och kvinnors och mäns företagande inom typiskt kvinnliga sektorer', in E. Sundin (ed.), *Om makt och kön – i spåren av offentliga organisationers omvandling*. SOU. Stockholm: Fritzes.

Swidler, A. (1986) 'Culture in action: symbols and strategies', *American Sociological Review*, 51: 273–86.

Symons, G.L. (1986) 'Coping with the corporate tribe: how women in different cultures experience the managerial role', *Journal of Management*, 12: 379–90.

Tewksbury, R. (1993) 'Male strippers: men objectifying men', in C. Williams (ed.), *Doing 'Women's Work': Men in Nontraditional Occupations*. Newbury Park, CA: Sage.

Thomas, A. and Kitzinger, C. (1994) '"It's just something that happens": the invisibility of sexual harassment in the workplace', *Gender, Work and Organization*, 1(3): 151–61.

Thomas, R. (1996) 'Gendered cultures and performance appraisal: the experience of women academics', *Gender, Work and Organization*, 3(3): 143–55.

Thompson, A.M. and Wood, M.D. (1981) *Management Strategies for Women, or Now that I'm Boss, How do I Run this Place?* New York: Simon and Schuster.

Thompson, P. (1993) 'Fatal distraction', in J. Hassard and M. Parker (eds), *Postmodernism and Organizations*. London: Sage.

Townley, B. (1994) *Reframing Human Resource Management*. London: Sage.

Tunstall, J. (1964) *The Advertising Man in London Advertising Agencies*. London: Chapman and Hall.

University of California at Los Angeles/Korn-Ferry International (1993) *Decade of the Executive Woman*. Los Angeles: UCLA.

Valdez, R.L. and Gutek, B.A. (1987) 'Family roles: a help or a hindrance for working women?', in R.L. Valdez, B.A. Gutek and L. Larwood (eds), *Women's Career Development*. Newbury Park, CA: Sage.

Van Maanen, J. (ed.) (1995) *Representation in Ethnography*. Thousand Oaks, CA: Sage.

van Vianen, A. and Keizer, W. (1996) 'Gender differences in managerial intention', *Gender, Work and Organization*, 3(2): 103–14.

Ve, H. (1989) 'Kvinnor, byråkrati och välfärdsstat', *Sociologisk forskning*, 4: 3–17.

Wahl, A. (1992) *Könsstrukturer i organisationer: kvinnliga civilekonomers och civilingenjörers karriärutveckling*. Stockholm: Ekonomiska Forskningstinstitutet.

Wahl, A. (1996) 'Företagsledning som konstruktion av manlighet', *Kvinnovetenskaplig tidskrift*, 17(1): 15–29.

Walby, S. (1990) *Theorizing Patriarchy*. Oxford: Basil Blackwell.

Watson, T. (1994) *In Search of Management*. London: Routledge.

Weedon, C. (1987) *Feminist Practice and Poststructuralist Theory*. Oxford: Basil Blackwell.

Weick, K.E. (1979) *The Social Psychology of Organizing* (2nd edition). Reading, MA: Addison-Wesley.

West, C. and Fenstermaker, S. (1995) 'Doing difference', *Gender & Society*, 9(1): 8–37.

Whittington, R. (1993) *What is Strategy – and Does it Matter?* London: Routledge.

Wikander, U. (1991) *Delat arbete, delad makt: om kvinnors underordning: och genom arbetet*. Uppsala University: Research Report no. 28.

Wikander, U. (1995) 'Some "kept the flag of feminist demands waving": debates at international congresses on protecting women workers', in U. Wikander et al. (eds), *Protecting Women: Labor Legislation in Europe, the United States, and Australia, 1880–1920*. Chicago: University of Illinois Press.

Williams, C. (ed.) (1993) *Doing 'Women's Work': Men in Nontraditional Occupations*. Newbury Park, CA: Sage.

Wright, R. and Jacobs, J. (1995) 'Male flight from computer work: a new look at occupational resegregation and ghettoization', in J. Jacobs (ed.), *Gender Inequality at Work*. Thousand Oaks, CA: Sage.

Young, E. (1989) 'On the naming of the rose: interests and multiple meanings as elements of organizational culture', *Organization Studies*, 10(2): 187–206.

Yukl, G. (1989) 'Managerial leadership: a review of theory and research', *Journal of Management*, 15: 251–89.

Index